NOURISHING LIFE

Food, Nutrition, and Culture

While eating is a biological necessity, the production, distribution, preparation, and consumption of food are all deeply culturally inscribed activities. Taking an anthropological perspective, this book series provides a forum for thought-provoking work on the bio-cultural, cultural, and social aspects of human nutrition and food habits. The books in this series bring timely food-related scholarship intended for researchers, academics, students, and those involved in food policy.

Volume 7
NOURISHING LIFE
Foodways and Humanity in an African Town
Arianna Huhn

Volume 6
THE DANCE OF NATURE
Negotiating Infant Feeding
Penny Van Esterik and Richard A. O'Connor

Volume 5
THE HERITAGE ARENA
Reinventing Cheese in the Italian Alps
Cristina Grasseni

Volume 4
FROM VIRTUE TO VICE
Negotiating Anorexia
Richard A. O'Connor and Penny Van Esterik

Volume 3
RE-ORIENTING CUISINE
East Asian Foodways in the Twenty-First Century
Edited by Kwang Ok Kim

Volume 2
RECONSTRUCTING OBESITY
The Meaning of Measures and the Measure of Meanings
Edited by Megan McCullough and Jessica Hardin

Volume 1
GREEK WHISKY
The Localization of a Global Commodity
Tryfon Bampilis

Nourishing Life

Foodways and Humanity in an African Town

Arianna Huhn

berghahn
NEW YORK · OXFORD
www.berghahnbooks.com

First published in 2020 by
Berghahn Books
www.berghahnbooks.com

© 2020, 2025 Arianna Huhn
First paperback edition published in 2025

All rights reserved.

Except for the quotation of short passages for the purposes
of criticism and review, no part of this book may be reproduced
in any form or by any means, electronic or mechanical,
including photocopying, recording, or any information
storage and retrieval system now known or to be invented,
without written permission of the publisher.

Library of Congress Cataloging-in-Publication Data

Names: Huhn, Arianna, author.
Title: Nourishing Life: Foodways and Humanity in an African Town / Arianna Huhn.
Other titles: Food, Nutrition, and Culture; v. 7.
Description: New York: Berghahn Books, 2020. | Series: Food, nutrition, and culture; vol 7 | Includes bibliographical references and index.
Identifiers: LCCN 2020018336 (print) | LCCN 2020018337 (ebook) | ISBN 9781789208894 (hardback) | ISBN 9781789208900 (ebook)
Subjects: LCSH: Food habits—Mozambique—Niassa (Province) | Diet—Social aspects—Mozambique—Niassa (Province) | Niassa (Mozambique: Province)—Social life and customs.
Classification: LCC GT2853.M85 H84 2020 (print) | LCC GT2853.M85 (ebook) | DDC 394.1/2096799—dc23
LC record available at https://lccn.loc.gov/2020018336
LC ebook record available at https://lccn.loc.gov/2020018337

British Library Cataloguing in Publication Data
A catalogue record for this book is available from the British Library.

ISBN 978-1-78920-889-4 hardback
ISBN 978-1-80539-724-3 paperback
ISBN 978-1-78920-890-0 web pdf
ISBN 978-1-80539-907-0 epub

https://doi.org/10.3167/9781789208894

Contents

List of Figures	vi
Preface	viii
Notes on Text	xvi
List of Abbreviations	xviii
Introduction	1
Chapter 1. Blood, Vitality, and Diet	28
Chapter 2. Labor, Reason, and Compassion	60
Chapter 3. Witches, Animals, and Humans	89
Chapter 4. Salt, Sex, and Fire	118
Chapter 5. Weight, Nutrition, and Body Size	149
Conclusion	175
Glossary	186
References	189
Index	208

Figures

0.1	Metangula, from the Sanjala hill looking north toward Mount Chifuli onto the neighborhoods of Seli and Nchenga.	9
0.2	Men repair fishing nets while seated on a beached canoe.	12
0.3	Vendors sell tomatoes and onions in the market.	15
1.1	Cigarette advertisement in Malawi.	31
1.2	Five-liter bottle of alcohol on sale in a Malawi supermarket.	32
1.3	A vendor sells oil in the market.	41
1.4	A group of men celebrate New Year's Day with beer and a meal of noodles mixed with beans.	53
2.1	Two women wash and sort the cassava they have just harvested.	67
2.2	Mustafa, surrounded by family in Micuio.	82
3.1	Bare-chested Chinese men are surrounded by curious onlookers in Michumwa.	91
3.2	A man accused of being a witch, recovering from his ordeal.	95
3.3	A dead, bloated hippo washes ashore.	108
3.4	A woman stirs the pot of *ntchima* she just removed from the cooking fire.	111
3.5	A child is handed a bread roll, and others immediately outstretch their hands for a portion.	113
4.1	Albertina prepares lunch.	122
4.2	A group of young men snack on sugarcane before school.	131

4.3	Filomena pours water through ash to produce *vidule*.	137
4.4	Asha, surrounded by several generations of her grandchildren and "feces grandchildren."	144
5.1	Women attend a nutrition-education seminar at the health center.	158
5.2	A group of men share a meal, each taking from a common dish.	162

Preface

"But Arianna, why have you come here?" Alima asked me this question one afternoon as we sat on the veranda of her home, facing the interior courtyard.[1] Aisha, a two-year-old grandchild, clung to Alima's leg, having heard someone say earlier that white people eat children. Alima swatted with a long, bamboo pole at ducks and goats trying to nibble the rice drying on a reed mat nearby. She had been largely immobile since a fall in her garden the previous year, and so this had become the way she passed the day. Kali, a teenaged granddaughter, hung laundry at the other side of the yard. She had just washed the clothing in the lake with soap I had brought them the previous week. "Alhamdulilah" *(praise be to God; Arabic)*, Alima had spoken softly while bringing both hands to cover her face and then lowering them in unison before taking the small gift from my hands. "I told you already," I replied. "I want to write a book about Metangula." She nodded in understanding, if not with a little disappointment that asking this question again had not revealed additional information to make sense of my presence. It was unusual to see mzungu—a white person, like me—in this part of Africa, and especially one who spent the day wandering about town to visit with people.

Alima was someone I had come to know over many years of visiting Metangula, a small town in northern Mozambique. The first time we had met was when she was serving as the convener of a girls' initiation ritual. It was my initial visit to Metangula, and I had little understanding of what was going on. Patrick, my cultural guide and interpreter at the time, asked Alima the questions that I had about the girls' seclusion and the rituals they underwent at night. But Alima did not provide much in the way of answers. The problem was more than one of translation and familiarity; it was one of trust. I scribbled very little in my notebook that year, beside that I thought Alima seemed hostile and unwilling or unable to elaborate on the ceremony she oversaw. Over time, we developed a mutual fondness as we delved deeper into each other's lives. Years later, that day on her veranda, Alima jutted her chin toward the notebook in my lap. It was opened to where I had been recording notes on our conversation about her time as a FRELIMO soldier, witches, emotional states, and the capacities *of ancestors to act in the world of the living. I had used up the last few pages and was trying to find a blank spot to record a few more notes. "Do you know why your notebook is full, Arianna?" she asked. I looked up, unsure how to respond. "Because you are someone who laughs with other people. Another person's notebook could be empty."*

I conducted the research that I present in this volume in the small littoral town of Metangula in northern Mozambique. I consider myself extremely privileged to have had the time and the support to do so, as well as to have happened upon a location for field research that was such a great match for my interests and my capacities for fieldwork. Not only did I enjoy my time in Metangula, but personal quirks and the peculiarities of the situations that brought me there also made it possible for me to find my footing relatively quickly. That I was willing to laugh with people, and to laugh at myself, and that I repeatedly left and came back again (having stayed for extended periods in 2005, 2006, 2007, 2008, and 2010–11) were essential, I would come to learn, to establish the relationships that allowed my research to take place. That I am a bit slow at learning new languages further necessitated spending long amounts of time engaged in one-on-one or small-group conversation to parse out the meanings of concepts, ideas, and vocabulary that were unfamiliar to me. This forced upon myself and my interlocutors the paced approach to interactions and the patience through which rapport and nuance most effectively emerge.

Limitations in the data that resulted from my time in Metangula must be acknowledged. For example, local decorum where men and women are most always separate from one another meant that I tended to spend most of my time with women. As a result, my research most clearly reflects women's experiences and perspectives. Though I have no reason to suspect that women's cultural knowledge is much different from that of men's on the topics presented in this volume, the paucity that I do see resulting from this gender segregation is that for an ethnography about a lakeshore town, there is remarkably little information about fishing—a man's domain. I have no doubt that fishing is ripe for analysis in ways that are complementary to the ideas I have set forth in this volume, and the work of Jennifer Lee Johnson (2014; 2017) along the Ugandan shore of Lake Victoria suggests as much to be true. However, the study of fishing in Metangula awaits another time. In addition to spending the majority of my time with women, I also focused on the processing and consumption of food rather than its cultivation. I thus do not have much to say in this volume about fields, planting, and harvesting or related issues such as land allocation and disputes. I concentrate instead on the purchasing, cooking, distributing, and eating of foods as I observed and engaged in these practices while seated on verandas, hovering around market stalls, relaxing at bars, or crouched down near the cooking fire.

While the resulting observations may be incomplete, I would like to think that even with these limitations I was able to produce a rich analysis of the foodways in a single African town. That being said, I do not presume that what I have written here is all there is to say, nor that my words will serve as final proof of the subjects explicated. This is especially true given that very little scholarly attention has been accorded the Nyanja population along the eastern shore of Lake Niassa. Scholars have, in fact, conducted very little research in the broader Niassa Province at all. This seems to be a product of the region's remoteness and inaccessibility, in combination with a colonial administration suspicious of the intentions of social scientists, a postcolonial regime that worked hard to downplay ethnicity and race in an effort to promote national unity, and nearly thirty years of war that made research almost anywhere in Mozambique a precarious endeavor (West 1997, 199, 201). Several dozen explorers and colonial officers traveled through the region that would become Niassa, mainly in the late nineteenth and early twentieth centuries, and their notes provide some observations about the local inhabitants. But there are no examples of extended ethnographic attention given to the peoples of Niassa Province before 1964, when Nuno Valdez dos Santos published his appropriately titled *O desconhecido Niassa* (Unknown Niassa). Only one nominally ethnographic account has been written specific to Mozambique's lakeshore Nyanja, Helen E. P. van Koevering's 2005 polemic focused on promoting the role of women's church groups in combating female subordination. Academic research on Mozambique has also broadly focused, until very recently, on a narrow set of topics: the colonial period, the "civil war," and economic development (Gupta and Rodary 2017). All of this means that there is a lack of precedent and somewhat of a lacuna of comparative material for the present work.

The remoteness of Niassa continues to detract many individuals and organizations, foreign and Mozambican, from venturing into the region, unless they have to. The province has a national moniker as "end of the world" (*fim do mundo*) for reasons that include its low population density (less than 27 persons per square mile, in comparison to 72 nationally), lack of infrastructure (in 2010 there were 326 miles of paved roads to service Niassa's 49,829 square miles of land, an area around the size of North Korea), and history of non-incorporation into the Mozambican nation.[2] In the 1980s, the government's infamous "Operation Production" forcefully relocated urban citizens engaged in various perceived social ills (e.g., crime, alcoholism, vagrancy) to Niassa, among other remote areas of the country, for "reeducation," but also as punishment (Machava 2019). The northern provinces of Mozambique have a more recent reputation for violent Islamist insurgencies and, at least among expatriates, for being a "land of *bandidos* [bandits]," brought about by illegal mining and timber operations that create a sense of trepidation and the need to tread lightly lest you upset the wrong powerful person when passing through. Northern Mozambique is not, in other words, an easy place to live for anyone, and especially for a foreigner to work in a sustained manner without constant harassment and logistical challenges. And yet, there are signs that Niassa is becoming less of a research hinterland. This volume is the third ethnography on Niassa in as many years, joining Devaka Premawardhana's (2018) volume on Pentecostalism among the Makhuwa and Jonna Katto's (2019) cultural historical analysis of women ex-combatants in relation to emotion and landscape among the Yaawo. These two works, together with my own, collectively demand that Niassa be taken seriously as a part of Lusophone Africanist scholarship.³ The parallel attention of each of these volumes, directly or in spirit, to affect and relationality is reflective of the region's capacity to draw anthropologists in with the spirit of its peoples and the deliberateness with which everyday life is pursued.

I came upon Niassa myself purely by chance. Julio Mercader, an archaeologist then at George Washington University, later at University of Calgary, was looking for a graduate student to join him at the site of a Middle Stone Age excavation. He hoped to construct a museum that would contribute to development and keep artifacts local. I was a master's student in museum studies, and I jumped at the chance to return to Africa after previous academic, research, and travel experiences in West Africa. I first came to Metangula with Mercader in 2005 and again for the three summers that followed, helping with a project that culminated in the opening of Museu Local (Local Museum) in Metangula in 2007. From my first field season, I developed a fondness for Metangula. I applied to PhD programs as somewhat of an excuse to keep visiting and learning more about the people who lived there. This is why I call myself an accidental academic, and I am fully indebted to Mercader for the trajectory of my career. As for the museum, we handed the building and its exhibitions and collections over to the local government in 2008. The institution has, since that time, waxed and waned in the resources and the attention it has been afforded.

The research that I have conducted in Mozambique could not have been possible without the warm generosity, congenial conversers, and open hearts of the people I came to know in Metangula. I am particularly grateful to the following persons and their families for their valuable assistance in my physical and cultural navigation of the town: Abudo Chaibo Micaia; Albertina Salimo; Asha Saide; Benedita Bonifácio Machinga; Benjamin Kazule; Faustino Constantino; Elisa Chungo; Fatima Saide; Fernando Saide; Idalina Julio; João Tandamula; Lúcia Jorge; Lúcia Kambeu; Maria Chisindo; Maria Mayendayenda; Martha Amado; Mustafa Makwinja; Mwema Aissa; and Patuma Saide. The vast differences between the lives of researchers and research subjects in rural Africa create and reflect uneven power relations. This makes it perhaps naïve to assert that the individuals listed here became my "friends." I can definitively say, however, that I came to deeply care about these individuals and their families, and I would like to think they cared about me, too. Researchers often create inadvertent problems for their interlocutors (Howell 2017). By inserting myself into the lives of these and other individuals in Metangula, I do hope that I have not harmed any of them, and particularly those whose thoughts and experiences directly inform this book.

I extend special thanks also to Helena Augusto and Judite Franco Kakhongue, who carried out dietary and demographic surveys on my behalf, and to Lourenço Thawe, who held down the fort between field seasons and faithfully and gently reminded me of the formalities and expectations of good relations. I also graciously thank the 102 households that participated in the dietary survey (especially the 97 that hung in through the end); the local chapter of Organização das Mulheres Moçambicanas (OMM), which accepted my attempts to dance as a contribution toward Mozambican nationalism; the Estamos *activistas* (activists), for their tireless health education campaigning, at which I never ceased to be surprised; Inácio Minícua and Beatriz Jaime in the Lago office of the Ministry of Education and Culture, for attending to my unusual requests and also defending me from periodic immigration inquiries; Chilombe Barnabe Mpalila, the former chief of Metangula, for granting permission and ensuring support for the work to the extent of his capacities; and the staff at Metangula's health center, for patiently obliging when I popped in for a chat.

Outside of Metangula there were many individuals I encountered in Mozambique and also in Malawi, primarily in university settings and government offices, who helped me in gaining access to materials that influenced the development of my research agenda, who acted as sounding boards for preliminary ideas, or who offered logistical support. Among these individuals I would like to especially thank Hilário Madiquida, Mussa Raja, and Armindo Ngunga at Universidade Eduardo Mondlane (UEM) in Maputo; Marcela Libombo and Gustavo Mahoque at the Maputo office of Secretariado Técnico de Segurança Alimentar e Nutricional (SETSAN); Anacleto Machava at the American Embassy in Maputo; and Ermelinda Mapasse at Universidade Pedagógica in Nampula. Special thanks are also due to inadvertent Maputo liaison Drew Thompson; Justin and Sofia Sondergaärd, for their hospitality in Lichinga; gracious overseas communications coordinator Andreas Zeman; and Maya Litscher, along with her many nieces and nephews at Mbuna Bay, for their generous hospitality. Additional support in Malawi came from Vuwa Phiri, François Nsengiumva, and Paul Kishindo at the University of Malawi, Chancellor College; Veronica Jana at the Society of Malawi Journal library in Blantyre; Experencia Madalitso Jalasi and Daimon Kambewa at Lilongwe University of Agriculture and Natural Resources (then University of Malawi, Bunda College); Menno Welling of African Heritage Research and Consultancy in Zomba; and Baptist missionary Ian Dicks.

Attending graduate school in Boston, I was lucky to have a cadre of Africanist mentors who facilitated some of the above contacts. I thank especially Jeanne Penvenne and Pauline Peters, for sharing their figurative rolodexes with me and for their more general support of my doctoral journey and beyond. Boston also gifted me Parker Shipton, who continues to amaze me with his capacity to be more efficient than Google Scholar for finding literature and who is unparalleled in posing questions that get people thinking deeply and creatively about anthropological subjects. I must make special mention, too, of James C. McCann, who inadvertently steered me in the direction of investigating local foodways when he expressed such shock that there was a pocket of cassava eaters in the middle of the African maize belt and who thoughtfully expanded our graduate seminar's thinking about Africa's "glutinous balls." My initial doctoral research project would have had me investigating local responses to a South African vacation home development project, a venture very much in line with trends of monetizing conservation in Mozambique (Diallo and Rodary 2017), but one that fell apart and left me floundering for direction just as I was entering graduate school. McCann guided me to use intellectual curiosity in picking up the pieces. Joanna Davidson taught me to step back and look at what was on the table once I had fit those pieces together. I would be remiss to not also mention here the influence of James A. Pritchett in guiding my choice of Boston University for graduate training. He knew that I needed the camaraderie and community of the African Studies Center to grow as a scholar. Who I have become is a direct result of how easy it was to trust him. Some of the ideas represented in this book developed in conversation with Laura Ann Twagira, Casey Golomski, and Shelby Carpenter through a Boston-based writing group that pushed us all to the limits of our academic productivity. I also received valuable feedback on earlier drafts of this research from Robert Weller, Kimberly Arkin, En-Chieh Chao, Ceren Ergenc, Eric Kelley, Lucia Huwy-Min Liu, and Mentor Mustafa. I wish to also express gratitude for my broader cohort at Boston University, especially Melissa Graboyes, Alfredo Burlando, Andrea Mosterman, Masse Ndiaye, Lynsey Farrell, Natalie Mettler, Andrew Armstrong, Abel Djassi Amado, Christopher Annear, and Lilly Havstad.

Research and writing are expensive. I am grateful to have received financial support for this project from DDRA Fulbright Hays, the United States Ambassador's Fund for Cultural Preservation, and a Foreign Language and Area Studies (FLAS) fellowship. I received additional funding from the Cora DuBois Charitable Trust and from the Boston University Department of Anthropology, African Studies Center, and Office of the Dean. At California State University San Bernardino (CSUSB), the Office of the Dean and the Office of Sponsored Research supported a return trip to Mozambique in 2017. The CSUSB Center for International Studies and Programs partially financed the time it took to write this book. The Institute for Child Development and Family Relations and the Faculty Center for Excellence at CSUSB support the Writing Accountability Group (WAG), through which I was able to find the motivation to write and revise this volume. I hope that the contributions I make here are found to help further the missions and goals of this diverse array of supporters.

I have previously discussed some of the ideas that appear in this book in chapters published in the edited volumes *Cooking Cultures: Convergent Histories of Food and Feeling* (Banerjee-Dube 2016) and *The Routledge Handbook of Medi-*

cal Anthropology (Manderson, Cartwright, and Hardon 2016), as well as in my articles "The Tongue Only Works without Worries: Sentiment and Sustenance in a Mozambican Town" in *Food and Foodways* (2013), "Enacting Compassion: Hold/Cold, Illness and Taboos in Northern Mozambique" in *Journal of Southern African Studies* (2017), and "¿Qué es Humano? Tabús Alimentarios y Antropofagia en el Noroeste de Mozambique?" in *Estudios de Asia y África* (2015). I thank the anonymous reviewers who provided feedback on these manuscripts and the editors and publishers who brought them to print, along with those for the present volume. I am also deeply indebted to Experencia Madalitso Jalasi, for her assistance with transcriptions and translations and also for her very helpful feedback on an earlier draft of the present text. While the final tome would not have been possible without all of the persons, funders, and institutions mentioned above, I alone take full responsibility for any errors and misrepresentations in the resultant manuscript.

I must also be indulgent in recognizing my family for providing the nourishment, in all senses of the term, that I needed to persist in bringing this book to publication. Steve, my spouse, helped with data entry while we lived in Mozambique. He, along with Nathan and Corinne (the children who came after we returned), also patiently allowed me the space and the time that I needed to complete this volume. My mom and dad, Gail and George, along with my sister, Julianna, have also bore with me through all the transportation mishaps, medical scares, and minimal communications for months at a time as I traveled in and resided on the African continent, and too often while at home in the United States as well.

Finally, I dedicate this work to two people: Patrick Chimutha and Cecilia Kazule. They are dearly missed. *Kaka ndi dada, ndikuthokoza. Tikukupemphani kuti mupitilize kutipenyelera ndi kutipatcha mtendere.*

Notes

1. I use pseudonyms throughout this volume to protect the identities of individuals whose lives are depicted. Exceptions include individuals whose identity is essential to their specialized knowledge or wisdom as a subject expert, project employees, and one man who explicitly asked that I use his real name in the hope that disseminating his story might help him to find his father.
2. Population density and paved road statistics calculated by converting data available in the Mozambican National Institute of Statistics' Statistical Yearbook for 2010 (INE 2011, 13, 72) into imperial units.
3. Earlier ethnographic works focused on Niassa include two volumes commissioned by the country's Cultural Heritage Research Institute (ARPAC), the first on dances (Tamele and Vilanculo 2003) and the second on marriage and other life-stage rituals (António and Omar 2007). Francisco Lerma Martinez's (2009) ethnographic inventory of the Makhuwa provides particular insight on local cosmology, as does João Baptista Amide's (2008) trea-

tise on the history and culture of the Yaawo. Additional ethnographies geographically centered in northern Mozambique include works by Harry West (2005) on memory, Liazzat Bonate (2006) on matriliny, Harri Englund (2002) on permeability and manipulation of national borders, Singe Arnfred (2007; 2011) on gender and sexuality, and Daria Trentini (2016a; 2016b) on religion and spiritual insecurity.

Notes on Text

The research for this ethnography took place in the Lago District in Mozambique's Niassa Province. The predominant language in this region is Chinyanja, a Bantu language closely related to Chichewa. Residents in the Lago District recognize three local dialects of Chinyanja, geographically distributed along the eastern coast of Lake Niassa. For the most part, this book records Chinyanja as it is spoken in the town of Metangula—a dialect known locally as Amalaba Chinyanja, which is also spoken north through to the village of Ngoo. North of Ngoo, lakeshore residents speak the Ahuti dialect, and south of Metangula through Meluluca, residents speak the Amalimba dialect. South of Meluluca, lakeshore residents speak Chichewa.

Chinyanja does not have a standardized orthography. In transcribing Chinyanja, I have modeled my spelling on the orthography of Chichewa, an official language in Malawi. There are exceptions, however, such as where phonology clearly diverged from Chichewa's standardized forms. An example is the staple food of the region, pronounced *ntchima* in Chinyanja, but *nsima* in Chichewa. Other examples include the verb "to wake up," which is *kuuka* in Chinyanja and *kudzuka* in Chichewa, and the noun for "intelligence," which is pronounced *njeru* in Chinyanja and *nzeru* in Chichewa. I have also retained place names as they are spelled in Mozambique, for example "Cóbuè" rather than "Kobwe" (the letters "k," "w" and "y" have only recently been added to Portuguese, the national language in Mozambique). A Portuguese orthography for the transcription of Chinyanja, while perhaps a step forward in Mozambican nationalism, would make awkward reading for regional scholars and for residents in Lago, who are familiar with reading in Chichewa due to the import of products from Malawi.

Chinyanja, like Chichewa and other Bantu languages, uses noun class-based conjugation for verbs and adjectives, as well as a host of suffixes, prefixes, and infixes that will be unfamiliar structures to many readers. When encountering the Chinyanja terminology included in this volume, keep in mind that subject and verb are combined into a single word. For example, take the root verb *-pita* (go). "I go" would be *ndipita*, and "you go" would be *mupita*. Verbs in the infinitive form begin with *ku-*; for example, *kupita* is "to go." It is also worth noting that adjectives are modified in Chinyanja (again, as with other Bantu languages) dependent on noun class and number, and that noun number (singular, plural) is marked through a prefix. For example, the root adjective *-kulu* (big) would be conjugated *munthu wamkulu* (big person), *mtengo waukulu* (big tree), *chinthu chachikulu* (big thing), *mbuzi yaikulu* (big goat), but also *anthu akulu* (big people), *mitengo yaikulu* (big trees), *zinthu zazikulu* (big things), and so forth. Thus, the same word (in the aforementioned example, "big") appears in multiple formulations.

I have selected to leave several foreign words in their non-English form throughout this volume. I use this technique only where the approximate English equivalent cannot evoke the appropriate set of meanings. These terms, and other common foreign-language terms and place names frequently used in this volume, are included in the glossary.

Abbreviations

AMETRAMO	Associação dos Médicos Tradicionais de Moçambique, Association of Mozambican Traditional Doctors
ARPAC	Arquivo de Património Cultural, Cultural Patrimony Archive
BMI	Body mass index
FRELIMO	Frente de Libertação de Moçambique, Liberation Front of Mozambique, originally a militia group fighting for independence from Portugal, later a major political party in Mozambique (Frelimo)
HIV/AIDS	Human immunodeficiency virus / acquired immunodeficiency syndrome
OMM	Organização das Mulheres Moçambicanas, Organization of Mozambican Women
RENAMO	Resistência Nacional Moçambicana, Mozambican National Resistance, originally a militia group fighting against Frelimo in a sixteen-year post-independence "civil war," later a major political party in Mozambique (Renamo)
SETSAN	Secretariado Técnica de Segurança Alimentar e Nutrição, Technical Secretariat of Food Security and Nutrition
STD	Sexually transmitted disease, used here as inclusive of their precursor sexually transmitted infections (STIs).
UMCA	Universities' Mission to Central Africa
WHO	World Health Organization

Introduction

Monica was a slender woman in her early forties—or maybe her late forties. She was not sure. She sat on the back porch of her home, folding small quantities of baking soda into scraps of paper ripped from a child's school exercise book. She would sell the packets to neighbors and perhaps turn a small profit. Monica's sister Elisa sat next to her on a woven reed mat. She was combing her hair in preparation for tying small tufts of it into braids or knots. The two women looked out from the porch into the inner courtyard of their compound. They had swept the earthen ground that morning, as they did every morning, to remove the debris of meal preparation, the fallen leaves, and the loose layer of soil deposited by the wind since the last go-around the day before. Several chickens pecked about—selling them was another small business venture Monica had started.

The yard was at the center of a rectangular property, framed on three sides by small homes made carefully of mud bricks and thatched roofing and on the fourth side by a fence fashioned from bamboo and twine. The three buildings each had a veranda facing the courtyard, which was where most of the day's activities took place. Monica and Elisa sat near the door to the home where Monica stayed along with her four youngest children. Hers was the only building in the compound that was whitewashed—the edifice smeared in a mixture of lime and water—making it stand out starkly against a rural African landscape dominated by browns and greens. Monica's surname was etched into the lime coating just to the left of the front door—Salimo. To the right of the same door was an electricity box that the government had installed the previous year, as they did throughout the town of Metangula. Only a small percentage of households had the funds to activate the connection. Monica's was not one of them.

Directly across the courtyard from Monica's home used to be the kitchen and stockroom, but she had converted them into a living space by adding sheets across the two doorways and relocating the pots, buckets, and basins that used to be stored there into the front room of her own home. When I arrived in Metangula in February of 2010, I remember watching one of the sheets billow back and forth with the wind, hiding and revealing that Diana was inside, content and in awe of a belly that was growing with pregnancy. Diana was the daughter of Filomena, a woman whose home was a few hundred yards closer to the lakeshore than Monica's. Filomena had formerly lived in Micuio, a small and tight-knit neighborhood separated from the rest of Metangula by several miles of lowland fields where townspeople grew cassava and increasingly maize, interspersed with small plots of cowpeas, bananas, and a handful of other crops. The father of the child in Diana's belly was Erasto, Monica's "nephew"—a cousin of Agostinho, a minibus driver whose route plied the seventy miles between Metangula and the provincial capital Lichinga, back and forth, transporting passengers and their goods along the deteriorating tarred road. Agostinho slept at the Salimo household when nightfall found him in Metangula or when his vehicle required repair before making the return trip to Lichinga. Monica had begun hosting Agostinho when they struck up a friendship, and she had taken in Diana and Erasto when they decided to cohabitate after realizing they would have a child together. The third building, situated between the two previously described and opposite the fence, was where Monica's sister Elisa lived with her two young daughters, Andrea and Amelia. Elisa had just moved to Metangula from Lichinga, where she was raised from a young age by an aunt. She had recently divorced, and with nowhere else to go, she had moved in with Monica. The sisters were usually pleasant to one another when face-to-face, but Monica was also prone to complaining that Elisa was not contributing her fair share to maintaining their homestead and that she acted selfishly. She also suspected that Elisa had AIDS.

That day on the porch Monica and Elisa joked, bantered, and gossiped as usual, about their families and their friends, occasionally taking a moment to explain the background details they thought pertinent for me to follow the conversation. There had been a fire at a neighboring house the previous week. Monica playfully suggested that this made her apprehensive about using her own new cooking hutch, a small earthen shelter with a grass roof in the corner of the yard. Elisa had heard that Patuma, a traditional healer living on the hillside, had gotten into a fight with Clara, the woman a few households over who walked with a limp, when one removed the other's water jugs holding her place in line at the pump. To yell at one another about the incident was important, Elisa explained to me, so as to clear their hearts. Only a witch would hide their anger, just smiling and carrying on as usual while secretly plotting revenge. Avoiding suspicions of witchcraft would be especially important for Patuma, given her profession—some healers were rumored to use the label of sing'anga (*traditional healer*) as a cover for nefarious or occult leanings—but also for Clara, whose barrenness put her at risk of losing her husband permanently to his other wife, who was pregnant and dangerously overdue.

When the subject of conversation got around to Monica's appearance, Elisa drew my attention to the fact that her sister had recently rubbed oil onto her skin as a moisturizer and asked a neighbor to braid her hair. I had actually noticed myself that Monica seemed to be glowing as of late, a far cry from her usual sunken cheeks, ashen complexion, and unkempt hair. Elisa explained very empirically that the transformation in Monica's appearance had come about because Monica had recently "found a husband," meaning a serial sexual partner. This implied a reliable source of income and food. Monica often lacked these things. Though she sold baking soda and the occasional chicken, or sometimes small cuttings from the roll of tobacco Agostinho had given her as a gift, she earned only a meager amount with which to purchase necessities to complement the rice and cassava she grew on a lowland farm. Elisa looked at me directly and added in a quiet but jovial tone that Monica was no longer lacking in vitamina *(vitamins)*. I assumed that she was referring to Monica's improved diet. Only later would I learn that she was euphemistically referring to a different sort of "eating."

Food in Anthropology and in Africa

Monica Salimo lived in Metangula, a small town located on the eastern shore of Lake Niassa in northwest Mozambique. This book is not about Monica, though my experiences with her and her extended family influenced what I present on the pages that follow, and they are featured in vignettes throughout the text. The focus of the volume is, instead, food as a thread for stitching together the everyday practices through which people living in Metangula defined, debated, and pursued a nourishing life in the opening decades of the twenty-first century. By using the term "nourishing" I intend to evoke both the act of provisioning substance for growth and wellness and the quality of that substance itself. "Nourishing" as both verb and adjective inherently maps onto alimentation. But I concentrate in this volume on neither the biologically nutritive attributes of food nor the acute effects on health and development that access to food entails, though these are both critically important inquiries and are, at opportune moments, engaged. While sustenance is integral to survival of the physical self, my attention in this volume is nourishment of the metaphysical and moral person. This is an organic result of my investigation, through which it quickly became apparent that I could only elucidate why the people of Metangula ate what they ate by first understanding their motivations for eating at all. Foodways—those beliefs and behaviors surrounding production, distribution, preparation, consumption, and definition of food (Counihan 1999)—were profoundly and inextricably bound up with personhood—the ideological forces and expectations that give reason, order, moral guidance, and meaning to (but do not determine) social life and lived experience. As a result of this approach, I devote much more ink to issues like ontology, cosmology, epistemology, and affect than topics perhaps expected in a volume focused on African food, like agriculture, land ownership, market access, nutrition, and food security.

To summarize ideas presented in the pages that follow, I found that humanity in Metangula—in the sense of humans as a biological species distinct from other animals, their benevolence, and the social status earned or enabled through the life course—entailed multidimensionality. As is common throughout sub-Saharan Africa (Beattie 1980; Fortes 1987; Jackson and Karp 1990; Menkiti 1984; Ogude 2018; Riesman 1986), human "persons" in Metangula were conceived as composite beings, where relationships with others are fundamental. Here the individual self emerges through embeddedness and affinity, rather than being conceived of as independent, separate in function and self-actualization from others, and with powers restricted to single bodies. Where this volume builds on extant studies of African personhood is in its ethnographic attention to practices of "unfoldment" (Ramose 1999), or the active and continuous work through which individuals deepen humanity (both their own, and the totality of human beings') through everyday (quotidian) and every day (the inexorable constancy of) pro-social, unifying, and revitalizing acts. Throughout the volume, I aim to make clear that this orientation was not a matter of rote habitus or instinctual preference. It was, rather, an individually executed and unrelenting choice at a perpetual series of crossroads. This implies that there was always the possibility and attraction of choosing a more insular orientation through actions that privileged, for example, selfishness, greed, and apathy.

Humanity was thus not as much a permanent state as it was a perpetual process of becoming that demanded the crafting, maintenance, and deepening of life-enhancing relationships through generative acts. In this light "nourishment" emerged as much through eating as it did in richly layered and experienced foodways. The connection of food and self thus extends in this volume beyond alimentation, for example to the obtaining, cooking, and sharing of meals—each performed in ways that demonstrated capacity for reason, compassion, and consideration of others, along with a broader constitution of the self as interdependent, performative, and relational. These were traits that distinguished persons from their alters, namely animals and witches. Upon the intentional and cultivated prioritization of these characteristics, humanity was conceived to depend. In the pages that follow, I describe how embodiment of the "everyday" and "every day" project of being and becoming human was bound up with food classification and taboos, physiology, market principles, exchange relationships, cooking, meal etiquette, evaluation and understanding of body size and weight, and the management of malnutrition, among other manifestations. Through these examples, I aim to demonstrate the work involved to establish, preserve, revitalize, and nourish humanity.

In addition to making a deeply ethnographic and food-focused contribution to the rich history of African and Africanist thinking and writing about continental patterns in personhood (sometimes subsumed under the term Ubuntu, elaborated in chapter 2), this volume rests on the shoulders of an extensive body of scholarship known as "food studies," particularly the holistic analyses of eating and drinking around the world that have been contributed by anthropologists.

To attempt a review of this vast literature would be out of place. It is worth noting, however, that the origins of the "anthropology of food" are often traced to southern Africa, and specifically to Audrey Richards's ethnographic studies of the Bemba in what is today Zambia. While her *Hunger and Work in a Savage Tribe* was published in 1932, it is her later *Land, Labour and Diet in Northern Rhodesia* (1939) that is better remembered for its intricate detailing of the production of food (what and how), its consumption (and attendant contexts of distribution, reciprocity, and hospitality), and the nutritional impact of these practices. In her focus on physiological needs (here, food) at the root of social institutions, Richards's work was clearly functionalist in its orientation—the dominant theoretical lens for anthropologists at the time. The trajectory of anthropological studies of food has since proceeded in tandem with the discipline as a whole—with contributions from structuralists, materialists, and political economists, for example, as well as thematic foci on topics such as gender, identity, and globalization.[1]

Among this diverse and burgeoning body of literature, Richards's volumes continue to be upheld as exemplary for their comprehensiveness, as well as for their blending of symbolic and biological considerations. Today the former is most often taken up as the "anthropology of food" (food as a system of communication and praxis that provides meanings and reveals patterns in social behaviors), and the latter as "nutritional anthropology" (food as biological imperative, impacted by social processes, but resulting in health outcomes to be studied through a combination of methods from nutritional science, medicine, and anthropology). Adherents of both approaches lament their continued separation (Chrzan 2013; Dirks and Hunter 2013; Ham 2017; Holtzman 2009)—mind and body, mental and material, utility and reason, apart, each pairing split for separate inquiry. The present volume contributes to dismantling this Cartesian divide, but less through a blending of the two anthropological approaches than in its attentiveness to the inextricable entwining of their foci. While not precisely "multisensory" (Howes 2019) or "tasteful" (Stoller 1989) ethnography, nor "gustemology" (Sutton 2010), affect scholars will take interest in this volume's attention to vitality as experienced with the body *and* the mind, in tandem and riposte, and to taste as both culturally situated and unconfined to the carnal senses. These contributions build on previous studies of the sensory experience as an entry point for exploring other aspects of culture (Howes 1991; Korsmeyer 2005; Sutton 2010). Entering directly into debates about affect theory is not, however, among my own aims.

This book also contributes to a rich literature attentive to food as it folds into relationality. Anita von Poser (2013), for example, offers a carefully detailed consideration of foodways as a realm for making and undoing ties of kinship in Papua New Guinea. Through exchange of sago, the staple crop, individuals show that they are "watching others and being watched," entwining planting, cooking, and sharing meals with the expression of empathy and transparency of feelings through which relationships become binding. Janet Carsten (1995) similarly assesses exchange of nourishment and commensality as enabling individuals to become persons in Malaysia through their full participation in social relations, thus processually making them into kin. Miriam Kahn (1986) also found food to be integral to relationality in Melanesia, with a focus on the asymmetry and ambivalence between men and women, and the use of "hunger" as a metaphor for the repression of greed, which was the outcome of failures to invest in social relationships. Shifting back to Africa, Ramah McKay (2018) takes a different approach, providing a forceful critique of the ways in which food aid in Mozambique operates as if health and wellness are located in individual bodies. Instead, she asserts, persons are inherently relational, and the distribution and consumption of food thus integral to the performance and expansion of networks of care. For McKay, these networks provide an important safety net in times of need. Paul Wenzel Geissler and Ruth Jane Prince (2010) instead conceive of the connectivity between individuals as integral to their very being. The pair's ethnography on "touch" among the Luo in Kenya focuses on the intertwining of persons through shared substance (for example, through food) and how these encounters enable life to continue in a manner that makes possible the transformative growth through which individual and collective life continues.

In their metaphysical approach to commensality, I find much kinship with Geissler and Prince's volume and also with the broader body of Africanist literature on substances, flows, health, and relatedness on which their work builds and to which it contributes (Devisch 1991; Myhre 2018; Setel 1999; Taylor 1992; Weiss 1996). Of these works, Brad Weiss's (1996) analysis of Haya (Tanzania) cosmology is of particular interest for its attention to "moral gastronomy," through which lived worlds are "made" and embodied through production, exchange, and consumption of food. In his attention to the shifting grounds on which foodways are performed and evaluated, Weiss's volume was also a predecessor to Jon Holtzman's (2009) ethnography on Samburu (Kenya) foodways as a complex site for thinking about, expressing, and experiencing the ambiguities, ambivalences, and contradictions of historical and emergent changes to social relations, particularly as they align with gender and age. Holtzman's richly detailed volume is also noteworthy for its assertion that food is not an arbitrary domain for the meeting of history, meaning, and practice. It is the simultaneity of food as material, social, and symbolic and the sensuousness and embodiment associated with eating that give it a special (though not unique) ability to tie everyday experience to broader cultural patterns and to link morality with memory.

Kristin D. Phillips (2018) is likewise interested in the "moral landscape" of patronage, reciprocity, and mutual support as it plays out in rural Tanzanian foodways. Mindful of the paradoxical and simultaneous existence of scarcity and abundance, she explodes the singularity and the banality of "hunger," finding that the experience of being without food patterns relationships between individuals, approaches to God, entanglements with government, and everyday life more broadly. In her consideration of morality and relationality as driving food-related ideas and practices, Phillips's approach is quite similar to mine. But where Phillips is attentive to the social experiences and material conditions through which a pro-social moral compass has emerged, my own work frontloads mutuality as reflective of long-standing ontological engagement in questions about the nature of being and becoming human, which in turn guide social experience and material condition.

The present volume additionally builds upon a growing and hearty stock of food-focused ethnographies about peoples and cultures of Africa.[2] It is important to note that this wealth of anthropological studies, however, makes up only a small, almost negligible, fraction of works attentive to African alimentation. The production, preparation, and consumption of food in Africa is more often written of—in scholarly, as well as gray literature from nonprofits and government entities—in relation to core themes like nutrition (how it is lacking), food policies (strengthening or changing them), food security (causes and coping mechanisms for famine), and agriculture (systems for controlling and improving crop outcomes).[3] While these topics are each important and deserving of attention and their analyses often insightful, the predominance of these perspectives can lead to a portrait of the continent's foodways as dictated by or even restricted to the project of survival. In popular culture the same is true—bookstore sections on cookery are noticeably thin in their representation of Africa in comparison to other world regions, and laypersons are more likely to associate Africa with famine than with cuisine. These realities have the impact of sidelining, in the words of historian James C. McCann, "Africa's fundamental energy and creativity in the history of cooking, and the way the flavors and textures of food adds character and quality to life's daily rhythms" (2012, 199–200). The affective experience of African eating, in other words, is elided, along with the potential for African agency and cultural meaning. The lens of Africans as victims and of African societies as deficient, passive, and timeless (whereas those in the global north are righteous, modern heroes engaged in beneficence; Phillips 2018) further contributes to the perpetuation of widespread misconceptions and stereotypes about the continent as inferior and in need of foreign interventions in order for its countries to develop and its peoples to civilize (Keim and Somerville 2018; Wainaina 2005).

Lack of public awareness of the complexities of African cuisine is understandable. The majority of the sub-Saharan African population relies on small-scale subsistence farming (Hanson 2018), poverty is pervasive (World Bank 2018), malnutrition is widespread (Akombi et al. 2017), and dietary staples are repetitive and calorie dense. Traditional meals for the African subcontinent are almost always made up of a stodgy mass of flour and water that serves as the main source of calories, accompanied by a side dish with ingredients that vary little except with environmental and financial seasonality (Osseo-Asare 2005). The consistency, constancy, and bland (or sometimes pungent) flavors of African diets make them not only unpleasant to many unaccustomed consumers, but also incomprehensible. Why anyone would voluntarily eat such fare is easily conceivable as little more than the product of limited resources. But evaluations of African diets in this manner ignore the fact that many Africans *do* perceive variety in their "simple" dishes, mild spicing arguably allowing for an appreciation of intrinsic flavors and texture variations that are both likely underappreciated by foreigners whose palates are not trained to perceive these subtle differentiations (Ikpe 1994; Lentz 1999; Messer 1984). Research has shown that many Africans also evaluate their culinary fare as being in no way lacking or inferior (de Garine 1997; Lentz 1999) and that Africans with the financial and logistical means to adopt completely new food styles often choose not to (de Garine 1997; Ikpe 1994; Hansen 1999; M. Johnson 2016).

What I aim to put forth in the present volume, then, at its most basic level, is that simplicity and necessity need not indicate total focus of alimentation on meeting biological needs. Planting crops, harvesting produce, processing raw foods, and preparing meals, in other words, garner carbohydrates, fats, and proteins, yes. But nutritive ends are rarely the full extent of what these processes and products accomplish, anywhere. Sustenance, the seemingly universal rationale for eating, does not drive all alimentary behavior. This is true even where local diet might seem to an outside observer to be oriented toward little more, and even when the vocabulary of nutrition has been taken up (as it has been in Metangula) as the language through which motivations for and results of eating are discussed. My more complex aim is to provide a detailed case study of foodways as a matter of nourishing life, for in Metangula it was only through performing generative acts that enhanced the wellness of others (in this volume, as focused on alimentation) that a person could experience the fullness of humanity. Understanding the dimensions of nourishment—inclusive of, but also beyond nutrition—in Metangula requires an ethnographic lens, a willingness to retrain one's gustatory palate, and above all the intimate engagement of the place and its people.

Bem Vindo Metangula (Welcome to Metangula)

The Mozambican town of Metangula, where this ethnography is based, stretches approximately two miles east to west and about five miles north-to-south as the bird flies, but much of this area is either water or mountain terrain. The town itself is situated along a thin strip of habitable land, where a majority of the residents reside in six densely populated neighborhoods (Seli, Michenga, Thungo, Sanjala, Chipili, and Micuio) sandwiched between the bays, rocky outcrops, and sandy beaches of Lake Niassa on one side and the steep foothills of Mount Chifuli on the other. The undulating landscape between is covered in the remnants of semi-deciduous miombo woodlands and dotted with towering baobabs

Figure 0.1. Metangula, from the Sanjala hill looking north toward Mount Chifuli onto the neighborhoods of Seli and Nchenga. Photo by the author.

and expansive mango trees. A small peninsula juts into the lake, supporting additional residences and much of the town's government infrastructure. Metangula is the capital of Lago District, the westernmost district in Niassa Province, which itself sits in the far northwest corner of Mozambique and borders both Malawi and Tanzania. Metangula town is also the administrative headquarters for the Municipality of Metangula, a decentralized local governing unit that includes its own six neighborhoods and also six surrounding villages (Chuanga, Chigoma, Michumwa, Mpeluca, Capueleza, and Mifungo).[4] At the time of research, government presence included district and municipal offices, along with a naval base, police headquarters, and a level-one health center (one tier below a hospital). Metangula also proudly boasted a community radio station, an expansive Catholic church, and the only gas station west of the provincial capital of Lichinga.

Lago District gets its name from Lake Niassa. *Lago* means "lake" in Portuguese. It was David Livingstone who named the lake "Niassa" when he mythically became the first foreigner to set eyes on the body of water while on a circuitous tour of the region that resulted in his quest to end the east African slave trade (as well as the epigram "Dr. Livingstone, I presume").[5] The body of water had before that time been known to the outside world mainly through hearsay and marked vaguely on maps with names such as Zaflan, Zambre, Hemozura, Maravi, Nyanja Grande, Nyinyesi, Sumba, and Uniamesi (Ransford 1966, 11). Of course, the local population had known of the lake for as long as they had been living in the region, which by most accounts was, at the time, several hundred years. Others, probably hunter-gatherers known locally as "Batwa" or "Akafula," had been living there for about two thousand years before that (Morris 2016), and they had surely noticed the body of water, too. When Livingstone spied the vast inland lake—the third largest in Africa and eighth largest in the world—during his travels, he asked what it was called. A porter reportedly told him that it was "Niarra," which meant "lake" or "large body of water" in his language. Livingstone heard "Niassa," and so he called it "Lake Niassa," creating, as with so many other geographic features in Africa, a repetitious proper name derived from a common noun (here, "Lake Lake"). When the Nyasaland Protectorate, for which the lake served as an eastern border, declared independence from Britain in 1964 and became Malawi, the new government renamed Lake Niassa as "Lake Malawi." Tanzania and Mozambique, which border the body of water on the opposite shore, however, continue to call it "Niassa," though Tanzania spells it "Nyasa," giving the lake three official names. In this volume, I will use the label preferred in Mozambique—Lake Niassa.

I would like to stress at the outset of this book that I have depicted the town of Metangula at a particular moment in time, hovering around the year 2010. To respect and reflect that reality, I have written in the past tense about the beliefs, values, activities, and organizational structures that I engaged with. This feels a bit awkward. While avoiding some of the pitfalls of depicting a people and place as existing in an unchanging and ahistorical "ethnographic present" (Fabian 1991), writing in the past tense at the same time freezes temporality in a way that suggests that it is no longer in existence (Archambault 2017, 21). At least some of what I have written about here no doubt continues into the present, making use of the past tense feel like a slight. But this choice seemed necessary in order to acknowledge culture as something more than a set of static behaviors and beliefs—mandate, resolute, and unresponsive to a world where the parameters of living shape-shift over time. Culture is best conceived of as principles used to negotiate acceptable and tenuous solutions to contemporaneous contradictions, ambiguities, and circumstances. These things are ideally explored in a contextualized space and time. And so, here we are.

Engaging with a place—whether past, present, or future—requires the capacity to envision it. To give you, the reader, the ability to imagine the lakeshore town of Metangula as the setting for this ethnography, allow me to paint a picture of what it was like there when my research took place. It is a June morning, let us say, which means that it would be the drier and cooler of the two seasons. The air would be crisp, but not cold. Being near to the equator, the sun would begin to lighten the sky above the mountains around 5:00 a.m., as it would year-round. Those with a charged cell phone or a functioning watch might have referred to their formalized timepiece to know the exact hour of sunrise. Most residents of Metangula, however, did not own such luxuries. "Come back when the sun is like this," they would tell me when I came calling and they were busy with other matters, signaling when I should return with their arm held out at an angle that indicated where the sun would be in the sky when they would be ready to receive me.⁶ The day would be punctuated with other reminders that time was passing—a rooster's crow, prayer calls from one of the mosques, mobs of uniformed schoolchildren coming from and going to morning or afternoon classes, and the predictable onset and cessation of scheduled radio programming.

On this morning, like any morning, there would also be a steady stream of residents walking the radiating dirt paths that organized households along rough thoroughfares and connected the neighborhoods of Metangula. Many of the women would be walking with infants or small children strapped to their backs with colorful *capulanas*, versatile cloth panels commonly used throughout Africa as a sling for carrying small children, but also as women's clothing by wrapping it around the hips or above the chest and securing it with a tug in one direction and a tuck in the other. These women would be greeting one another using teknonymy, referencing individuals by their children's names, or substituting kin terms like *titia* (auntie, from Portuguese *tia*) or *kaka* (brother) for a personal name. Such practices are common in societies that emphasize the importance of relationships for developing individual identities. In their encounters, these women would ask about one another's wellness: *Mwauka bwanji amake Fani?* (How did you wake up, Fani's mother?); *Ndauka, dada* (I awoke [well], sister). Most residents in Metangula spoke Chinyanja as their primary language. Government offices and schools in Metangula, however, operated in Portuguese, a reminder of Mozambique's history as the colonial-era territory of Portuguese East Africa. The nation has been free of Portuguese rule only since 1975.

Chinyanja speakers are typically identified as culturally Nyanja, and they share much affinity with others grouped in the "Maravi Cluster," a label describing Bantu-speaking matrilineal peoples in southeast Africa north of the Zambezi River, south of the Rovuma River, and east of the Luangwa River, predominantly living in the modern nation-states of Malawi, Mozambique, and Zambia. Other groups typically labeled "Maravi" include the Chewa, Mang'anja, Chipeta, Mbo, Nsenga, and Zimba.⁷ Cultural affinities are also strong with the Yaawo, Makhuwa, Sena, and Tumbuka. Key shared (though not unique) characteristics of Maravi populations include an emphasis on the importance of sibling relationships; marriage bonds that are initiated and dissolved with few formalities; expectations of sexual fidelity within recognized marital unions; importance placed on physical reproduction; childhood initiation ceremonies, especially for girls; a male-only secret society; and a decentralized political organization featuring leaders primarily concerned with arbitration and spiritual matters. While it is important to remember that each population has experienced distinct historical trajectories, environmental pressures, and political alliances, ethnographic observations and analysis from one group are often useful in working through data from another. Throughout this volume, I reference case studies from a variety of Maravi groups for context and comparison, especially drawing from works on Chewa populations living in Malawi, with whom many in Metangula felt more affinity than they did with their Mozambican compatriots.

Some of the women we left behind exchanging morning greetings might have had trousers underneath their waist-wrapped *capulana*. This would be helpful when making their way into the hills to gather firewood (for cooking) or grasses (for roofing or fence making). They would return home balancing neatly bundled, incredibly heavy loads of these materials atop their heads and without wearing their *capulanas* (which were too restrictive for the quickened trot necessary to make the journey as short as possible). The men would be busy with other tasks, if they were awake after fishing the previous night. Some would be heading to the mountains along with the women, looking for bamboo to sell or to use to construct a home or repair a fence. Others might be trolling the streets dressed smartly in trousers and a collared shirt, in search of piecemeal day labor. Many would be sitting on verandas, performing various tasks related to preparing and

Figure 0.2. Men repair fishing nets while seated on a beached canoe. Photo by the author.

maintaining fishing gear. There would be plenty of people also taking their breakfast of tea, perhaps along with a small bread roll, a bowl of porridge, a roasted sweet potato, or a boiled portion of pumpkin or maize.

Other women would be leaving home balancing basins of dried maize or cassava atop their heads. They would be on their way to a local mill, where these staples could be ground into flour for afternoon and evening meals of *ntchima*, a polenta-like stiff gruel. Previous generations had processed maize and cassava (and before that, finger millet and sorghum) using a mortar and pestle. While mills reduced the workload, women still soaked, dried, and sifted flour by hand, to ensure the final product was going to taste right. These tasks also occupied the mornings of many women. Others would be among the crowd at the pumps, along with children, extracting buckets and jugs of water for their homestead's use that day. Canalized water had already been available in Metangula for several years by 2010, but few households could afford the cost of a connection, let alone the monthly bill. As a result, the service was primarily restricted to the neighborhood of Sanjala, where government buildings and employee residencies were located. Even then, the pipes were nearly always dry. For tasks that required a lot of water, like washing dishes and clothes, or for bathing, most in Metangula headed for the lake. Large sex-segregated crowds peopled the shores from dawn until early evening. It was young girls who tended to wash dishes. Older girls and women typically took care of the clothes and bathing young children, who might be playing soccer or sitting idly in the sand nearby as their bodies dried. Locations with large rocks atop which clothes could be pounded clean and heels scraped smooth were especially coveted.

On this morning we would also surely find many men, women, and children making their way to the main market in the neighborhood of Seli to buy or to sell staple goods. The lifeblood of the market was in two central blocks of market stalls. In one, hawkers purveyed breakfast-related and snack items like sweet potatoes, bananas, pumpkins, breads (wheat, banana, and maize), and boiled maize. Others sold *bolos* (fried dough fritters) and *gelo* (plastic vials of frozen or chilled orange, raspberry, pineapple, or cola-flavored Jolly Jus powder mixed with water) for one metical each (about three cents), making them popular items with schoolchildren milling about before classes at the nearby secondary school. "*Mili, mili*" (thousand, thousand—from the Portuguese *mil*), the vendors would call out to entice customers with the cheap price. This recitation was an old habit from the years before July 2006, when the government responded to hyperinflation by lopping three zeros off from the metical and issuing a new currency, turning one thousand (*mil*) meticais into one metical "nova familia" (new family), abbreviated MZN and henceforth referred to in this volume simply as "meticais." The move was a bid to promote integration in the world economy and stimulate economic growth. At the time of research, the United Nations Development Programme ranked Mozambique the fourth poorest nation in the world—behind only Congo, Niger, and Burundi (Klugman 2011). While exchange rates fluctuated during research, sometimes dramatically, the American dollar fetched on average about thirty meticais in 2010. A day's minimum wage for those who were employed in "unskilled" labor might be only twice that amount, or around two American dollars.

In the second block of market stalls, vendors sold common items for afternoon and evening meal preparation—beans, leafy vegetables (like chard, rape, and mustard greens), tomatoes, onions, and peanuts, mainly. Other seasonal items might include sorghum, sesame, the occasional green pepper, carrot, or avocado, and every so often the palm-sized mushrooms that grew on termite hills. Once I saw a pineapple. Outside of this second block of cells was a patchwork of sandalwood, bamboo, and tarpaulin where a group of vendors regularly sold the culinary staples needed for meal preparation: oil, sugar, salt, tomatoes, and onions. The municipality was constructing a third block of stalls for sellers of meat and fish, who otherwise spread out on tarpaulin-covered bamboo tables just outside the formal market. The meat was usually goat, sometimes live chickens or ducks, and very rarely a slaughtered cow or pig sold in one kilogram portions (around two pounds each) from a wheelbarrow. The availability of particular species of fish was dependent on the time of year, the wind, and positioning of the moon, but offerings usually included *usipa*, a small sardine-like fish, and *utaka*, a small bony cichlid. If it were indeed June, there would also likely be *bonya*, young *usipa* fish so small that vendors sold them in dried, clustered masses. Catfish and *chambo*, which both make for an excellent fillet, made their fair share of appearances in the market as well, along with other varieties of seafood—Lake Niassa boasts more than five hundred species. Vendors, who typically bought their fish in the morning directly from fishers, had a busy task of shooing flies with whisks, particularly as the day wore on and their stock began to lose its freshness.

Over time, the two original blocks of market stalls had become surrounded by a sea of individual concrete bunkers, creating the mazelike market that is so common in African towns and cities. Customers would weave through the narrow passages to find the nonperishable products they were after: plastic goods, electronics, packaged foods, tools, seeds, school supplies, cleaning supplies, toiletries, clothing, and shoes emerged from these stalls afresh each morning. Colorful *capulanas* hung from wooden slats, and televisions flickered with images of Brazilian soap operas, Nigerian films, and American pop music videos. If this morning were like any other during harvest season, there would also be trucks unloading maize hauled in from highland farms. The de-cobbed kernels might be sold by the sack, but more likely by the twenty-liter bucketful, just outside the southern market wall. Prices fluctuated with supply and demand. When the harvest was in full swing, as it would be in June, the price was low, maybe ninety meticais per bucket. During the planting season the price might reach double that amount. One bucket of maize could be ground into enough flour to make the *ntchima*

Figure 0.3. Vendors sell tomatoes and onions in the market. Photo by the author.

that would feed a family of five for about two weeks, if they received no visitors. But there were always visitors.

At the opposite side of the market, a few men, women, and children might be gathered in the hope that northbound transportation would become available that day. Such a scenario was unlikely, and they would soon begin to walk if they hoped to reach destinations like Chuanga, Messumba, Chia, Ngoo, Cóbuè, and Ngofi—sparsely populated villages dotting the coast, where many had family and friends and some had farmland. The farthest locations would take several days of travel to reach by foot. Those on their way to Lichinga, the only sizable city in Niassa, and other eastbound destinations could hail one of the minivans, busses, or pickup trucks regularly trolling the streets looking for passengers in the early hours of the morning. The journey to Lichinga took only an hour and a half since the government tarred the road. Before that, it took upward of three times as long—that is, when the route was navigable at all; in the rainy season it sometimes took three days. Those traveling north, or west across the lake, could also do so via the MV Ilala, a converted steamer ship with a one-hundred-ton carrying capacity, plying the waters of Lake Niassa since 1951 (Cole-King and Chipeta 1987, 40). The ship called into port at Metangula on Tuesdays and Saturdays when it was on schedule (and, more often, Wednesdays and Sundays when it was not), its booming horn eliciting gleeful calls of "Eee-lah-lah" from any child within earshot and some wayward adults. The route north stopped in the town of Cóbuè before heading over to Likoma and Chizumulu, Malawian islands completely surrounded by Mozambican waters, and then to the mainland Malawian town of Nkhata Bay. The route more directly west from Metangula docked in Malawi at Nkhotakhota before proceeding to other destinations south. This journey cost the same as the land route to Lichinga when purchasing a ticket in the ship's hull, where passengers jostled for space amid sacks and sacks of maize, dried fish, and other products being transported as gifts or for sale.

As the sun rose higher into the sky each day, Metangula would become abuzz with activity and gossip. Women would be passing the day much as they did the morning: attending to the tasks of meal preparation, household maintenance, caring for children, and otherwise ensuring the resources with which to live. They would also visit friends and family to chat, to gossip, and to pass along news of funerals, impending visitors, and local dramas, as well as to make requests for help on constructing a home or purchasing beans for the evening's meal, and such. Some would be making their way to lowland gardens, where they tended crops such as cassava, rice, pumpkins, cowpeas, beans, leafy greens, and a handful of other edibles, dependent on the season and which seeds they were able to obtain. But many did not have fields, and so they were dependent entirely on the market and gifts for their sustenance. To earn the funds with which to purchase foods and other goods, they engaged in petty trade and piecework. Men, for their part, might also spend the day farming or earning money through day labor. Many men, though, spent much of the day walking around town, politicking, drinking alcohol, or attending to fishing gear in need of repair. At least, these were my observations when I did encounter men. Sometimes it seemed to me as though Metangula's men simply disappeared between meals.

When school was not in session, and when they could evade chores, children were everywhere in Metangula—playing marbles, cards, jump rope, hopscotch, or an alarmingly violent game of tag in which a ball was hurled between two players at a third trying to stack bricks or fill an empty glass bottle with sand. Boys might be playing soccer in pitches or any other clear space they could commandeer. They would pass between them balls handmade from condoms filled with air, covered in layers of plastic bags, and laced together with twine. Other young boys would be busy modeling clay or wire cars, constructing playhouses from grass and very small bricks they had previously crafted and dried in the sun, or wandering around town in a "minibus" fashioned from several reeds tied onto a length of bamboo. Girls meanwhile bundled small handmade clay dolls against their backs with their *capulanas* to carry them like children and formed small globs of mud they served to one another as "meat" and "*ntchima*." Some nearing puberty practiced practical culinary skills by gathering twigs to start a cooking fire and making small meals from maize bran or whatever other scraps their mothers provided or they stole from kitchen stocks. The girls did not venture as far from home as boys in their play, as they were generally expected to come home immediately whenever their names were called. In their play, then, the girls and boys would be honing skills and behaviors and learning expectations that would characterize their gendered, adult lives—women at or near home and directly caring for others, men out and about engaged in politicking and provisioning, though in reality this division of labor operated along much fuzzier lines.

Around 5:30 p.m., the sunlight would have begun to fade. Within what always felt to me like a matter of minutes, the sky would be black, with the first hints of the Milky Way overhead, so brilliant that it could be mistaken for billowing noctilucent clouds. The streets would become quieter as girls and women worked at preparing the evening meal at each hearth and as boys and men bathed and waited for supper. After mealtime, children would be back at play underneath the few streetlights with functioning bulbs or around the edges of several bars that filled with men and women, mostly men, imbibing in boxed wine, gin, and bottled brews. The brightly colored Triângulo was especially popular for such activities. Occupying a prime location at the intersection of two main roads and proffering cold drinks (via gas-powered generator before the arrival of electricity) and a variety of snacks, this was a favorite spot for those who were lucky enough to have a few extra meticais to spend and plenty who did not. Groups of young men would likely be crowded around single bottles of twenty-five-metical gin, while the more economically advantaged patrons might consume a full bottle of beer (costing thirty-five meticais) on their own. Others with fewer resources drank the home brews of *kacholima* (spirits) and *kabanga* (beer) while seated on oil jugs, metal car parts, brick molds, and wooden benches in a neighbor's backyard. A mug of *kabanga* cost five meticais, the same price as a double shot of *kacholima*. The sound of music from the Triângulo and other gatherings would drift with the wind across Metangula until late in the night, long after most had gone to sleep and the fishermen had set off on their nightly excursions, in preparation for another day tomorrow.

Methods

Between 2005 and 2017 I made six trips to Metangula, each varying in length but totaling together about two years of residency. The longest of these trips lasted fifteen months (February 2010 through April 2011), and it is my formal research during this period that makes up the backbone of this book. During my first four visits to Metangula I was focused on transforming a run-down schoolhouse into a museum and library as part of Projecto Património Arqueológico e Cultural (Archaeological and Cultural Patrimony Project), spearheaded by archaeologist Julio Mercader at the University of Calgary. Monica, with whom I opened this introduction, lived near that schoolhouse. We struck up a friendship when she began to send me cooked sweet potatoes to snack on while I worked on curating and fabricating the museum's exhibits. Later she would be key in facilitating my access to local events. On subsequent trips to Metangula, Monica introduced me to her sister Elisa and then to sixteen-year-old Diana, though I had known Diana's mother, Filomena, for much longer. I truly dreaded seeing Filomena for many years; she was confrontational, intrusive, and frighteningly sharp. The first time I met her was when she called to me from the outer veranda of her home in Micuio, her voice booming and deep. She commanded that I take her picture with my camera, and I obliged. Each time I saw her thereafter she demanded a printout of the image. When I repeated the excuse that I lacked a printer she became increasingly indignant. When I finally did bring her the photo on my next trip, she eased up a bit in her demeanor and generally exuded less malice toward me. Over time, she showed herself to be a very patient interpreter of the intricacies of local customs and the Chinyanja language.

In all, during my time in Metangula I maintained regular, close contact with several dozen individuals and their respective households. Many of these individuals I met through snowballing (as with Monica, Elisa, and Diana), but it was also often that I would meet two people independent of one another and later find out that they were friends or family (like Diana and Filomena) or sometimes enemies (like Judite, my host mother, and Jose, a traditional healer, both of whom you shall meet in the pages that follow). Such was life in a small town of about ten thousand people. Of these close contacts, there were several individuals that I visited more often than others—"key informants," as anthropologists once called the persons on whom our discipline relies especially for gaining access to local events, individuals, and understandings. Some now prefer the term "collaborator" to acknowledge the active contributions that these persons make to the formation of anthropological insights and analyses. Indeed, I could not have collected these data or come to the conclusions presented in this book without the contributions of individuals like Monica, Elisa, Judite, Jose, and Filomena. I would like to extend the idea of agency evoked in the term "collaborator" and envision that these acquaintances and I chose one another for the ethnographic work we engaged in together—they were among those who graciously invited me to join them on their verandas or to chat at their places of work, and I was attracted by their openness to answering questions, frankness in discussing sensitive topics, thoughtfulness and thoroughness in offering explanations, and availability.

Ultimately, for both parties, the interactions came down to an intellectual curiosity to think about everyday life from a new perspective—and also, good rapport. This was honed through repeated visits, reciprocal gift giving, and shared meals that not only helped to situate my observations for analytical purposes, but also allowed me to conduct the research at all. Mutuality, or entwining one's life with that of others, was considered a normal part of everyday life in Metangula, but also a necessity. Those who did not regularly chat with friends were assumed to be mentally disturbed or perhaps even nefarious witches. The research method of regular, informal, intermittently directed conversation with confidants was thus necessary to be accepted as a functioning, human person, and I was directly told on many occasions that my interest in talking with people and my ability to laugh and make jokes with them is why "my notebook was full," as recounted in the vignette that opened the preface to this volume. This does not mean that I was ever accepted as, or that I ever suffered from delusions that I was, a full-fledged community member. In Metangula, regardless of the chorus of "Arianna" calls that I heard as I went about my business each day, I would and will always be an outsider.

More than simply chatting, my principal research method for this project can be characterized as long-term, situated, unstructured interaction with the local population. The technical term for this is "participant-observation," which means that I lived among the people I was researching, and I actively engaged alongside them in the activities that made up their lives. Such emulating of and integrating myself into everyday life in Metangula attuned both my senses and my intellect to the daily experiences of local persons and exposed me to a broad range of situations that piqued my curiosity. This is largely what the discipline of anthropology intends in basing its research methodology in grounded theory— rather than explicitly beginning with and testing extant theoretical frameworks and hypotheses, analysis emerges for an anthropologist through collecting data inductively and iteratively. This produces contextualized understandings and insights that often nuance, and sometimes unravel, the patterns and universals that other disciplines specialize in defining and explaining.

In addition to everyday life, I bore witness during my time in Metangula to ritual events such as initiation ceremonies (*nzondo, jando, chiputu,* and *chisamba*), funerals and remembrance ceremonies (*sadaka*) of assorted religious traditions, national and global holiday celebrations (Valentine's Day, Women's Day, Children's Day, Independence Day, Family Day, and New Year's Day), religious festivities (Ziala, Eid ul-Fitr, Christmas, Lent), and political gatherings (which included my dancing with a local women's organization when Armando Guebuza, the president of Mozambique, was in town). I also regularly attended tri-weekly lectures on health-related topics and occasional cooking demonstrations organized by local health centers. Opportunities for conversation emerged organically on these sorts of occasions and also in small one-on-one discussions or informal focus groups at the market, at the homes of those who called me over to chat while waiting for the minibus to Lichinga, and so forth.

Those I interacted with in Metangula were aware that I was always documenting their thoughts and actions in writing and that I would use our conversations to help me to write a book. In doing so now, several years later, I have given my acquaintances pseudonyms when I discuss and analyze their lives. This will surely be curious for readers in Metangula, as many of the people and events that I write of will seem familiar but misattributed. I assure them (and other readers) that this has been done only with a heavy heart, not a "big" one (which in local parlance means something akin to selfishness and arrogance, rather than its English connotation of generosity), because of disciplinary ethics and the ease with which individuals can be contacted (and harassed) with the aid of internet technology. I have not, however, changed the name of the research site, as the contextual circumstances of Metangula are so particular and my own association with it so undeniable that it would be impossible to disguise. As a matter of respect, I have also used the real names of individual elders who have passed away and who are quoted for their expertise, authority, and wisdom.

I did not financially compensate anyone for their participation in my research, though when visiting homesteads I did on occasion bring with me small gifts like salt, soap, cloth, tea leaves, or *bolos* from the local market. I also provided money for seeking medical treatment or "buying sugar" when my acquaintances or their family members were sick. Additionally, I tried to help with whatever chores individuals were engaged in while I conversed with them. These were usually food-related tasks—shelling corn, peeling cassava, removing the fibrous veins from pumpkin leaves, and such. The entertainment value of my clumsiness was probably of more value than my contribution to diminishing the workload in such scenarios. My ineptness at a variety of tasks seemed to have been widely enjoyed in fact. It is very possible that if you were to travel to Metangula and encounter somebody who remembered my time there, they would clap their hands together or slap their leg as a way to emphasize the great joy they took in watching my "mannish" way of walking (explained to me as walking with a purpose, rather than carefully and cautiously, as if balancing something on my head), listening to my nasalized speech (along with, my language teacher in Malawi would surely tell you, a tendency to confuse words that, to me, sounded similar—like *chimwewe* [happiness] and *chiwerewere* [promiscuity], or *mawere* [sorghum] and *mabere* [breasts]), and witnessing my illogical fear of fire (local women would manipulate burning firewood with their bare hands, which I was apprehensive to do myself).

I conducted this research primarily in Chinyanja, which was the first language of approximately 80 percent of people in Metangula, according to the 2007 census. Mozambique had not yet pushed for the standardization of local languages into written scripts, and the Chinyanja spoken along the lakeshore during my research boasted the variation and dynamism expected of any predominantly oral communication system. Swahili, Chiyaawo, Chitumbuka, Chingoni, Arabic, Portuguese, and English all contributed to the vocabulary of Chinyanja, and it was not uncommon to receive two or more words of various origins when eliciting a translation from Portuguese into "the" local language. Portuguese and Chiyaawo were also the primary language in a significant number of Metangula homes (13 percent and 7 percent, respectively).[8] In daily affairs, I rarely heard Portuguese outside of the more affluent Sanjala neighborhood, where many government officials (often migrants to Metangula) lived with their families. Those living in Metangula's other neighborhoods, while they could speak Portuguese at levels that ranged from rudimentary to expertise, tended to use the language in their daily interactions only rarely. This was changing, however, as the town was becoming more diverse and as uppity children began refusing to speak anything but Portuguese with their parents.

In addition to participant-observation, I consulted for the purpose of this research several archives and special collections in Mozambique, Malawi, and the United Kingdom.[9] The documents, unpublished reports, and student theses I encountered helped me to better understand the meanings of beliefs, practices, and circumstances I witnessed in Metangula and to contextualize my research within regional patterns and historical trends. For quantitative data on alimentação, I also developed and implemented a dietary survey. There were ninety-seven Metangula homesteads that participated in the survey for at least ten of thirteen months (April 2010–April 2011). Participants were selected by first mapping the town of Metangula and assigning each homestead a unique number, then using a list randomizer to generate an order in which to visit them to request participation until one hundred homesteads were enrolled. Two part-time, paid research assistants, Helena Augusto and Judite Franco Kakhongue, collected the dietary survey data by visiting each enrolled homestead two to three times per month, on a randomized schedule that I provided. Upon each visit, they would ask the primary cook what she had prepared the previous day, using which ingredients and cooking methods, how each ingredient was obtained, and who among homestead members and guests had consumed the foods. They also tracked down as many homestead members as possible and asked them individually what they had consumed outside of the home the previous day. My spouse reviewed the surveys for quality control and entered these data into a computer for quantitative and statistical analysis. To enable correlation of dietary scores with health proxies, I personally measured the body mass index (BMI) of survey participants over five years of age using a portable scale and tape measure. My research assistants also collected demographic information for all survey participants. I employed Steven Schuster while he was a PhD student at Boston University to use these data to estimate socioeconomic level based on standard principal component analysis, with results grouped by *k*-median clustering.[10]

Orientations

I have written this volume envisioning an audience made up primarily of readers interested in food studies, anthropology, public health, and Africa. To make my ideas as accessible as possible for nonexperts and scholars of these diverse fields, I do not assume prior knowledge of central concepts, I avoid technical language and unnecessary jargon, and I aim to mimic in my organization and presentation the inviting prose characteristic of storytelling. These strategies should not be mistaken for "dumbing down" the content. As Ian Bogost (2018) wrote in *The Atlantic* to encourage academicians to frame our research for audiences not primed to grasp the material, "The whole reason to reach people who don't know what you know, as an expert, is so that they might know about it. Giving them reason to care, process, and understand is precisely the point." Precisely. This book will also serve for most readers as an introduction to the Nyanja people living along the eastern shore of Lake Niassa in northern Mozambique. This is because it focuses on a population largely absent from the annals of academic research. My goal in writing this account should not, however, be mistaken for filling an ethnographic gap. Thus, I do not take pains to spell out in detail social institutions, cultural norms, community beliefs and behaviors, and historical trajectories of "the Nyanja," except where such discussions are explicitly pertinent to my central concerns.[11] Each of the chapters of the book begins as this one did, with an event or a conversation reconstructed from my field notes and elaborated with later insights, presenting some set of circumstances through which I encountered the meaning and making of foodways in Metangula. The vignettes that open each chapter are printed in italics in order to mark them as moments of ethnographic storytelling that introduce subjects that are analyzed in the text that follows. I have taken this corpus of vignettes, along with other events, out of their chronological order to enhance my ability to underscore specific points. All of the events and conversations that are depicted in the vignettes, and in the broader volume, however, actually happened—these are not fictitious fabrications or ethnographic amalgamations.

Following these introductory remarks, there are five chapters in this volume, each offering a themed glimpse into the foodways of Metangula, capped off by a conclusion. The ordering of these chapters is intended to introduce concepts like building blocks, to equip you, the reader, to journey with me to explore and to see the intricacies of Metangula's foodways and, through foodways, the pursuit in one African town of the universal endeavor to constitute humanity. With chapter 1 we begin by looking at the composition of the local diet, concentrating on the importance attributed to four ingredients: oil, onion, tomato, and sugar. I explain that these foods, more than others, were consistently reported to me as provisioning consumers with "vitamins." This word, however, had a different meaning in the context of Metangula than it does in its biomedical use, and I adopt the Portuguese word *vitamina* to mark this distinction when elaborating my findings. I examine *vitamina* as intimately tied with cultural knowledge of the way the body works, with a particular focus on the importance of *vitamina* for individuals' *thanzi*, or vitality, the energy and motivation for living. Chapter 2 then takes up in more detail the use of these capacities for partaking in the life-enhancing and pro-social labor through which individuals contributed to the care of others. I situate these findings within broader African models of composite personhood, through which life is made meaningful only in mutuality and interdependency with the living and the dead. I additionally elaborate the importance assigned in Metangula to reason, forward thinking, and compassion as capacities that were integral to being and becoming human, and I examine how these principles are evident in both historical accounts and more recent market behavior.

In chapter 3, I then take up the alternatives to humanity—engaging in witchcraft or acting as if an animal. The chapter begins with a brief introduction to witchcraft as it was envisaged in Metangula to be a nefarious activity aimed at undermining the basic principles that define humanity. While the reader may have doubts about the factual veracity of witchcraft, I hope to make clear the very real social importance of distancing oneself from the occult, lest an individual face social ostracism or physical harm. I go on to examine local understandings of witches as cannibals and to elaborate how the desire to avoid *seeming* cannibalistic can help us to understand taboos on certain meats that resemble humans in form, emotion, and spirit. I also detail in this chapter the distinctions and similitudes people in Metangula saw in comparing humans and animals, focusing on their alimentary manifestations and implications. The chapter is followed by an in-depth consideration of everyday rituals related to pouring salt, an essential ingredient for meals to be culturally edible. Chapter 4 explains the parameters of these rituals, and the illnesses for third parties that resulted where the prescriptions were violated. My analysis suggests that following the precise rules was less important than adhering to their underlying expression of concern for the well-being of others and establishing oneself as part of a collectivity with the living and the dead. Such relations of mutuality demanded continuous revitalization. I additionally consider the similarities between potash and *dawa* (a broad category of substances with the capacity to heal or to harm) to enhance attention to precarity and ambiguity as aspects of being human that were lived with, rather than resolved, in Metangula and as a broader condition of humanity.

Chapters 1 through 4, then, build upon one another in a progressive argument: foods were eaten to garner the *vitamina* that fed vitality and living (chapter 1), this energy and motivation was necessary to engage in properly human endeavors related to care work, reason, and empathy (chapter 2), being human was a better alternative than being a witch or an animal (chapter 3), and humanity was deepened through revitalizing relationships of unity and belonging (chapter 4). All of these points manifested through local foodways, in which individuals supported, enacted, and sometimes negated principles deemed culturally necessary to lead a nourishing life. Chapter 5 builds upon these points but considers several practical implications for public health—namely in relation to child nutrition, dietary interventions, and sexually transmitted diseases. In order to contextualize these points, the chapter also details local knowledge that connects body size to individual potential rather than quantity or quality of a person's diet, and decouples body size with weight, along with elongating the dependence of reproduction on sexual activity.

The book as a whole thus presents an ethnographic accounting of how the people living in Metangula in the opening decade of the twenty-first century conceived of nourishment as dependent on enacting interdependence, cooperative labor, compassion, and moral intelligence and where this positioning was both evidenced in and lived out through local foodways. The conception of humanity as dependent on mutuality, sociability, and kindness is not unique to Metangula. Scientists from a variety of disciplines have found increasing evidence to suggest a species-level evolutionary disposition that favors morality based on empathy, cooperation, and justice (Bekoff and Pierce 2009; Boehm 2012; Breithaupt 2019; Pagel 2012). And yet, humans also have the capacity for true evil (van Beek and Olsen 2016) and incomprehensible violence (Wrangham 2019). It seems, in other words, that humanity is inherently precarious and unstable; not a matter of being either (good or bad, social or antisocial, giving or greedy, sociocentric or egocentric), but having the potential for both. It is this universal predicament of ambiguity and impermanence that makes human life "always risky and at risk," as phrased by anthropologist Michael Jackson (2005). While we might be primed (biologically or culturally) for pro-social orientations, then, they still must be chosen amid other possible dispositions. In this volume I provide an ethnographic study of a population living with rather than resolving these ambiguities, with a focus on the alimentary practices through which individuals consciously and constantly cultivated, rather than achieved or enacted as a matter of rote habitus, a nourishing life. Humanity was, in other words, conceived and pursued not as an ascribed or stable state of being, but as a lifelong task of perpetual becoming. Complicating this daily work were constraints similar to those experienced across Africa in the early twenty-first century. These included limited resources with which to carry out a pro-social agenda (Klaits 2010) and emergent formulations of success and well-being that competed and sometimes clashed with those upheld as superlative in the past (Ferguson 2013). This meant that agency in cultivating humanity was at times restricted not only by the human condition, but also as a result of the context of globalization, capitalism, and the uneven economic development of global north and south.

In moving away from the more traditional Durkheimian approach to morality as a given set of explicitly formulated rules, external to the person and determinative of what we are or are not to do—as Jarrett Zigon (2008) notes, "a convenient term for socially approved habits"—we can thus see pro-sociality through a more Foucauldian lens, or morality as a matter of the processual formation of inner subjectification, produced by individuals in accordance with their pursuit of and inquiries about what constitutes humanity. Morality was, in other words, not a matter of following rules, but a continuous feedback loop shaped and reshaped through lived experiences, evaluation, and decisions for action (Fassin 2012). This shift in focus from defining moral systems to a study of moral values and practice amid uncertainty enables a nuanced look at the everyday, and every day, moral lives of actual, living people. This is often missing in philosophical considerations of the contours of humanity, and it marks the potential for a uniquely anthropological contribution to the study of moral living (Zigon 2008).

This book, then, documents the dimensions and confines of humanity, the simultaneity and the attractiveness of alternative orientations, and the active practice (rather than mere evolutionary outcome, rote habitus, moral decree, or static achievement) of being and becoming human as these things played out in one African town at the beginning of the twenty-first century. Before moving on, I want to directly address the fact that writing this volume at times made me feel out of step with current trends in the field of anthropology. Surely some readers will remark that my approach to the research (interrogating cultural knowledge), my analysis (heavily reliant on locally contextualized meanings), and the focus on a single geographic area (in an increasingly interconnected world that necessitates interrogation through multi-sited ethnography) represents an orientation to "the field" that no longer defines the discipline. Indeed, despite pop-culture depictions of ethnographers discovering (or inventing) unknown peoples in remote places, anthropology is certainly not confined to distant travels, the ritual of extended and extensive fieldwork, and depictions of culture as a cornucopia of the bizarre. Sociocultural anthropologists study corporations, sports fans, drug addicts, doctors, and college students, along with just about any other social group, identity, or activity that humans partake in. Even then, the relevance for the discipline is, for some, born specifically out of utilizing the anthropologist's tool kit to comment on the cultural milieu of the digital age, late capitalism, and other aspects of the Anthropocene.

But there are people out there, too—a lot of them—who live in "small places" (Kincaid 1988) and who are doing small things. These small things continue to be meritorious of recording, too, as giving meaning and structure to lived life.[12] Sometimes these small things are also big things. While it may not be apparent on the surface, this volume, with its focus on the ethnographically and historically contextualized beliefs and behaviors related to foodways and humanity in one peri-urban African town, is as much motivated by the present moment as are works explicitly devoted to the problems of our era. Specifically, we are living in a time where many feel as though we are fighting—amid massive corporate greed, consumerism, xenophobia, and digitally induced anomy—for the survival of the planet and of our species. In the face of psychic numbing to daily tragedies that leaves many searching for answers, for understanding, and for guidance on how to lead a meaningful life, it is useful to consider what it is that truly makes us human. While I am not so naïve as to suggest that Metangula holds the answers to these conundrums, the case study of a people that lives the daily work that it takes to maintain mutuality does offer an important opportunity for critical self-reflection. And, it is precisely in elucidating the in situ lived experience of a shared humanity that contemporary ethnography, as grounded in empathetic connection and moral witnessing, stands to recover its cultural point (Hannig 2017). Locating the playing out of ontology, cosmology, and epistemology through something as quotidian as food—rather than relegating their engagement to philosophy or to sacred, religious spaces—should help every reader ask what it is that you do (yes, you), or what you want to do, and what you can do—within the minutia of your own everyday and every day life—to consciously, purposefully, and meaningfully practice, rather than to merely be a part of, humanity.

Notes

1. Reviews of the anthropology of food and nutrition are periodically published in journals and edited volumes, for example Dirks and Hunter (2013); Messer (1984); and Mintz and Du Bois (2002).
2. Fran Osseo-Asare (2005) provides a geographically organized assessment of how foods are grown, cooked, and eaten across the African subcontinent (along with recipes). A sampling of ethnographies of food in Africa include Osmund A. C. Anigbo's (1987) attention to the "drama" of Igbo commensality as a symbolic event to be decoded; Tuulikki Pietilä's (2007) exploration of the commoditization of food at markets on Mount Kilimanjaro; Gracia Clark's (1994) deep ethnography of market women in Ghana; Susanne Freidberg's (2004) assessment of the impact of European anxieties on African growers of baby vegetables and green beans for export to Britain and France; the work of Karen Coen Flynn (2005), Eno Blankson Ikpe (1994), and Kwaku Obosu-Mensah (1999) on urban foodways in Tanzania, Nigeria, and Ghana, respectively; Alex de Waal's (1997) and Mary Howard and Ann V. Millard's (1997) critical assessments of the famine relief industry; and Kathryn M. de Luna's (2016) linguistically inspired but multidisciplinarily executed analysis of technology, the organization of labor, and environmental knowledge as central to understanding subsistence strategies as multiple and shifting over time. Additional contributions to the studies of African foodways that are more squarely historical in genre are reviewed by James C. McCann (2012).
3. The political economy of food in Africa is also treated ethnographically. See Parker Shipton (1990) and Mamadou Baro and Tara F. Deubel (2006) for reviews of anthropological contributions to the study of food security and famine. Seminal analyses include Johan Pottier's (1985) *Food Systems in Central and Southern Africa* and Jane Guyer's (1987) edited volume *Feeding African Cities: A Study in Regional Social History*.
4. The towns and villages listed here are sometimes spelled differently, for example "Mechumua" for Michimwa, "Caphueleza" for Capueleza, and "Chiwanga" for Chuanga.
5. Some scholars argue that other explorers or traders arrived at the Lake Niassa shore before David Livingstone or that Livingstone never arrived in person at all (Jeal 2013; Reis 1889; Thompson 2013).

6. In addition to residents of Metangula lacking formal timepieces, a wealth of anthropological literature also makes clear that temporality is conceptualized and experienced differently around the world. See Nancy Munn (1992) and Roy Ellen (2016) for a review of such literature, or see the classic work of E. E. Evans-Pritchard (1939).
7. See Elizabeth Isichei (1997, 113), Brian Morris (2000, 16–19), Mary [Tew] Douglas (1950), and Matthew Schoffeleers (1968, 103) for additional discussion of "the Maravi."
8. Statistics for Metangula's language use reflect unpublished, disaggregated data from the national census in 2007, which I obtained directly from the Instituto Nacional de Estatística (INE).
9. I conducted formal archival research at Museu Local in Metangula, reviewing a collection of oral histories I collected along with Patrick Chimutha in 2007 (LAG Oral Traditions collection), and at Oxford's Bodleian Library (home to a collection of documents related to the Universities' Mission to Central Africa, which operated churches along the Mozambican lakeshore). Additionally, I read student theses to find unpublished material that could help to contextualize my own findings. I obtained these works in Mozambique from Universidade Eduardo Mondlane (Maputo) and Universidade Pedagógica (Nampula) and in Malawi from Chancellor College (Zomba), University of Malawi College of Medicine (Blantyre), Lilongwe University of Agriculture and Natural Resources (Lilongwe, formerly Bunda College), and Kamuzu College of Nursing (Lilongwe). Additional repositories where I found both obscure and unpublished materials include the Chancellor College Social Research Documentation Centre and the libraries of the Malawian Ministry of Health, the Mozambican Ministry of Health (MISAU) Nutrition Department, the Mozambican Institute of Statistics (INE), and the Mozambican Technical Secretariat for Nutrition (SETSAN).
10. Additional information on the dietary survey, including survey instruments and preliminary data analyses, is provided in my doctoral dissertation (Huhn 2012).
11. For a more thorough introduction to the history of Niassa, consider *Historia de Cabo Delgado e do Niassa (c. 1836–1929)* by Eduardo Medeiros (1997), along with Luis Wegher's two-part *Um olhar sobre o Niassa* (1995; 1999).
12. For additional perspectives on the danger of anthropologists failing to pay attention to social experiences as they are valued by Africans themselves, see Francis B. Nyamnjoh (2001), Todd Sanders (2003), and China Scherz (2018).

CHAPTER 1

Blood, Vitality, and Diet

One afternoon, while walking down the peninsular hill on which the neighborhood of Sanjala is situated, I was called over by António, a man I had met many times before. Most times that I encountered António he was inebriated, and this day was no exception. He was at a local shebeen imbibing in kacholima, *a gin-like drink made with fermented sugarcane. Individuals selling* kacholima *signaled that spirits were available by arranging an overturned small plastic bottle somewhere near the entrance to their homestead. Here, at the home of Carolina, a* kacholima *maker and seller, a Sobo bottle hung on a stick that was planted in the grass fence surrounding her yard. António was standing near the front veranda of the main house, holding onto the handles of his bicycle. Samuel, a government employee, stood next to him. Yusif, a middle-aged man, and Carolina sat on the veranda of the house, in the shade of an overhanging grass roof.*

"I am sick," António said to me while arranging his bicycle to depart for home. "I am thinking too much." I asked what he was thinking about, and he told me money and work. He would go north to Michumwa the next day to look for both. I asked Carolina if women do not also become sick with "thinking." They do, she said, but not as much as a man. "A woman only becomes ill like this when her husband is not providing for her or when she is afraid he may soon stop providing. Otherwise a woman is not really thinking; the man is just providing for her." The others agreed. I tempered my feminist impulse to argue for equality and turned again to António to ask how thinking so much caused a person to be sick. "Blood," he said in response, "is things that taste good" (mwazi ndi zinthu zokoma).[1] *Samuel, having recently swallowed the contents of his glass, licked his lips and looked askance at António. "There is a difference between things that* are *good, and things that* taste *good," Samuel said in a lecturing tone. "For example, if you go to the market you can ask which fish is 'good.'" By "good," he meant fresh or edible. He continued, "But that does not mean that the fish will taste good to the tongue." To summarize his point he concluded, "Taste linguistically refers only to food."*

The others clucked their tongues in disagreement, "la," and shifted their weight in discomfort with Samuel's ideas. António stared off into the distance with a wide grin on his face, and Carolina looked toward the fence with pursed lips. After a moment of gathering his thoughts, António turned back to Samuel. "Tastiness," he said, looking Samuel square in the eye, "is life." He continued, "If there are problems in the house, people in that home do not eat. They have no appetite. Nothing tastes good to them." He gave a more specific example then, saying that if he were happy, beer would taste good to him even though it is bitter. If he were sick or otherwise distressed, however, the beer would not be tasty, though there are of course people not able to stomach beer regardless of their circumstances. Lack of appetite, then, was an ominous sign, such that if someone ate just a little and said that they were full, it would be a clear indication that they were distressed, not in good health, and lacking blood.

Returning to my question, and perhaps taking pity at my look of confusion—as I did not yet understand taste as a matter of context, feeling, and emotion, rather than gustatory perception, nor could I grasp health as a manifestation of blood quantity and quality or vitality—António turned directly to me and pointed to a wound on his right elbow, which had scabbed over after a fall from his bicycle the previous week. He asked, "Why, when we wound ourselves, do we bleed blood and not water?" When I professed ignorance, he answered the question himself: "Because hurting ourselves is painful." He continued, pulling the various components of the conversation together for me and summarizing, "Painful things are things that do not taste good, and so you lose blood." Things that taste good, he went on to explain, do so because we are well, and when we are well this is reflected in our blood. António looked at me directly and said, "Blood is a big thing. This is because blood is the same thing as life. Without blood, we are not in good health, and there is no tasting of good things."

Helena, one of two research assistants administering a dietary survey on my behalf, had meanwhile joined the gathering when she saw me at Carolina's house. She had heard much of António's explication and took her turn to address the group to support his conclusions, repeating many of the same points and then adding her own. "Even sugar," she said, "would taste bitter to someone who has problems." António, Carolina, and Yusif nodded in approval. Samuel, a slight man with a broad face who was wearing a light-blue collared shirt tucked into a pair of oversized khaki pants cinched in at the waist with a faux-leather belt, had a look of incredulity on his face. Helena continued, "The tongue only works when a person is without worries." Samuel, looking at Helena, blinked slowly, his inebriation beginning to show in the pace and coordination of his movements. He handed his shot glass back to Carolina with a smirk, turned to take his leave, and silently trudged back up the Sanjala hill to his government office, oblivious to the irony of gin no longer seeming pleasurable to consume in an environment that felt hostile.

There are two reasons that I begin my first chapter on Metangula's foodways by recounting this impromptu focus group at a Sanjala shebeen. One is that such happenstance events and everyday conversation were how the topics that guided my research emerged. Beginning each chapter with one such vignette, then, feels both natural and appropriate. The other reason is that this particular encounter with António, Samuel, Helena, Carolina, and Yusif was especially formative in spurring the analysis presented in this ethnography. It was at the base of the hill that afternoon that I palpably came to realize the dissonance between my own understandings of what food is and how it impacts the body and prevalent local knowledge that ordered cause and effect and paired eating with health, blood, and energy in very different ways than I was used to. It was in particular António's attention to taste as a product of external, non-gustatory conditions impacting circulatory processes that helped me to see that there was something missing when I assumed that concepts like "blood" and "vitamins" had universal denotations. I imagine that many readers come to this book having the same scientific conception of biomedicine-as-fact with which I myself entered into the field. It is thus important at the outset of this volume that biomedical formulations are positioned as just one of many culturally elaborated systems of understanding the body's organization and functioning and the making and meaning of health.[2]

This chapter focuses on the connections that people in Metangula drew between food, emotion, the senses, feelings, nourishment, and wellness. I use the word *vitamina* (Portuguese for "vitamin," but used in a plural sense more like "vitamins") to highlight the circumstantial nature of alimentation's contributions to well-being in Metangula, such that a food's ability to confer energy and health to its consumers could not be stated definitively, in the way that micronutrients like vitamins are in biomedical formulation. Instead, the capacity of a food to nourish was dependent on bodily response, which varied between individuals, by location, and across time in ways that reflected both relationality and affect. Eating was, as such, only able to impart *vitamina*, a fuel for the vital force and energy associated with blood, when done in circumstances that were themselves nourishing—sanguinity paired as a physical and an emotional state, and vitality and wellness as mutually affirming. To make these points, I consider in particular three foods that people in Metangula almost invariably assigned *vitamina*—tomatoes, onions, and oil. A closer look, however, suggests that these foods' positioning as *vitamina*-rich was not absolute and that their capacities to proffer *vitamina* were, like other foods', dependent on circumstantial experience and embodied response. Likewise sugar, and I use a discussion of sweetness to elaborate flavor terminology as reflective of the cultural construction of taste as perceived with the entire body rather than the tongue alone. I continue with a consideration of foods and circumstances that negated *vitamina*, stymied the body's capacity for strength, or otherwise "sucked blood," identifying again the same principles at play. The chapter as a whole makes clear a cultural knowledge of what food is and what it does to the body that was distinct in many ways from biomedical standards. The connections between circumstance, energy, emotion, and alimentation laid out in this chapter also provide the scaffolding upon which, in the chapters that follow, I will layer morality and personhood as mutable, intentional, and everyday pursuits that played out in the realm of foodways.

Before diving in, it is necessary to address the fact that the word *vitamina* is of Portuguese origin. While Portugal's footprint dates back several centuries in Mozambique, part of what is wrapped up in *vitamina* dates back much further. This is most readily apparent in the Chinyanja/Chichewa word *thanzi*, used for describing the energy that a person feels when their blood is infused with *vitamina*. This animating vitality and motivational impetus to contribute to enhancing life was distinct from just being alive, or "life" (*moyo*). To illustrate this difference, consider descriptions of two products, as observed in Malawi in 2010. First is a small billboard advertising Pall Mall cigarettes, emblazoned with a Ministry of Health warning that read, "*Kusuta kumaononga moyo*," translated formally into English on the billboard as "Smoking is hazardous to health." Literally, the Chichewa phrasing means "Smoking ruins life." If you smoke, you are increasing your risk of death—for example, through stroke, emphysema, lung cancer, and heart disease. By way of contrast, a Malawian liquor manufacturer warned on its five-liter jug of Kadansana 40 percent alcohol that "*mumwa mowa mopitiliza muyezo kumaononga thanzi la munthu*." This translates as "too much alcohol con-

Figure 1.1. Cigarette advertisement in Malawi. Photo by the author.

Figure 1.2. Five-liter bottle of alcohol on sale in a Malawi supermarket. Photo by the author.

sumption can ruin a person's vitality." One who drinks alcohol to excess, in other words, runs the risk of being unable to perform normal tasks (through inebriation) and potentially to pursue a productive life at all (through addiction). Such an individual would also be less likely to have the appetite for meals or the physical capacity to consume them. Comparing the two products, smoking cigarettes had the potential for ending life as a physiological state (*moyo*), whereas drunkenness and alcoholism impaired the substance of life—one's motivation, energy, and pursuit of generative labor (*thanzi*).

While *vitamina*, then, may have been a relatively new word in local vocabulary, the idea of an animating energy as distinct from biological life has a much longer history. This is true not only among Chewa/Nyanja populations, but across the African continent, often in association with blood and food. For example, Sharon Hutchinson (2000) writes of blood among the Nuer of South Sudan as a substance both powerful and mysterious in its capacity to illuminate the connections and boundaries between people, and natural tensions between vitality and vulnerability. Blood, while not life itself, was that from which life was conceived to emerge through the powers of divinity, and (together with milk, semen, and sweat) it was the source of all human energy. Blood was generated from food, and the oneness of blood (through kinship and blood brotherhood) was marked through regular commensality. Brad Weiss (1996) also records blood as a "generative fluid" among the Haya of Tanzania, where the substance fluctuated in volume and in its potential to energize a person due to changes in diet and activity, but also in response to broader engagement of individuals with other persons and objects. Blood was not only a *signal* of the body's capacity to act, but the very potential for the body to act, which was itself an index of well-being. Paul Wenzel Geissler and Ruth Jane Prince (2010) also identify a connection between blood, eating, and relatedness among the Luo in Kenya, such that those persons with whom an individual ate came to share substance and (so) become their kin. It was in commensality and other practices of momentary unification through touch that the creative potential of transformative processes was enabled or stymied.

These three case studies are but a few of those recording quality and quantity of blood as related to content and context of alimentary consumption in Africa.[3] Research into historical panics about vampires and other forms of blood theft (Isichei 2002; L. White 2000) additionally index the serious regard with which blood has long been engaged in Africa. The language of *vitamina* (and, in Malawi, *vitamini*), however, is clearly of more recent origins. The scientific discovery of vitamins dates back only to the early decades of the twentieth century, with attention to vitamins quickly thereafter coming to underscore medical practitioners' efforts to combat health disparities in Africa (Quinn 1994). Both Victoria Quinn (1994) and Cynthia Brantley (2002) provide assessments of how these ideas played out in colonial-era Malawi, where, despite survey findings evidencing neither nutritional deficiency nor widespread nutrition-related diseases, the colonial government placed emphasis in local health programming on reducing "ignorance" by improving dietary content (rather than more sorely needed attention to food security). Missionaries operating in Mozambique's Lago District, who were more closely aligned with the British government than they were with the Portuguese and who for many years offered the only biomedical health interventions in the region (Good 2004), were most certainly influenced by this orientation, along with broader trends in pathologizing African bodies in association with empire building (Arnold 1988; Comaroff 1993; Vaughan 1991; Wylie 2001).

It is quite plausible, then, that in the course of their interactions with missionary medical practitioners in the first half of the twentieth century, the population in Metangula would have been exposed to the concept of vitamins as essential for wellness.[4] This does not mean that biomedical knowledge and practices replaced whole cloth traditional approaches to health and healing (inclusive of cultural knowledge about blood, vitality, and nutrition), nor that in incorporating the term *vitamina* into Chinyanja the local population necessarily took on the concept's underlying logics. Across the continent, scholars have recorded African approaches to health management as syncretic, plural, complementary, and otherwise "messy," rather than singular or exclusionary (Littlewood 2007; Ranger 1982a; Whyte 1989). It seems very possible, then, that renderings of "vitamins" as essential for health added to older conceptions of blood-based life force and vitality as essential for living, producing an "intermingling of therapeutic worlds" (Feierman 2000) that spurred the concept of *vitamina* that I recorded in the twenty-first century. As Caroline H. Bledsoe observed in her studies of aging and fertility in the Gambia, such worlds can be "deceptively commensurate," especially where they share vocabularies, eliding perceptions of difference (2002, 4). It is as such that ethnographic contextualization is necessary to parse out what people in Metangula meant when they used a Portuguese term as a part of cultural knowledge about wellness, diet, and bodily function.

Vitamina and Circumstance

"Blood is a big thing"—those were the words of António as he readied his bike to depart from Sanjala in the vignette that opened this chapter. "Blood is the same thing as life." These statements might appear trite—an individual without blood coursing through their veins and pumping through their heart is lifeless. António's words are all the more seemingly self-evident when we consider the prevalence in sub-Saharan Africa of malaria, a blood-borne illness passed through mosquitoes that feast on blood they extract from the human body, and HIV/AIDS, a sexually transmitted disease that infects the blood. Both of these sicknesses have potential consequences for mortality and morbidity. But blood, in António's formulation, did more than transport energy and waste to and from the body's cells. Blood reflected, measured, and constituted an animating power, or vitality (*thanzi*) through which humans had the capacity to make life meaningful. For António, and for most of the people of Metangula with whom I interacted, blood was simultaneously reflective and constitutive of health and wellness, making physical our psychological states and emotional experiences. The ways that António and others in Metangula conceived of the physiological processes through which blood is augmented and depleted and the manner in which they related blood to vitality are key to understanding the foodways of Metangula, for it was through eating that a person accessed *vitamina*, and it was *vitamina* that enabled (a) nourishing life.

During my stay in Metangula, the word *vitamina* peppered conversations everywhere I went. Whether due to my prompting or of their own accord, people debated the *vitamina* of new foods or combinations of foods. They also blamed paltry *vitamina* for reduced energy levels and sickness, often glossed as "anemia." Patuma, a traditional healer (*sing'anga*) born in Malawi and living at the time of my research in a small house on the Thungo hillside with her husband and children, explained the matter with an analogy: The heart is like an engine, and the blood its gasoline in constant need of replenishment. Where there was not sufficient *vitamina* in the body, blood would become watery (*madjimadji*) and weak (*ofowoka*) or otherwise less voluminous and effective. The heart, as a result, would pump more quickly and the body would "cool" (*kuzizira*). In this state a person would feel mental, spiritual, and physical inanition, and they would as a result only be able to passively observe, not participate in society.

Siphons of blood were diverse and naturally occurring. Blood loss could happen due to injury, menstruation, lochia, or uterine discharge following miscarriage, for example—physical and visible loss of blood from the body. Blood could also be internally redirected for bodily processes—like the production of semen in an excessively sexually active man or of breast milk in a lactating woman. Monica one day suggested that milk was, in fact, the same thing as blood. She held up as proof a baby bottle left in the sun, causing the breast milk contained within it to turn red (a process biology would attribute to bacterial colonization). The consistency of blood could also thicken or thin in ways that were deleterious to its function. Spending time in the sun, for example, would cause the liquid component of blood to evaporate, leading to coagulation. People took pains to avoid direct sunlight where they could, and I regularly witnessed children scolded for their prolonged sitting or standing in the sun or for allowing a younger sibling to do so. It was also common for people in Metangula to manipulate trees with weights and trellises, so that the branches grew outward to offer more shade. Houses in Metangula almost always had a wraparound veranda and overhanging roof, ensuring that there was a place to evade the sun at all times of day. Particularly prone to blood loss through sun exposure were newborn babies, who had very little blood to begin with. Family regularly met postpartum mothers at the hospital bearing an umbrella that the woman would use to protect her newborn from the sun for their first several months of life.[5] Regardless of preventative measures, however, blood would always be subject to depletion through the activities of everyday life and thus required constant replenishment in the form of *vitamina*.

Given the differences between local cultural knowledge and biomedical formulation of blood and circulatory processes, it should be unsurprising that *vitamina* was distinct from the "vitamins" from which the concept linguistically, and perhaps in part conceptually, derived. Whereas vitamins in biomedical formulation are organic compounds that impact the body in predictable ways—such that eating a banana provides the consumer with the niacin that reduces cardiovascular risk, and a glass of orange juice guarantees vitamin C that acts as an antioxidant, for example—the relationship between food and *vitamina* in Metangula was more situationally determined. *Vitamina*, in other words, was not a property inherent within specific foods. Instead, *vitamina* was produced through circumstances of eating that revitalized the metaphysical person. It was António who introduced this point at the shebeen, after Samuel departed, when I naively asked which foods were good to eat when a person was anemic. António responded that there were no particular foods that a person could eat to increase their blood quantity and quality—whether a food provided *vitamina* depended on if it tasted good. But tastiness was not a property of gustation alone. "Tastiness" depended on context.

António explained his point by way of example, suggesting that in a remote village there would be few options for ingredients with which to cook a meal and few resources to supplement them. Thus, typical fare might consist of the staple food *ntchima* with an *ndiwo* side dish of wild greens cooked in water and seasoned with nothing but salt. "In the bush" (*ku tchire*), António said to emphasize the remoteness of a person living in the circumstances he was describing, "a person can be healthy eating like this, with just salt and water, because they do not have any thoughts." By "thoughts," António meant both the anxieties that stem from the inability to care for dependents (like his own worries about money and work) and the experience of exclusion when witnessing neighbors and friends enjoy their lives or even comparing one's current situation with those previously experienced oneself. A person living in a remote village, in other words, would be satisfied with a diet of basic foods seasoned with only salt because that would be what the individual had always consumed and that was what was consumed by their fellows. Thus *these* foods, for *these* individuals, would taste good, and so they would enable *vitamina*. But, António continued, someone living in a town would find the same diet paltry, dissatisfying, an embarrassment, and (therefore) not tasty. He explained, "They would be comparing with their neighbors, and they would say, 'This is not food.' They would think of the *ndiwo* that they ate yesterday, which was stewed with tomato and oil and onions, and they would just think their food today is not good." That same food that could lead to *vitamina* in the bush, then, would not do so in a town. *Vitamina* was contingent, and taste perception varied by individual circumstances external to the body and experienced through affective response.

This point was driven home when I passed through the neighborhood of Thungo one afternoon and came across a small family preparing greens for lunch. They sat on the front veranda (an odd place to cook) fanning a fire sandwiched between two earthen bricks, upon which a small pot of frothing phosphorescent green stew bubbled. A stack of denuded stems sat in a neat pile on an old maize sack to the right of the pot. As I was in the habit of doing as a conversation starter when I came across people engaged in food preparation, I asked the woman with the stirring spoon in her hand what she was cooking. It was *kaminga*, she told me—a wild-growing, edible leaf that I had heard of through free-listing exercises, but I had never before recorded being cooked or consumed. I took a whiff and asked if *kaminga* tasted good. The woman responded with a simple phrase: "Are we not eating our problems?" (*Sitikudya thabu?*). The answer, in other words, was obvious—because they were reduced to eating wild leaves, rather than greens that had been cultivated or purchased, the family was experiencing a hardship. They were unable to rely on family, friends, or neighbors for help with foodstuffs, and so they found themselves collecting wild greens and experiencing negative emotional states. Wild greens were a tangible product and symbol of disparity, hence the question of flavor being both inapt and inept (and perhaps also why they were cooking on the front veranda, to publicly announce their dire straits). The *kaminga* leaves could not taste good, and for anyone who found themselves in circumstances that required consuming wild greens when there was opportunity for other fare, the meal would taste unpleasant. This meant a continued deficit in *vitamina*, and so also in vitality and wellness.

Back at the shebeen on the Sanjala hill, I wanted to be sure that, in his description of the discrepancies between *vitamina* properties of a food consumed in both "bush" and "town" contexts, António was not describing some sort of inherent difference between "bush" and "town" *peoples*. So I asked what would happen if a baby born in Metangula to parents from Metangula was moved to a "bush" location at an early age to be raised by some other family member. If this happened immediately after the baby was born, António explained, the baby would be fine with "just salt and water," meaning the most basic of alimentation. "That baby would look at oil and think, 'This is not food; this was not eaten by my grandparents.'" But, he continued, a baby of three or four months "has begun to eat *ntchima*, and so the baby would cry in the bush with only salt and water. Their life would not be very good." Indeed, I often saw small portions of *ntchima* dipped into the *nsuni* (liquid stew) of *ndiwo* side dishes and placed into an infant's mouth, where it was worked for several moments with the tongue and then emitted in a stream of drool. In António's description, such experiences would generate expectations for an infant as to what food should taste like. And without those expectations being met, the infant would perceive him- or herself to be suffering. This would prevent the child from building *vitamina*, and they would not be in good health. Context and affect, in other words, mattered more than the specific content of a meal, and the tongue was perceptive to more than just flavor.

The point finds good company among the observations of other food scholars who document intersections of food and memory (Holtzman 2009; Sutton 2001) and taste as conditioned through expectations rather than a matter of pure gustatory experience (Korsmeyer and Sutton 2011). Many with whom I discussed *vitamina* in Metangula provided anecdotes and explanations that concur with such analyses and with António's account, suggesting duress, deprivation, shame, anxiety, and anomie as pathogenic emotions that negated the capacity of alimentation to arouse *vitamina*. This was in large part because eating is not enjoyable to those who are suffering, like the family cooking *kaminga* leaves on their front veranda. Food would not taste good and meals would not be satisfying where an individual was unwell. Undesirable circumstances could also impact an individual's appetite, such that mental fixation on a problem might lead to skipped meals or the diminished desire to eat at all. This also resulted in deficient *vitamina*. Paolo, a man of mixed Portuguese and Mozambican origins, for example, told me that he was in ill health because he had last seen his father around at the age of three. His mother had been in a relationship with a Portuguese soldier stationed at the naval base in Metangula during the War for Independence, during which Paolo was conceived and born. As an adult, Paolo found it distressing to be saddled with no father and, what he said was worse, not knowing whether his progenitor was alive or deceased. Paolo was employed as a guard at a local maize mill and said that he spent most of his idle time there crying. When I would find him there or at his home on the foothills of Mount Chifuli, his shoulders were often hunched, and as we spoke he would sporadically lose his train of thought and stare intensely into the distance. Paolo told me that he often refused meals because he lacked the appetite to consume them—he was preoccupied with thoughts about his father. And even when he did eat, nothing tasted good. This was why he was often unwell. By not eating, and not enjoying his meals when he did consume food, his blood was lacking *vitamina*.

Filomena also lacked an appetite. Introduced briefly in the preface as an acquaintance and then again in the introduction as the mother of Diana, who took up residency in Monica's kitchen while pregnant, Filomena was a strong and proud woman, "one of only two individuals with disabilities in Metangula who farmed," she often reminded me. Filomena once recounted for me that which she had heard from family—that she had been a beautiful child, which had made an aunt jealous. The aunt reacted by bewitching her, disguising the *dawa* (in this case, a substance for inflicting harm) in the form of a polio vaccine. The morning after Filomena had gone to receive the shot, her feet began twisting awkwardly and she writhed in pain. Her mother responded by burying Filomena's legs in the sand, in the hopes of straightening them out again. She also consulted with multiple *ang'anga* (traditional healers; singular, *sing'anga*), through which she obtained knowledge of who was to blame for her daughter's condition, but she could find no cure. The young Filomena's lower legs and feet soon lost their full functioning, and she was forced to locomote by crawling on hands and knees. As an adult, she traveled by way of a dilapidated, three-wheeled, hand-pedaled wheelchair the government provided to her—that is, when the tires were not flat, the chain was not broken, and the dirt paths were not too muddy.

Filomena was someone I frequently visited, and I could often convince her to help me cook foods that others were unwilling to help me to prepare, like wild roots and leaves, but also inventions of my own curiosity like *ntchima* made from wheat flour or from the maize pericarp (*gaga*) that was usually fed to goats. It was not unusual for Filomena to abstain from eating much when we sat down to try the results. I initially blamed this on the oddity of the fare, but she did the same when we were together for more standard meals as well. She explained her lack of appetite with the difficulty of her circumstances. As the mother of seven children, with a home near coveted amenities like the lake, a water pump, and the market, and a healthy plot of land on which she grew cassava, Filomena had by many standards a good life. But she was also married to an alcoholic man who sold their belongings to the highest bidder when he needed money to imbibe, often squandering Filomena's meager earnings from selling banana bread, peanuts, *bolos*, and chili peppers in the market. On occasion he physically beat her with the pump she used to inflate her wheelchair tires. Not only did the family lack financial resources, but because Robert was a recent immigrant from Malawi and Filomena was physically disabled, they also did not have much in the way of political clout. Robert's daughter from a previous marriage had also recently been ejected from Robert and Filomena's home, accused of dabbling in the occult just like her twin brother had been when they lived in Malawi. All of this was distressing, but not unexpected: financial windfalls came and went, domestic abuse was commonplace and, while disapproved of by many, widely tolerated, and witchcraft was common. What was most troubling to Filomena was her neighbor, Paulina, a woman near her own age who had made it a routine to announce loudly from her veranda how much better her own life was in comparison to Filomena's.

One September morning Filomena was feeling particularly anxious about Paulina's tirades, which Filomena told me had first begun when she herself had successfully made over 10,000 meticais selling peanuts the previous year. She had used the money to purchase a fishing net for her husband and had temporarily been able to buy more than five pounds of meat for one meal. She laughed a hearty guffaw as she recalled the meals they had eaten when she was selling peanuts, smiling and declaring very matter-of-fact, "We ate very well." But she also made certain to point out that even at present, when the peanut money had long since been exhausted, there was no hunger in her home. "How can a person with *ntchima* be poor?" she asked me, responding indirectly to her neighbor's accusations of penury. "Even so much that the *ntchima* is 'sleeping' until the next day." With this last statement, she uncovered an aluminum pot containing leftovers from the previous evening's meal. This was something that would be reheated for breakfast in some households, but more often fed to chickens and goats. That food remained (or had "slept") until morning was intended to indicate that nobody was wanting for food in her household.

But there was more. Filomena tilted the pot toward me and indicated that I should look closer at the *ntchima*, pointing out that the two dough masses were swimming in an unusual-looking, faintly colored, and partially coagulated liquid. As I looked up and met her gaze, Filomena's eyebrows raised and she slowly nodded, as if to confirm what I should be thinking. She replaced the lid and put the pot aside, explaining that she suspected the strange appearance was due to Paulina pouring *dawa* into the cooking pot during the night, with the intention of causing illness when Filomena consumed leftovers the next day. She sucked her teeth lightly and her head quivered, as if trying to shake negative thoughts out of her mind. She took up a more serious tone than I had previously heard her use. "Neighbors," she said, "cannot be enemies." It was the thought of Paulina as her nemesis that made Filomena lose her appetite and so, even if she did manage to consume something, to be lacking in *vitamina*. It was as such that sanguinity physiologically manifested, and back again. Likewise, emptiness. In both cases, this occurred regardless of the specific content of one's diet.

Oil, Onion, and Tomato

If *vitamina* diminished where an individual was unsatisfied with their meal, or where they lacked an appetite, it stands to reason that satisfying and appetizing meals would precipitate *vitamina*. Indeed, this seemed to be the case. Cooking such *vitamina*-assuring meals, though they might take on diverse forms, typically required three specific ingredients: oil, onion, and tomato. These three foods, as such, had seemingly stable and consistent nutritive properties for everyone. Not only this, the trio of ingredients were spoken about as if *necessary* for health, operating more like sources of vitamins than *vitamina*. It would seem, then, on the surface at least, that these three foods were incorporated into cultural knowledge about the body and wellness in ways that were distinct from all other foods, which were more mercurial and dependent on affect in their capacities to enable *vitamina*. Digging deeper, however, feeling and experience were at play for tomatoes, oil, and onions as well. In this section, I make the case for these three edibles as both special in their *vitamina*-stable classification and at the same time wholly ordinary, as a closer look reveals that their ability to provision *vitamina* was contingent, just like that of other foods', on corporeal response. Specifically, the stability of these three ingredients' *vitamina* attribution seemed to be a product of their predictable capacities to physiologically satiate, visually and olfactorily stimulate the appetite, and produce socially meaningful meals. Though still dependent on affect to enable *vitamina*, the reliably positive experience of eating onions, tomatoes, and oil, particularly where mixed together to form a hearty *ndiwo*, meant some assurance of both precursory and resulting wellness.

It should be unsurprising, then, that oil, onion, and tomato were among the foods most commonly consumed in Metangula. In the yearlong dietary survey I designed, administered, and oversaw during my field research, oil, tomato, and onion were among only a handful of ingredients that nearly every participating homestead reported consuming (100 percent of households for oil, 99 percent for tomato, and 97 percent for onion). The only other foods that were consumed over the course of the year in at least 90 percent of homesteads were *ntchima* made from *ufa woyera* (ground, soaked-maize flour, with the pericarp removed), sweet potato, pumpkin, beans, mango, *utaka* fish, and *chai* ("tea," but in local parlance meaning simply hot water). Oil (with 3,536 recorded instances of consumption), tomato (3,428 instances), and onion (2,308 instances) were also among the ingredients most frequently reported as used in the survey, outnumbered only by flour. There were only a handful of other foods for which I recorded even more than 1,000 instances of use over the course of the survey: sugar (1,512 instances), *chai* (1,471 instances, about 86 percent of instances including tea leaves), and beans (1,197 instances), along with the all-important additive salt (5,751 instances), which will be addressed separately in chapter 4.

A pass through the Metangula market would also demonstrate the centrality of these ingredients for the local diet. The same tomato and onion sellers (often one and the same) sat every day, from sunup to sundown, at semi-permanent, staked, bamboo, sandalwood, and tarpaulin tables (with sun shades, of course), interspersed with oil, salt, and sugar vendors—creating a one-stop shop for these five ingredients, four of which (onion, tomato, oil, and salt) were often combined to flavor and form the *nsuni* (stewed, liquid base) of *ndiwo* side dishes, to which fish, greens, meats, or occasionally mushrooms (whether fungi or the dried, textured soy also called *bowa*) were added. I often passed the afternoons in this section of the market, conversing with the vendors and on occasion being placed in charge of selling when someone had to step away. Amado was a salt and oil vendor who was often willing to share his wooden bench with me, perhaps because he knew that it was likely that I would purchase a snack and that if I did, I would share it. During my visits I noted that Amado, like the other vendors, would receive among his customers family or acquaintances expecting a small discount in the form of a *basera*, or "gift," like an extra tablespoon of loose salt when they purchased a cup's worth. One day an elderly woman who came to purchase salt protested that Amado should provide her with oil free of charge. While she had the money to pay for it, she explained, holding out her hand with a ten-metical coin inside of it, she still needed to purchase tomatoes and onions for making dinner. Ten meticais certainly would not go a far way to do that, relegating her to purchase perhaps a single, small onion and a small pile of tomatoes. Amado not only acquiesced to the request for free oil, but he provided her with twice the amount of salt she had paid for. When I inquired about the motivation for his kindness, Amado reported that the old woman was a witch who could cause him to die if she was angry. While offered in jest (I think) before explaining that the

Figure 1.3. A vendor sells oil in the market. Photo by the author.

woman was his grandmother, the incident underscores the perceived seriousness of the necessity of tomatoes, onions, and oil (as well as salt) as culinary additives, the negative feelings that could erupt where a person was denied them, and the idiom of kin for making and fulfilling requests for care.

This ethnographic snippet from the marketplace, in concert with my observations in backyards and on verandas while cooking and eating in Metangula, and with the statistics produced through the dietary survey, makes clear the centrality of tomato, oil, and onion in the local diet. The question, of course, remains as to the rationale for this abundance. When I asked various acquaintances why these three ingredients were so important for cooking *ndiwo*, they repeatedly told me that onion, tomato, and oil made meals rich in *vitamina*. Their combination in the cooking pot, in other words, had the capacity to impart healthful properties to any food with which they were combined and so to enhance the vitality of consumers. It was such that when I attempted early on in my research to undertake a simple survey to find out which foods had *vitamina* and which foods did not, the most common response I got (besides a blank stare) was "How is the food prepared?"

Maria, an older woman in the neighborhood of Nchenga, entertained my questions one day as we sat on overturned mortars in front of her home. She had mentioned that she was feeling "anemic"—which she, like others, explained as lacking blood from insufficient *vitamina*. This was because she had not been eating very well lately. "Beans for lunch, beans for dinner," she complained in a common refrain that I heard in Metangula regarding dietary monotony, particularly during the rainy season when there were few ingredients for sale in the marketplace beyond legumes, not much to be harvested aside from pumpkin leaves, and little the fishers' nets brought ashore besides *usipa* fish. I took the opportunity of Maria discussing her condition to ask whether fish had *vitamina* or not. "Well, what kind of fish?" she inquired. She caught me off guard. "*Usipa*," I tried, thinking that perhaps I had finally stumbled onto a stable *vitamina* classification system. She qualified her response in a way that I did not expect, "A fried *usipa* fish has *vitamina*, but one that is roasted on an open fire does not." Frying in oil, in other words, made the fish (and any food, I would come to understand) have *vitamina*, as did stewing *usipa* with tomatoes, onions, and oil, it would turn out. But direct contact of the fish (and other foods) with fire meant that resultant fare did not have *vitamina*.

This line of reasoning finds good company in the history of anthropological theorizing about food and foodways, Claude Lévi-Strauss (1969) having given much attention to the matter of cooking technologies in his oft-cited *Mythologies* series. One structural model he proposed for an analysis of Amerindian myth links different states of food substances (raw, cooked, and putrid) and type of cooking (roasting, smoking, and boiling) with nature or culture. He saw cooked foods, for instance, as representing a cultural form, in opposition to both putrid and raw, which were natural forms. At the same time, raw was opposed to putrid because the latter is transformed and the former is not. This represented for Lévi-Strauss an abstract triangle, onto which a concrete triangle of cooking techniques could be transposed and similar oppositions drawn, marking some cooking techniques as more clearly representative of culture than others. Roasting, for example, in cooking food through direct exposure to fire, and boiling, through indirect exposure, marked the former as representative of nature and the latter as representative of culture. And so goes a host of binary oppositions mediated by presence or absence of air or water, length of cooking time, uniformity of cooking, and, in some instances, the simple imposition of human myth. Lévi-Strauss' "culinary triangle" has been called "obscure but interesting" by Alan Barnard (2000, 130), a "farrago of nonsense" by Stephen Mennell (1996, 9), and a "game of acrostics" by Edmund Leach (1989, 29), suggesting mixed opinion by more contemporary anthropologists on its utility as an analytical tool. Anne Murcott provides a fairly balanced approach to the matter, noting that recognizable similarities in the ways people think about food cross-culturally suggest Lévi-Strauss was onto something. But, she concedes, "sorting out the worthwhile and the far-fetched is no easy matter with Lévi-Strauss" (1988, 10). Lévi-Strauss himself even admitted in the introduction to *The Raw and the Cooked*, from which the culinary triangle is extracted, that his interpretations very well could have been a product of the workings of his own mind (1969, 13).

If a scheme like the culinary triangle were to be used to interpret *vitamina*, we might note that those states that align with "culture" (boiled, stewed, fried, and also cultivated and purchased) were more likely to be associated with wellness, strength, vitality, and health than those that were not. Be that as it may (or may not), what is interesting about Maria's distinction between fried and roasted *usipa* fish for the present analysis is that a single ingredient—oil—made a difference in *vitamina* attribution. This distinction was not unique to fish. People in Metangula, for example, snacked happily on fried dough fritters (*bolos*), said to have *vitamina*. But bread rolls, made with the same ingredients as *bolos*—wheat, water, yeast, sugar—sans oil, had no *vitamina* and were in fact designated as "sucking blood," a categorization somewhat the opposite of *vitamina*, discussed below. While the significance of oil for *vitamina* may have been in part gustatory, there is significance to be found also in the fact that oil was one of the most accessible and certainly the most common source of fat in the local diet. And, without fat, it is difficult to feel physiological satiation. Because feeling satisfied with a meal was integral to its enabling *vitamina*, it would seem that oil operated very much like any other food: capacitated to impart *vitamina* in concert with positive corporeal response. Foods into which oil was added or foods cooked in oil were satiating, and thus they provisioned *vitamina*.

Besides oil, another major source of fat in the Nyanja diet was meat. And, like many African societies, people in Metangula expressed a distinct liking and periodic craving for it. The food was among the most expensive in the marketplace, and in the dietary survey many households served meat—inclusive of beef, goat, duck, chicken, and on very rare occasion pork—on holidays, without which the meal simply could not be festive. My own host household on several occasions undertook long journeys to neighboring villages just to buy a chicken (while there were many chickens in Metangula, owners were often loath to part with their fowl), and when a holiday was approaching it was common to see cars returning from Lichinga with live goats tied to their roofs. Meat was also an appropriate dish for special guests. This was the reason that I gave up vegetarianism early in my forays to Metangula, as I felt awkward declining food while knowing someone had made a financial sacrifice just for me to feel welcomed. This was also around the time that Julio Mercader, an archaeologist I worked with for several years in Metangula, decided to fly Lourenço, his project manager, to Maputo. Here Lourenço would participate in the process of project reporting to Universidade Eduardo Mondlane and the government and enjoy a bit of vacation. To honor Lourenço, we took him to Costa do Sol, one of the most beloved fish markets in Maputo, where consumers select from among a variety of sea creatures that are then cooked up fresh. Lourenço looked bewildered when we placed a feast in front of him—foot-long shrimp, succulent shark steak, pan-seared calamari. "*Nyama*," he said under his breath, eyes cast downward, as if in disbelief. "*Osati nyama*." Meat; it is not meat. Our attempts at hospitality had caused unintentional offense because fish was common fare, rather than the celebratory feasting associated with eating meat.

But despite all the proclivity for meat that I encountered in action, in speech, and in Lourenço's disappointment, it seemed to be less the flesh and more the associated lard and marrow that were regularly associated with *vitamina*. Fatty bits with bones were more prized than meaty ones when doling out portions, such that when trying to behave modestly at a meal with a chief, I ended up looking greedy by selecting a chicken leg over a breast. One of few foods besides meat for which I heard people express periodic longings was *malimbachala*—orchid root that has been pounded, boiled, and then dried.[6] People said the delicacy was "like meat" (*ngati nyama*), but the rubbery consistency and neutral flavor of *malimbachala* was more like fat than flesh. All of this seems to suggest that the most appropriate translation for the word *nyama* is not so much "meat" as it is (land) animal, and that Nyanja meat craving was at least in part the expression of a longing for fats. Equally, the word *mafuta* in Chinyanja, usually translated as "oil," is more appropriately "lipid" in a culinary context, for the category includes fats in liquid and solid forms, all of which acquaintances regularly classed as contributing toward *vitamina*.

If oil, then, derives its stable *vitamina* classification through its predictable association with physiological satisfaction, onion was awarded similar status for its role in stimulating appetite. The desire to eat was, in fact, very much tied up in the pleasant aroma that is emitted when an onion is being fried in oil, which both encouraged consumption and made eating a pleasurable (and so *vitamina* enhancing) experience. The connections between onions, appetite, and *vitamina* were voiced in a particularly clear manner in an encounter that I had with three women volunteering to help prepare porridge and bean soup as part of a nutrition program organized by the local health center. "Every ingredient provides nutrition," Beatriz, the health center's nutrition officer, told the volunteer cooks in a self-important tone. Beatriz was doing very little to help physically prepare the two dishes that would be served to women waiting to have their babies weighed and measured at their monthly screening. Beatriz took her leave to attend to some paperwork, and the three women continued chopping, peeling, pouring, and stirring. They needed little instruction to prepare the dishes, having learned to make them while previously working for Estamos, a local NGO funded by the Clinton Foundation. When the project's money had dried up, they found themselves out of work. Still, they continued at their previous duties when asked by the hospital to do so, in the explicit hope that one day they would receive remuneration for these tasks.

Given the context, it seemed appropriate to ask the women for their understanding of the nutritional properties of the dishes they were working to prepare. Both of the dishes, the women told me in turn, building off one another's comments and at one point explicitly translating into Chinyanja what Beatriz had said in Portuguese, "have *vitamina*." Rosa, the most talkative of the three women, elaborated on several of the specific ingredients. "For the porridge you can add peanuts or you can add oil," she explained as an example. "But you do not need both, because they do the same thing." While she could not name what that "thing" was, she had enough Clinton Foundation funded training to know that foods could be grouped by their nutritional properties. Not familiar myself with any bio-nutritional benefits to eating onion (which I would later learn include vitamin C, fiber, folic acid, calcium, iron, and protein), I asked what "thing" the ingredient added to a person's diet. Without missing a step, Rosa responded, "They smell good." Onion fried in oil, she continued, "will make a person want to eat." This property of appetite stimulation was the sum of an onion's dietetic benefit, equitable with fats, vitamins, and proteins as a nutritional property in and of itself, for it helped to ensure appetite, and so *vitamina* and vitality. I return to Beatriz, Rosa, and their public health campaigning again in chapter 5.

The importance of appetite stimulation for the nutritional attributes of *vitamina* can be seen in other ways, as well. Most notably, in the realm of vision—an element of taste elaborated by Carolyn Korsmeyer as assuring eaters of edibility, arousing desires to eat, and heightening taste through the anticipation of flavor (Korsmeyer and Sutton 2011). In Metangula, such effects were tied to the color red, especially in relation to *nsuni*, the stewed, liquid component of *ndiwo* side dishes. An *nsuni* that was not red would make for an aesthetically inferior dish and could not provide *vitamina*, because it did not stimulate the appetite. Cooks often achieved the red color of *nsuni* through the addition of tomatoes to the *ndiwo* cooking pot. Tomatoes were, however, too expensive for regular inclusion in the diet of some homesteads. Oil vendors like Amado responded to this reality by mixing a flavorless red powder (*colorão*, "coloration") into the small vials of soybean oil he sold for about ten cents. When I noticed one day that some of Amado's oil vials were significantly yellower than the others, I asked why. He responded matter-of-factly that he had run out of *colorão*. Having not previously recognized that the vials I sat behind all those afternoons contained coloration at all, I dug deeper. Amado reported that when he left the oil its natural translucent yellow color, it was "ugly." Individuals with limited financial means (like his grandmother) would be reluctant to spend money on this ugly, yellow oil because they would be thinking about the need also to buy tomatoes to produce a red-colored *ndiwo*. If the oil was already red, Amado reasoned, only one purchase would have to be made.

Once I trained my eye to recognize the difference between beautiful and ugly oils, I saw the distinction at the other vendors' stalls as well. Through inquiry I came to realize that adding *colorão* to small quantities of oil was standard marketplace practice. I did not, however, see coloring added to oil where it was sold in larger jugs from the more formal, bulk market vendors. When I reported this observation back to Amado, he explained that this was of course the case. It was unnecessary to color bottles of oil, because anyone who could afford to buy that quantity at once (about two American dollars' worth, or a full day's wage for unskilled labor) could probably also afford tomatoes. A similar logic of achieving red coloration to visually please and so stimulate the appetite of consumers also underlay the addition of baking soda to porridge where a household lacked money to purchase oil. Chemical reactions caused the mixture to redden (and so to resemble porridge into which oil had been added), making it visually appealing, appetizing, and (so) *vitamina*-rich. Aesthetic, and the emotions and feelings that it elicited by stimulating the appetite, thus seemed more important than foods themselves for provisioning *vitamina*. *Colorão* and baking soda themselves did not impart *vitamina*, according to those I asked. But their capacity to imitate red, viscous foods achieved the same effect.[7]

Tomatoes, on their part, in addition to providing red coloring to a meal, seemed to enable *vitamina* in large part because they allowed a greater number of individuals to partake in the fare. To explain, we must briefly consider how a meal of *ntchima* and *ndiwo* was typically consumed. While guests were often served their meals separately, it was typical in Metangula to find the members of a household eating in small groups—women and children encircling a mountain of *ntchima* with one or more dishes of *ndiwo*, and older boys and men around a second *ntchima* mountain and plates of *ndiwo*. To eat *ntchima* properly, a consumer pinched the large mass with their fingers to remove a small piece (*mbamu*) that fit nicely into the palm of their hand. A consumer then smoothened the piece by holding it in their palm, squeezing their hand shut, opening it, manipulating the position of the ball, and squeezing their hand shut again (*kukomata*), then repeating.[8] Once the piece was well condensed and shaped, the consumer might press their thumb lightly into one side of the ball, creating a shallow scoop into which pieces of *ndiwo* might fit. The individual then dipped their *mbamu* into the *ndiwo*. If the vegetable, bean, mushroom, fish, or meat was resistant to being removed through this action, the ball could be pulled up into the palm and the thumb and index finger used to remove a small amount of *ndiwo*, or the ball kept in place but the thumb used to pinch *ndiwo* against it. However, eating chunks of *ndiwo* with every bite was unbecoming, as it meant that the *ndiwo* would not last long. In my own household, when I could manage to get the family to let me eat with them (rather than separately, as a guest),[9] I would often see grandchildren scolded for consuming too much *ndiwo* proper and not enough of the stewed juices (*nsuni*), most often composed of tomatoes and oil.[10] When the *ndiwo* was disappearing too quickly, Judite, the head of household, would declare that the grandchildren were eating "like fish," and she would mime the way that the animals quickly open and close their mouths.

It was rare at one of these meals to run out of *ntchima*. There was usually something left over, in other words, of the main staple such that it could "sleep" until the next day, as Filomena declared to bolster her claims of not suffering from poverty amid her neighbor's tirades. But those gathered for a meal almost always finished their allotted *ndiwo*. And if they did not, it was typically consumed by someone else in the homestead, a neighbor, or a grandchild wandering between homes in search of something else to eat. *Ndiwo* was, in other words, the limiting factor in determining how many people could eat and how much *ntchima* could be consumed at a meal. When the *ndiwo* was gone, a meal was over. Adding more tomatoes to the *ndiwo* crafted a heartier, tastier, and more voluminous *nsuni*.[11] While perhaps less satisfying than the vegetable, bean, fish, and meat solids of *ndiwo* proper, the *nsuni* ensured that even those with meager resources could put something on the table that could feed a lot of people.[12] As I will take up in more detail in coming chapters, provisioning of and consideration for others was a key element of well-being. And where wellness is constituted by and constitutive of *vitamina*, it is very plausible that tomatoes consistently proffered *vitamina* at least in part for their capacity to engender compassionate care.

Besides sizzling onions, voluminous tomato stews, and satiating fats, appetite was also stimulated and satisfied in Metangula through dietary variety. Novelty prevented the boredom that might otherwise disincline a person from eating their next meal. I frequently heard complaints of dietary monotony along with self-diagnosis of anemia in the dry season months of June through November, when *ndiwo* selection was minimal and expensive. "All we are eating these days is rape shoots," one person said with a scowl; another, "Sweet potato leaves for lunch, sweet potato leaves for dinner . . ." Maria's complaint about beans was already noted above. Acquaintances would tell me they had skipped meals not because they were lacking food, or because they craved exotic foods, but because the idea of eating the same thing yet again was repulsing. Alima was complaining of hunger (*njala, njala* . . .) one afternoon as she swatted her stick at the goats in her yard. Yet, she was still immediately able to bring me a cooked plateful of cassava leaves to snack on when I professed a particular fondness for the dish. She was not lacking the ingredients or fuel to cook, but the appetite to consume. Reliance on a monotonous inventory of foods decreased appetite and so diminished *vitamina*.

Seemingly in response to such a conundrum, particularly well-off families in Metangula would sometimes offer two or more *ndiwo* at a single meal, allowing a person to select their preference rather than forcing consumption of a single dish that may not be enjoyable to all. For most families, however, simply having fish one day, beans the next, and greens the day after (for example) ensured that individuals would not experience ennui, did not feel deprived, maintained an appetite, and thus were able to strengthen their vitality with *vitamina*. This was also a reason, some said, that certain foods were reserved for festive occasions. When celebrating, it was appropriate and desirable to eat novel foods like noodles and cake and to drink *thobwa* (a grainy, cassava-based nonalcoholic beverage, sweetened with sorghum or millet), precisely because they were unusual in the local diet. In my dietary survey, 25 percent of noodle consumption occurred on holidays, all five instances of cake eating occurred on Christmas and New Year's Day, and there was no *thobwa* drunk outside of the celebration of Eid ul-Fitr. While financial means and time constraints also likely played a role here, festive foods being somewhat pricey and/or difficult to prepare, as one well-off acquaintance stated, "If we ate noodles every day, then what would we eat when we are celebrating?" Consumption would not *feel* special if it were a regular occurrence.[13]

Feel the Taste

The section above on onion, tomato, and oil adds depth to the shebeen vignette that opened this chapter by elucidating *vitamina* as related to feeling and experience, and taste as dependent on more than the tongue. I would like to expand upon these points here through a brief consideration of a fourth food that people in Metangula consistently mentioned as a harbinger of *vitamina*: sugar. Sugars were sometimes consumed in Metangula in the form of industrially manufactured cookies or soft drinks and increasingly as hard sucking candies (*masuwiti*) sold for a few cents from doorsteps in every neighborhood. But it was most often that sugar was purchased from the market raw in one-kilogram bags (about two pounds) for about one American dollar or, like the divvying up of bulk jugs of oil into smaller quantities for purchase by the less wealthy, in small plastic vials for a few cents. Raw sugar might be added to porridge or consumed by a child who snuck into the food pantry, licked their fingers, and dipped them in for a quick snack. But sugar was most coveted as an additive to *chai* (Swahili for "tea").

In local parlance *chai* indicated simply hot water. While many added loose tea leaves or lemongrass, and some added condensed milk, the key ingredient for a satisfying (and *vitamina*-rich) cup of *chai* was sugar, preferably several tablespoons worth. At a local shop where I purchased tea and bread for breakfast on days that I wanted to get going quicker than the pace my host household allowed for, I noted that it was only myself among the customers who was allowed to add the sugar to my cup of *chai*. Other customers' tea came to the table pre-sweetened, the owners assuming that otherwise patrons would take as much sugar as was offered—and with good reason. When Tina, the shop owner, once made the mistake of leaving a mounded sugar bowl on my table in a show of feigned hospitality—by this point she knew that I preferred tea without sugar (*chingabwe*, a perceived to be very odd behavior that people in Metangula associated with Malawians)—another customer took it when she was not looking. I watched him add ten teaspoons to his own pre-sweetened mug before the error was detected and Tina came to scoop the dish away. For my host family also, there were constant tensions between the heads of household and the construction workers we were paying to seal the house with concrete, each accusing the other of rationing sugar (and also occasionally jam and sweetened condensed milk) improperly. The workers argued that they needed the sweetness for *vitamina* to do their work. The family felt that the workers were being greedy and unreasonable, squandering limited resources.

In the case of sugar, then, we again encounter a situation (similar to onion, tomato, and oil) where it would seem that a specific food had intrinsic and immutable properties to impart *vitamina* to those who consumed it. But, like oil, onion, and tomato, contextual and embodied circumstances provide some nuance. Sweetness, let us consider, is the most universally liked flavor (Reed and McDaniel 2006), making it reasonable to expect that a person consuming sugar will find the experience of eating it pleasurable.[14] Because positive feelings when consuming a food translated into *vitamina*, sugar, by default, would almost always be *vitamina*-rich. It was, then, not the sugar per se, but the satisfaction felt while eating or drinking it that gave it a near consistent labeling as *vitamina* enhancing. Likewise, where a person was not primed to enjoy the sweetness—due to external circumstances and resultant internal states—*vitamina* would not be forthcoming. As Helena suggested at the Sanjala shebeen, "Even sugar would taste bitter to someone who has problems." The tongue only worked without worries. It would seem, in fact, that the word *kukoma*, usually translated as "to taste sweet," more broadly means "pleasantness," such that I recorded a well-salted *ndiwo* as labeled *chokoma* (sweet) as often as an orange-flavored Fanta or an orgasm. Comparable observations have been made elsewhere in the region. Beatrice Mary Chimwaza noted, for example, equivalent usage for a Chewa population in Malawi, where sour water added to *ndiwo* made it "sweet" (1982, 33). Jon Holtzman found similar applications among the Samburu in Kenya, and Brad Weiss among the Haya in Tanzania, the authors concluding that the local word for "sweet" in each context more accurately meant "tasty" (Holtzman 2009, 62) or "agreeable" (Weiss 1996, 94).

Likewise the verb *kuwawa*, usually translated as "to taste bitter," in my recordings more broadly meant "unpleasant," and the associated experience was not restricted to the tongue. As such, prussic acid–rich varieties of cassava, poverty, and the smell of gasoline were equally *chowawa*, as were *kaminga* leaves and any other wild food gathered out of necessity, the bitterness of the situation that led to consuming these plants seemingly transferred to the experience of eating them. The two categories of sweet and bitter, or, it would seem, pleasurable and unpleasant, could be used to describe almost any instance of alimentation, and they mapped onto *vitamina*. Hence sugary foods were almost always classed as *vitamina*-rich, regardless of their other properties, because eating sugar felt pleasant. More broadly, feeling well enabled any food to have *vitamina* (even wild leaves cooked with nothing but salt in the bush, as António indicated). Likewise, anything experienced as unpleasant—whether alimentary or circumstantial—indicated lack of *vitamina*. In sum, that which was pleasurable enhanced life in both the physical and emotional senses of sanguinity, while that which was not pleasurable or was painful diminished these traits.[15]

The association of sweetness with pleasure and bitterness with unpleasantness was in large part what made my preference for tea without sugar so perplexing for people in Metangula. While embraced by Tina, the tea shop owner, as a mechanism for her to retain additional profits, it simply did not make sense in local formulation—sweet things were pleasurable. But I prefer the taste of tea without sugar, making *chingabwe* (tea without sugar) *chokoma* (pleasurable) for me, and sweetened tea *chowawa* (unpleasant). My husband feels the same way. And yet, every morning for the year plus that we lived with our host family, they set out a bowl of sugar to accompany a thermos of hot water for our morning breakfast. Up through the end of our stay, when granddaughters, daughters, and nieces were sent to clear our dishes, I would catch them lifting the lid to the sugar bowl and, finding it untouched, looking up in awe. Upon a return visit in 2017 it was the same routine, though this time I was without my husband and the granddaughter charged with clearing my breakfast dishes, Solange, verbally confronted me to request explanation for the offense she had caused that led me to reject the sugar she put out. I explained my perception of tea without sugar tasting pleasurable, but this was not enough. Late in my stay, Solange requested that I teach her to bake the cookies we had made for Christmas in 2010. She was thinking that learning the techniques might provide her with skills to start her own business.

I obliged and hitched a ride with her uncle to Lichinga in order to purchase the ingredients that I could not get in Metangula—like vanilla, powdered sugar, and white sugar. We baked the cookies the next day in what had been her mother's *estufa* (a small, electric oven). Under my direction, Solange and her age-mates rolled the dough with an empty Coke bottle and cut out circles with an overturned mug. The day that followed, Solange brought the regular thermos of hot water to the table with a bit more skip in her step than usual. I looked up from writing my notes when she seemed to be making a show of adjusting the sugar bowl. She then lifted the lid to reveal that she had replaced the locally available turbinado sugar—large, brown crystals—with some of the refined white sugar left over from the cookies. "Now you will take sugar in your tea." She stated these words as a sort of declaration, not as a question, triumphantly solving the conundrum of my tea preferences—I must only consume refined, white sugar. When I encouraged her to take the dish away to try in her own tea, her broad smile quickly faded. She avoided my gaze as she carried the container out of the room, the thud of her bare heels forcefully striking against the concrete floor as she did so echoing throughout the house.

Full Bellies and Agentive Throats

While I was never able to fully convey my preference for tea without sugar, I did have some success in expressing my dislike of the sardine-like *usipa* fish. While I did not mind the flavor of *usipa*, I found that I could not muster an appetite for them (too many heads on one plate). Pleas that I "do not like" the fish had done nothing for months to stop the flow of them into the *ndiwo* that I was served. Individual disposition in accordance with likes and dislikes, despite the prevalence of such positioning in the global north (Lupton 1996, 86), was irrelevant here. But when I instead offered the explanation that "my throat rejects the food," my host family stopped serving *usipa* to me. By that point in my research I had discovered that the throat, in local formulation, played an important role in digestion. More than just a portal for food to enter into the body, the throat had some agency in determining what could and could not pass into the stomach. It was precisely in shifting my framing of dislike from personal predilection to corporeal response that I fostered understanding.

Where an individual's throat rejected a food, as mine did for *usipa*, they would sometimes feel a burning sensation, as if the food was still there, even after swallowing. I heard people say this of their throats most often in relation to boiled pumpkin and *ntchima* made from cassava flour (*kondowole*). In other cases, an individual's throat would make it so that they could not swallow the food at all. Lourenço, the archaeological project manager with a hankering for meat, for example, referenced his throat when explaining that he could not eat a common lake fish, *sanjika*, because it looked too much like a chameleon (which people in Metangula, sometimes with great effort, completely avoided). The attribution of negative food preferences to corporeal response, rather than personal dislike, has been noted by others—for example, Beatrice Mary Chimwaza (1982, 85) and Memory M. Mtembezeka (1994) in their studies of Malawian populations, though in these cases not associated with the throat. In Metangula, positive food preferences were also sometimes attributed to the throat, particularly where they were unusual (like snacking on raw okra). I never, on the other hand, heard anyone (besides myself) describe such food preferences in the realm of personal predilection ("I like unsweetened tea" or "I dislike *usipa* fish," for example). Penchant was, as such, placed squarely on somatic response and corporeal experience.

Cultural knowledge regarding digestion offers insight into other aspects of food classification in relation to embodied experience as well. For example, people considered foods that lingered in the belly or otherwise took a long time to digest to be "hard" (*-limba*). This was less a physical descriptor than a reflection of the foods' resistance to timely processing, which made a person feel full for an extended period. This might lead to skipped meals or constipation, both of which meant depleted *vitamina*.[16] People often referred to hard foods, like bread and boiled potatoes, as "ending" (*kutha*) or "sucking" (*kukhoka*) blood and considered them an impediment to wellness and vitality. Other "hard" foods included particular types of banana and *ntchima* made from cassava flour, which were best eaten only in moderation, as well as legumes—or at least their skins. I once came upon Maria carefully removing the fibrous coating of individual cooked beans to extract the tender insides for her lunch. She was feeling weak and feared that by eating the bean skins she might experience digestive problems that would keep her full for too long.[17]

Some hard foods could be more safely consumed with the simultaneous consumption of hot liquids or lubricants, with which hard foods "melted" (*kusungunuka*) more quickly in the belly. In the 606 instances of in-home bread consumption recorded in my dietary survey, for example, only a handful (6.8 percent) were not clearly accompanied by simultaneous ingestion of *chai* (tea) or an alternative lubricant like margarine. Though the survey did not record distinctions in breads, some of that consumed without a lubricant was likely handmade in the provincial capital Lichinga or industrially produced in neighboring Malawi. Unlike bread made in Metangula, those from Lichinga and Malawi were considered to be "soft" and *vitamina* enhancing, even without tea or margarine. Residents of Metangula had come to expect travelers from Lichinga to arrive with bread. This prompted minibuses to regularly stop at a bakery before leaving town, followed by an exodus of passengers scrambling for spare meticais to purchase a bag full of the large, doughy, ten-cent rolls that were more easily digested and less filling than bread from Metangula.

Contrary to what is often written of African diet, then, the primary goal of eating in Metangula was not to become "full." Rather, acquaintances explicated, it was important to eat until no longer hungry and in a manner that ensured that the stomach promptly emptied before the next mealtime. The distinction between being full and being satisfied can easily be lost on an observer who comes from a society where the meal is not complete until there is, colloquially, no room left in the belly. Even in Chinyanja, the same word (*kukhuta*) is used to describe the sensations of being without hunger, satisfied, full, and sated. But it is clearly the former two definitions that were preferred states in Metangula. My own tendency to overeat once sadly led me to have to decline a delectable snack of *topetope* (a sweet, fleshy fruit also known in English as custard apple, in Spanish as guanábana, and in the Caribbean as soursop) with the explanation that I was "full" (*ndakuta*). Monica looked at me confused, remarking, "But you have not even eaten it yet." Especially on holidays, people were wary of becoming too full. In addition to seeking out noodles and cake for their novelty, as discussed above, people also touted these foods as appropriately festive because they were not filling. Noodles and cake (and rice, cookies, and other "non-food" edibles) were ideal on holidays precisely because they could be eaten in large quantities

Figure 1.4. A group of men celebrate New Year's Day with beer and a meal of noodles mixed with beans. Photo by the author.

before feeling satisfied, enabling continued merriment without making the belly too full.[18]

In addition to hard foods, many people in Metangula considered lemons as particularly harmful to consume because of their impact on *vitamina*. I was first introduced to this strong negative prejudice on a sunny afternoon, early in my research campaign. I sat on a woven reed mat with Verónica, a middle-aged woman enrolled in the dietary survey. Two young women sat with us, Deolinda and Saldina. Several children played nearby in a small trash heap in the shade of a tree. The women and I were preparing pumpkin leaves for lunch. I had only recently met them, and we were all still feeling one another out. We made some small talk but largely stared at our own hands and went about the work in silence. After some time, Deolinda looked up and noticed that her child had left the trash pile. The young girl, about eight and wearing a dirtied dress that had once been white, had repositioned herself so that she was behind her mother and out of her immediate line of sight. When Deolinda seemed to be scanning the horizon looking for her daughter, I jutted my chin to indicate the girl's position. Deolinda glanced behind her. Catching sight of the girl, Deolinda turned back to her original position to drop the leaves she was working on, planted her left hand on the ground, and more fully swiveled her body to address the child. "What is that?" Deolinda asked in an accusatory manner. "A lemon!?" She amplified the word "lemon" (*ndimu*) in a frantic tone. The girl nodded slightly, her mouth too busy sucking on the fruit to respond verbally, and knowing that she was doing something wrong. "Throw it away!" Deolinda yelled, her manner giving the impression that this was a battle that the two had engaged in before, at which the mother had become exacerbated but expectant of the child's continued petulance.

The girl averted her gaze from her mother's and then turned her body away, continuing to enjoy the lemon with her back turned toward us. Deolinda returned to her work with the pumpkin leaves, shook her head disapprovingly, and clucked her tongue, "La." Not ready to give up, Verónica yelled at the girl also. "Hey you! Put that lemon down. It will make you skinny. You will not get fat. It will suck your blood!" The girl took the lemon from her mouth, glanced behind her at Verónica for a moment, and then returned to her former stance and her snack. Deolinda looked again behind her and then, with a huff, put the pumpkin leaves back down, got up, marched over to the girl, ripped the lemon from her hand, and threw it down into the trash heap. The fruit, now nearly folded in half and largely depleted of its juices from being sucked on so vigorously, landed in a pile of ashes. The girl started crying. Deolinda escorted her into Verónica's fenced yard, where she was left to her tantrum alone.

I watched this incident unfold with a bit of confusion. Not only were lemons, to me, an odd snack choice for a child, but the intensity of the offense that it caused both Deolinda and Verónica was perplexing. When Deolinda returned, I asked for additional explanation of what had transpired. Her response was delivered in a mix of Portuguese and Chinyanja. "When you eat a lemon," she said, "there is no appetite" (*opande apetite*). I would, over the course of the next several months, decipher that lack of appetite deprives the body of *vitamina*, and so blood, as I have outlined above. When recounting the lemon incident to others, I received explanations for Deolinda's reaction that were diverse, but all rooted in blood loss as the consequence of consumption. Some, for example, explained that lemon juice on an open wound stings and (so) dries blood, and it could be expected to do the same from within the body. In a similar vein, others offered that sucking on a lemon leaves the mouth feeling dry and so could be expected to dehydrate blood, stymying its movement. But many, like Deolinda also did, used the medical terminology of "anemia" (a biomedical disease, in which an individual lacks enough healthy red blood cells to carry adequate oxygen to the body's tissues) to explain the corporeal impact of eating or sucking on a lemon.

The connection between lemons and anemia, like that of vitamins and *vitamina*, evidences the messy mixture of local and biomedical knowledges of physiological processes. In this case, the blending may have been initiated by the health center itself via its nutrition specialist, Beatriz. When I went to her with the conundrum that local people were telling me they learned at the hospital that lemons caused anemia (whereas in more familiar biomedical formulation lemons and other citrus are touted as helping to combat anemia), she quickly and assertively replied, "But lemons *do* cause anemia." When I asked her to expand on the connection, she backtracked. Lemons do not *really* cause anemia, she explained, and in fact there were no health impacts from eating lemons at all, except that the acids cause you to lose weight. These are claims that I would later find no biomedical support for. Beatriz also suggested that lemon is fine to consume as juice. "But here in Metangula," she added, "they do not use lemons correctly. They just suck on them." She would tell people that lemons caused anemia, she explained, because this was a simple message that "the people" (*a população*) would understand. It would seem, then, that cultural knowledge and biomedical message had converged such that local perceptions of blood loss through foods that "suck blood" also induced anemia.

Conclusion

It was precisely the convergence of biomedicine and local knowledge that led to *vitamina* evading my attention, and my understanding, for much of my time in Metangula. In this chapter I have outlined what I eventually came to make of *vitamina* as an alimentary categorization distinct from biomedical "vitamins" in its dependence on corporeal feelings and emotions experienced during (though not necessarily stemming from) ingestion. While there were several foods in Metangula that could pretty consistently be counted on to rouse hunger and inspire contentedness with a meal (like onions, tomatoes, oil, and sugar), variability in individual reaction and the circumstances of consumption made *vitamina* a primarily personal and contextual rather than a definitive scheme. Individual life satisfaction could enable virtually any instance of eating to enhance *vitamina*, while unpleasantness, depression, anomie, repetition, and pain depleted *vitamina*, regardless of diet. The blood-based energy, or *thanzi*, enabled through eating thus resulted not so much from specific quantities or stable nutritional qualities of foods, but the experience of alimentation. This made the body not only a product of wellness, but a determinant of it, and blood not only a source of vitality, but a bellwether for the capacity to enact it. Sanguine persons and foods mutually constituted one another, while anything that caused pain, physically or contextually, "sucked blood" and depleted *vitamina*.

These associations seem to extend beyond Metangula, clues in the ethnographic record suggesting a more widespread regional salience. A report by the Mozambican Ministry of Health, for example, documented an equation of vitamins, energy, and blood circulation throughout northern Mozambique (Guzman 2006). This is echoed in the work of Sara Stevano, working in the same region almost a decade later. Stevano also found that food was evaluated as good for human health (or not) based on how it made a person feel, whether or not it tasted good, and if it had *vitamina*, though there was no consensus on the application of these criteria to specific foods (2014, 231–45). Further afield, Geissler and Prince (2010) wrote in passing of food as influencing the amount and quality of an individual's blood in Kenya among the Luo. Jon Holtzman (2009) noted, in Kenya also, that the Samburu used Guinness beer to build up blood supplies after childbirth. Weiss (1998) found that in Tanzania meat, leafy greens, and fish were classed as adding blood to the body and so enhancing well-being, while other foods like citrus and anything bitter tasting diminished blood.

Moving beyond East Africa, Jessica R. Ham concluded that a plant-based culinary additive used in Ghana was valued more for facilitating blood circulation and ensuring energy and strength than as a flavor enhancer (2017, 249). And, in a diasporic contribution, Michelle C. Johnson (2016) recorded that Africans from Guinea Bissau living in Portugal complained that "nothing tastes sweet," which she related to feelings of guilt at their abundance of expensive material objects, while others back in Africa suffered. As a result of this worry and stress, appetites became spoiled, food seemed tasteless, and what was consumed did not provide energy. Elisa Janine Sobo (1993) also reported that Afro-Jamaicans linked food, energy, and mental state—harmonious conditions ensuring vitality, and unhappiness correlating with lack of energy. Crucially, unhappiness came from disconnect with or being ostracized from one's community, which related to miserly, selfish, and other antisocial behaviors. Likewise, René Devisch wrote that among the Yaka in Democratic Republic of Congo, pent-up rage made a person withdraw from social circles, and in this anomie they suffered from "starvation" (1990, 128). Food, blood, well-being, and sociality—though not always the direct subject of ethnographic investigation—appear to commonly cluster in Africa and also for some diasporic populations with African ancestry. Likewise, where eating is about wellness as much as it is about sustenance, and well-being can only be achieved where a person feels fulfilled by their place in the world, then hunger becomes an intimate expression of dissatisfaction, exclusion, and anxiety—"starving on a full stomach," as Diana Wylie (2001) termed the lingering feeling of deprivation despite having plenty of food to eat from a biological standpoint. With this background, we can now turn more directly to the generative labor toward which *vitamina* was directed in Metangula.

Notes

1. Colleague Experencia Madalitso Jalasi has pointed out to me that António may have actually said *zokhoma* (aspirated "k") rather than *zokoma* (unaspirated "k"), a distinction that can be difficult for unaccustomed ears (like mine) to hear. *Kukhoma*, as a verb, means "to knock or hit." *Zokhoma*, as an adjective, can then mean "things that knock you down" and is used to indicate troubles, difficulties, pain, and other things that are negatively experienced. Given the context, this would mean that António's original statement was not that "blood is things that taste good," but rather something more akin to "blood is painful things" (personal communication, 5 January 2020). In my experience, pain was more frequently described in Metangula using the verbs *kuwawa* and *kupweteka*, both meaning "to hurt, have pain, or be painful." The manner in which the shebeen conversation I have recounted in the opening vignette unfolded suggests that while António may have initially used *kukhoma*, Samuel (a government employee who spoke Chinyanja but contributed to the conversation in Portuguese) heard *kukoma*, as I had. Given the way in which both pleasure and pain affect blood, both statements in Nyanja formulation are true: blood is things that taste good, and blood is things that are painful.
2. Non-biomedical systems for classifying, conceptualizing, experiencing, and treating illness and health are sometimes referred to with the term "ethnomedicine," coined by Charles Hughes (1978). The argument that biomedicine is also a system of ethnomedicine, entrenched in cultural logic as much as any other medical system, has since been advanced by a range of scholars. See Robert A. Hahn and Arthur Kleinman (1983) for an introduction to these ideas and Margaret M. Lock and Deborah Gordon (1988) for their seminal collection of essays laying bare the cultural scaffolding of biomedicine.
3. Sarah O'Neill et al. (2016), Jessica R. Ham (2017), and Eugenia Rodrigues (2014), among others, provide additional perspectives on the convergence of blood, vitality, and food in Africa.
4. Though I have not been able to recover any specific evidence of nutritional education programming or efforts to change local diet in Metangula or more broadly along the eastern shore of Lake Niassa, Agres Rennick (2003) records a variety of disparaging missionary remarks about lakeshore diet and feeding practices, and one missionary nurse did record a description of lakeshore diet as "practically without vitamins" (Universities' Mission to Central Africa 1952, 12).

5. While I have not come across descriptions of the sun being feared for depleting blood elsewhere in Africa, there is widespread association of shadows with a person's spirit, soul, or life essence. For additional information on this point, see the work of Anita Jacobson-Widding (1990).
6. Benjamin S. Platt (most likely via the observations of Margaret Read) noted the same hankering for boiled, pounded orchid root in colonial-era Nyasaland (present-day Malawi), where the dish was called *cinaka* (1939, 202). He also reported that people preferred the fat-rich belly and head of a fish over meaty portions (1939, 186). Primary documents related to his massive Nyasaland Nutrition Survey have been made accessible through Veronica Berry and Celia Petty's published collection (1992).
7. The resemblance of stewed tomatoes and colored oil to (oxygenated) blood, which *vitamina* had the capacity to "fuel," suggests a possible sympathetic connection between these substances. The legacy of Victor Turner's *The Forest of Symbols* (1967)— in which he utilizes ethnographic observations among the Ndembu to suggest a pan-African tripartite (red-white-black) color symbolism—makes a chromatic connection between blood, life giving, and red foods particularly enticing. However, such symbolic meanings did not directly pan out in my own research setting, and so they are not a part of my analysis.
8. Alternatively, someone eating *ntchima* would condense the *mbamu* (small piece) with only the tips of their fingers. Acquaintances associated this manner of eating with elders (*agogo*) and thought this manner of eating perhaps a habit retained from the common consumption of sticky cassava-based *ntchima* (*kondowole*) in the past, since replaced with *ntchima* made from de-branned, twice-soaked maize flour (*ufa woyera*, literally "white flour").
9. My American sense of obligation to artificially flatten the guest-host relationship by eating with the family (and perhaps their wariness to engage in regular commensality with a stranger) led to a lot of tension and awkward meals at the beginning of my stay. Eventually we settled into a pattern by which my husband and I ate together for breakfast, separate from the rest of the family, as we usually took our meal so much earlier than everyone else. For lunch and dinner I was invited to eat with the women and children if there were men around for my husband to eat his meal with; otherwise I was expected to keep him company.
10. Of note, Jessie Williamson (1954) records in her own studies of diet near Lake Niassa that the addition of peanuts to an *ndiwo* side dish was important for ensuring that the sauce had enough viscosity to stick to the *mbamu* (small portions) of *ntchima* dipped into it, adding another dimension to the importance of oil for a satisfying meal.
11. Paul Stoller and Cheryl Olkes (2005) provide an extended discussion of thickness versus thinness of sauces (the former an indication of social distance and the latter of social proximity among consumers) that could perhaps have resonance for Metangula, though the emphasis when discussing *ndiwo* in my own recording was on volume rather than consistency and on number of persons served rather than who they were. Elsewhere (Stoller and Olkes 1986) these authors contribute important insights into how the quality of a sauce can serve as social commentary and the expression of emotional states, making important "tasteful fieldwork" to grasp the situations into which an ethnographer is embedded.
12. The use of tomatoes to enable additional consumers to partake in a meal is reminiscent of Jon Holtzman's (2009) observation that milk—an increasingly scarce resources for the Samburu—was being added to tea in a way that enabled more individuals to share it.

13. It is important to note here, then, that meals in Metangula homesteads varied more in quantities than content. There was, in other words, no "low class" and "high class" cuisine, a common phenomenon where there is little social stratification (Goody 1982). And tomato, onion, and oil were regularly consumed in almost every household. Thus, while these three ingredients may have been valued in part for their status as commodities, a political economic analysis of the prevalence and positioning of these foods in relation to health does not feel organic or satisfying.
14. Deborah Lupton, however, points out that human preference for sweetness may be socialized rather than innate, a product of the sweetness of breast milk as most humans' first substantial introduction to food, paired with emotional and sensual responses to the food provider(s) (1996, 13). The work of Sidney W. Mintz (1985) also powerfully traces the history of sugar in relation to the spread of capitalism, and the symbolic importance of sweetness in relation to social status. Mintz's work serves as an important reminder that in addition to any innate or learned preference that humans may have for a food (sweet ones or otherwise), political-economic structures and strictures are also at play.
15. The binary of pleasure/pain parallels that noted by Judith Perani and Fred T. Smith in traditional African arts, where beauty is tied to effectiveness and goodness rather than necessarily to form (1998, 8), and also that formulated by Michael Jackson in his discussion of the Kuranko of Sierra Leone, who divide the world broadly into that which augments life and is therefore good and that which diminishes life and therefore is wrong (2011, 72), among other manifestations. Jennifer Lee Johnson (2017) notes also that in Uganda staple food without sauce does not qualify as food (*emmere*), but instead is known as *maluma* (pain). People who refuse to eat food without sauce will say, "I do not eat pain" (*sirya maluma*), which she suggests is a phrasing with widespread intelligibility across Bantu-speaking populations, indicating breadth and historical depth to the perception of pain as a negation of nourishment.
16. Concerns about blockages in digestive processes also resonate with regional concerns for unencumbered flows as requisite for health—for example, Chris Taylor's (1992) work in Rwanda, where liquid flows of beer and semen enabled social and cultural reproduction (thus making the use of condoms not a personal decision for protection from STDs and the prevention of unwanted pregnancies, but an affront to societal well-being). René Devisch (1991) suggests that stymied or unreciprocated relationships among the Yaka caused an imbalance between that which was flowing from the body and into the body. This disrupted a person's "body-self," by which the body mediated between the social and the individual and through which individuals became themselves, resulting in illness.
17. In Jessie Williamson's (1954) discussion of the cooking and consumption of legumes among the Chewa, she notes a preference for thin- and soft-skinned beans, as well as concerns that eating beans too frequently could cause digestive distress.
18. Several researchers have noted Maravi negative evaluation of fullness (Ali, Nyirenda, and MacLachlan 1998, 76; W. P. Johnson 1969 [1922], 34; Platt 1939, 152). Others, however, have placed equal emphasis on fullness for satiation (Morris 1998, 186–87; A. C. Williamson 1972, 49), suggesting that this is a topic on which additional regional research would be useful.

CHAPTER 2

Labor, Reason, and Compassion

One evening in July 2007, early in my forays along the eastern shore of Lake Niassa, I was relaxing in the village of Chia, situated about fifteen miles north of Metangula as the bird flies. I sat on the interior veranda of Chief Mayendayenda's house along with his wife, some of their children, the chief's mother, and Patrick, my cultural guide and interpreter as we traveled the Lago District collecting songs, stories, and personal histories to deposit in Metangula's museum. That afternoon Patrick had taught me how to say in Chinyanja, "What would happen if . . . ?" I decided to pass time in the fading light of another spectacular sunset by practicing the conditional conjugation. "What would happen if you did not bathe?" I asked aloud to nobody in particular. After some hesitation, one child quietly answered, "You would stink." Everyone laughed. After a few stumbles with the wording I managed to ask next, "And, what would happen if you did not sleep?" The chief's wife responded this time, "Your body would hurt." She answered quickly, as if slightly confused at the fact that my inquiries had such obvious answers in comparison to those I had posed earlier in the day. The next question that I asked was, "What would happen if you did not eat?" It was the chief's mother who answered this time, "You . . . would . . . be . . . tired." Her words came out slowly as she closed her eyes and leaned back, mimicking the results. I found this response to be curious—I had expected an answer of "You would be hungry" or maybe "You would die." I recorded the incident as a peculiar anecdote. It was only years later, in conducting multiple and varied discussions about food as a part of formal research, that the elder's words truly resonated. The primary function of eating was not to stay alive, for this was in the hands of God. Eating was instead necessary to fuel the energy with which to partake in living.

This chapter is about energy as essential for grasping not *what* people ate in Metangula (as was elaborated in chapter 1), but rather their motivations for eating at all. As indicated by Chief Mayendayenda's mother in response to my question all of those years ago, food was necessary for "living" as a matter of active engagement in the world around you—more so than "life" as a state of being alive. *Vitamina* fueled labor, and the work to procure ingredients, prepare dishes, and share meals was generative not only of nutrients, but also of mutuality. This chapter, then, helps to illuminate the central role of *vitamina* in the categorization, cooking, and consumption of foodstuffs in Metangula by offering a grounding in the central importance of the actions that alimentation enabled. Specifically, *vitamina* was wrapped up in facilitating the active care work that brought forth individual and collective humanity. The chapter begins by detailing interdependence as essential for (a) nourishing life in much of sub-Saharan Africa, including Metangula. Entanglement with others was, in fact, so integral to individual identity that mutuality was at the very heart of being a person. Once having established this point, I consider three essential elements of African personhood—labor, intelligence, and compassion—with special attention to how each played out in Metangula and its foodways. I utilize a mix of both historical and contemporary overview to support these ideas and to trace their adaptation from the subsistence economy of the past to the market economy of the twenty-first century.

The Principle of Participation

This volume is premised on the question of what constitutes humanity. Such inquiry has inspired generations of philosophers, and it is a foundational premise for the discipline of anthropology. And yet, for many, what and who is human is not a point of everyday reflection. The status of all human beings as human persons is, rather, conceived to be an obvious birthright, ascribed rather than achieved, and never mutable or questioned. But in many places around the world, the status of being a "person" is processual, cultivated, and earned over the life course. An individual, in other words, becomes a human person rather than coming into the world with this status intact. Becoming human might be aided through ceremonies, like birth rites or initiations, with which individuals are incorporated into their families, communities, and societies through ritual acts. But it is also possible that an individual's personhood is wrapped up in the performance of everyday acts through which they demonstrate and build their humanity as a constant project. In such cases, humanity is less of a final status than it is a "metaphysical beacon" of possibility (Peterson 2019, 89), contingent, mercurial, continually deepening through experience, and always incomplete. This is the case in much of Africa, where the conditionality of being (or, more appropriately "becoming") human is wrapped up in the "principle of participation" (Kanyike 2004).[1] This guiding precept takes as self-evident the fact that individuals, in broad form, do not first exist and *then* socially interact. Rather, they are symbolically and literally constituted *through* their mutuality. The idea is often summed up with a quote from philosopher John S. Mbiti, "I am because we are; and since we are, therefore I am," or the proverb (as popularized by Archbishop Emeritus Desmond Tutu) *umuntu ngumuntu ngabantu*, which roughly translates that a person is a person only in relation to other persons (quoted in Ogude 2019a, 4). Academicians, along with politicians, often use the term Ubuntu to refer to pan-African ideals of interdependent ontological orientation as the basis of humanity—reflective of the root *-ntu* and similar cognates used in many Bantu languages (of which there are hundreds) as the basis for words like "humankind," "humanity," and "person."[2]

That the principle of participation is a cornerstone of personhood and broader humanity as articulated, and arguably as lived, in African contexts should not be mistaken for an assertion that individuals and individuality are nonexistent. The principle of participation is, in fact, dependent on the coming together of separate entities. It is the "otherness" of others that makes this coming together possible and meaningful. The principle of participation, in other words, is premised on an interrelation and codependence of community and individual, mutually constitutive, rather than one being prioritized over the other.[3] It is for these reasons that philosopher Niels Weidtmann asserts that community is valued in Africa as a consequence of Ubuntu, rather than the other way around (Weidtmann 2019a). Bringing individuals together through unity and consensus (notably, not unanimity and communalism), Weidtmann argues, unleashes transformative potentiality and a sense of multidimensionality, or belonging within a web of human relationships that extends from the past into the future, that makes life fuller, deeper, and more generative (2019a; 2019b). This point is concretely demonstrated in the ethnographic work of Paul Wenzel Geissler and Ruth Prince (2010), where they focus on the powerful potential of sharing physical substances—food, sweat, semen, spit, and bodily closeness. It was in these momentary encounters, where togetherness enveloped division, that creative processes (such as conception, cooking, fermentation, digestion, plant and animal growth, healing, and rain) that connected the living, the dead, and the land were enabled. Philosopher D. A. Masolo premises such merging and separation of individuals as more broadly nourishing the human spirit—a constant unfolding of potential "through the formation and execution of self-cultivation and realization" (2019b, 61). It is for a combination of these reasons that John Comaroff and Jean Comaroff (2001) highlight the importance of *becoming* human as a social process of growing, developing, and building oneself by producing people and things. The alternatives, being static or autonomous, are the equivalent of social death.

Masolo and Weidtmann were part of an interdisciplinary group of scholars who convened over the course of several years with the explicit purpose to deepen understandings of the concept of Ubuntu. Led by James Ogude and funded by the Templeton World Charity Foundation, the collaboration produced a flurry of publications that simultaneously extend and condense thinking on African relationality and its applications for human relations in the twenty-first century (Ogude 2018; 2019b; Ogude and Dyer 2019; Müller, Eliastam, and Trahar 2019). While each contributor to this project emerged with their own conclusions, the group of publications as a whole forcefully advances the idea that Ubuntu is best conceived not as an African tradition or a culture-specific model of personhood. Rather, Ubuntu is one manifestation of the universal potential to be empathetic, kind, and compassionate with others (Ogude 2019a, 17). Inserting Ubuntu into global discussions of humanism thus has the potential to enhance the fullness, richness, vitality, and wholeness of life for everyone (Ogude 2019a, 14) by denaturalizing assumptions about what it means to be a person in a community and in the world and articulating a morality premised on connection, caring, and responsibility (different from and complementary to predominate models based on rights, freedoms, and autonomy). This collection of works, as such, not only mollifies portraits of Ubuntu as static and culturally bound, but it also asserts with vigor the potential for African cultural knowledge to make a valuable, and some would argue necessary, contribution to the revitalization of social relations in the twenty-first century.

My aim in this volume is not to argue for African exceptionalism, nor is it to promote African essentialism. But my analysis in this book does rest heavily on the reality of a principle of participation underpinning everyday life in Metangula, much as it does across the African continent (Beattie 1980; Fortes 1987; Jackson and Karp 1990; Menkiti 1984; Ogude and Dyer 2019; Riesman 1986). This principle encourages cooperation, compassion, and self-abnegation as virtuous, fathoms these orientations and their negation as affecting transformative potentialities, and conceives of humanity as inseparable from membership in and contributions toward the maintenance and perpetuation of generative relationships. Productive agency, in other words, emerges through intersubjectivity. This does not, of course, mean that these principles are always upheld, that they are enacted by everyone the same, nor that they are maintained selflessly and without disputes or transformations in different circumstances and over time. But, in broad form, African orientations toward self and other prioritize mutuality over independence, personal power, and possession in reconciling and giving reason, order, and meaning to the lived experience of human persons and their capacities to carry out action in the world.

Negotiation of personhood in the alimentary realm is much of what this book is about. Foodways are not, however, alone in embedding a principle of participation in the cultural fabric of African societies. Events and experiences that enhance connections and interdependencies receive special cultural elaboration across the subcontinent, for example in commensality, sexual intercourse, and other instances of mutual sensorial interaction that dissolve physical boundaries between individual persons (Devisch 1991; Geissler and Prince 2010; Jackson and Karp 1990). Likewise, reciprocal exchange relationships involving livestock, material goods, persons, and money are socially privileged for intertwining individuals, families, generations, and communities with one another, temporarily and in perpetuity (Shipton 2007). Traditional African economies are generally characterized as being governed by a "wealth in people" approach, rather than the "wealth in objects" standard of capitalism (Miers and Kopytoff 1977), with an "economy of affection" (Hyden 1980) that values dependencies over the accumulation of goods and purchasing power, and premises transactions on crafting relationships that connect people to other people through obligations, rather than linking people to objects alone. As Devaka Premawardhana (2018, 133) observed of the Makhuwa language spoken in northern Mozambique, and the same can be said of Chinyanja, the verb "to have" (in Chinyanja, *kuli ndi*) literally translates not as a term of possession in the sense of private ownership, but as a statement of mutuality, "to be with."

Choosing to reject the community through individualism, singularity, materiality, egoism, or independence in Africa can result in being ostracized. In a context where the essence of life is found in and through interconnectivity, such exclusion is akin to secular notions of death—an end to existence. To maintain relationships, conflict is at times suppressed, and tranquility promoted. Persons learn how to control their emotions, avoid temptation, sublimate self-interests, remain silent, and concede to proper authorities for resolving disagreements rather than taking arbitration into their own hands. Julie Livingston's work on disability in Botswana (2005) and Julie Archambault's work on cell phone use in Mozambique (2017) collectively point to the importance also in choosing to hide aspects of oneself that are "ugly" (physically for Livingston, and figuratively for Archambault) as a matter of respect for others' and one's own sense of self. In both cases, this allows room for those around you to choose not to see characteristics that would disrupt mutuality. Of special threat to fellow feeling in Africa can also be negative emotions like jealousy, envy, and spite, frequently cited as instigation for witchcraft, sorcery, cursing, the evil eye, and otherwise diminishing or destroying social relations rather than enhancing them, as will be addressed in more detail in chapter 3. A continental history marred with conflict and violence confirms, however, that while peaceable values may be upheld as ideal, reality often requires compromise and carries with it the possibilities of both agency and imposition (Salo 2018; Wiegink 2013).

The importance of interdependence is not only espoused in sub-Saharan Africa, but it is also embodied. This is no clearer than in matters of personal health. Across the region, individuals and communities conceive of interpersonal relations as contributing to physical wellness, while anomie and negative emotion are pathogenic. Following social rules provides protection from illnesses with origins in relational disruptions. Likewise, healing frequently involves uncovering and addressing social tensions, rather than or in addition to attending to viruses, bacteria, and other microorganisms (Feierman and Janzen 1992; Janzen

1978). Such was the case in Metangula when, for example, Filomena blamed her aunt's bewitching of a polio vaccine for her resultant disfigurement or when Clara found cause for a debilitating asthma attack in her husband's taking of a second wife. The location of experience within (rather than opposed to) the body and synthesis via corporeal participation (rather than the body as the site of incidents that happen to a person and metaphorically reflect them) are additional commonalities in descriptions of African personhood (Karp 1997). Affect and feeling become, as such, elements of cognition, and the body a site for negotiating individual being in relational contexts. This of course dovetails with the previous chapter's discussion of food categorization as intimately tied to somatic experience and situational contexts as they reflected the capacity to fulfill relational obligations and to maintain interdependence with others. The remainder of this chapter extends the exploration of the principle of participation for the alimentary realm and beyond by outlining associated moral values of productivity, intelligence, and compassion.

Persons as Economic Beings

Relational interdependence in Africa is often tied up with productivity (Nyarwath 2019, 83). As summarized by Augustine Musopole in his discussion of Chewa theology:

> Productivity, refers to the enrichment of one's life and that of the community through work. Whether through economic, biological, social and educational undertakings, it is a valued index of assessing the essential *uMunthu* [humanness] of someone. To be unproductive is to refuse to be human because it is not to care about personal or communal life. It is to abdicate responsibility. This is why laziness or slothfulness is a sin. To be a human parasite is to feed on the life of others. . . . A person who has *uMunthu* strives not only to feed him/herself, but in the process of feeding him/herself, he/she feeds the community as well. For the wellbeing of the community, this concern for one's own well being [*sic*] and that of the community has to be mutual. They are complementary concerns. To be *Munthu* [a person] is to be an economic being. (1998, 29)

John Comaroff and Jean Comaroff also place stress on the importance of productive agency (a capacity that can be stymied by those with more power) for the making of persons among the Tswana in South Africa. Through labor, individuals created value in the form of persons, things, and relations, thus simultaneously producing for oneself and for entitlement to personhood. "Work," they write, "in short, was the positive, relational aspect of human social activity, of the making of self and others in the course of everyday life" (Comaroff and Comaroff 2001,

273). To continue producing (both the products of one's labor, and so oneself) was to avoid social death. Labor, the self, and the social, then, were mutually constituting.

Musopole's description and the contours of the Comaroffs' study ring true in Metangula, where someone with no desire or ability to effectively plan or perform work was often teased or mocked into productivity, lest they be shunned. Take for example Mwai, a young woman of sixteen years living in the homestead next to my host family in Metangula. A jag in the fences between the two yards allowed an easy flow of traffic, perhaps the remnant of earlier days when the two homesteads engaged in more cooperative and mutually sustaining interactions. At the time of research, however, Mwai's parents were not present. Mwai was thus left in charge of herself, her younger brother, and her newborn son. But rather than taking on the charge of head of household seriously, Mwai noticeably spent much of her time idle or playing with children, instead of caring for others, tending to fields, or enacting some *programa* (Portuguese, literally "program") to earn money to support her family. She also came over at least several times a week to beg for an *ndiwo* side dish to accompany the *ntchima* she had cooked. A common occurrence among neighbors, what was unusual here was Mwai's need for assistance due to her own non-productivity. "You watch out," my host family's daughter-in-law, Albertina, yelled one day as Mwai disappeared sheepishly back into her own yard, clutching a reluctantly provided plate of fried *usipa* fish. "Tomorrow I am coming to your house to beg for *ndiwo*." The threat was empty, but the irritation was real. A child could be expected to take resources without working to also contribute to the maintenance of relationships. But a grown woman, with her own child? The outrage was not rooted in an economic logic of return so much as it was Mwai's unwillingness to engage in work. As articulated by Aloo Osotsi Mojola in the context of human dignity broadly, in refusing to labor Mwai was failing to exhibit the "values that constitute, sustain, and ensure the existence of human community" (2019, 23). Her visits became unwelcomed, and one day, soon after the confrontation over *usipa* fish, I came home to find the jag in the fence had simply been patched over. Mwai had been literally and socially shut out.

Unlike Mwai, most adults whom I encountered in Metangula were intentional and deliberate about working to contribute toward the material needs of themselves and those in their relational networks. Families were largely self-sufficient, to be sure. But they also contributed to the cooking pots, storerooms, and emergency expenses of neighbors, friends, and extended relatives and received such help themselves in return. These commitments required a seriousness and diligence in daily labor that we might readily define as "industrious" if that term were not so caught up in historically racialized evaluations of worth (Shih 2008; Ranger 1982b). During my residence in Metangula, I was conspicuously surrounded by individuals engaged in physical activity that included farming, fishing, shucking, cooking, caregiving, washing, building, and so forth. The thud of a woman pounding her wooden pestle into a concave mortar, the scraping of metal on mud as a man erected a brick home, a girl sweeping a bundle of dried branches along the dirt to clear the yard of debris, the squeak of a long-unoiled bar being raised and lowered by a schoolboy to release a stream of water into a bucket below the pump . . . the soundscape of Metangula was awash with labor. Notably, I was never able to find a native term to characterize or label such "industrious" behavior. As Musopole asserts, to labor was simply to be human.

This point is enshrined in the Nyanja creation myth as told to me on various occasions by Metangula elders and as I have encountered it in published form attributed to Chewa or broader Maravi origins (Kaspin 1996; Schoffeleers and Roscoe 1985).[4] The story generally proceeds with the following elements: God created humans. God lived together with humans on earth, along with animals, until humans invented fire. The smoke from this fire irritated God, and God fled into the sky. The animals also ran deep within the forest to escape the conflagration. As a result of this literal and figuratively incendiary act, God declared that humans would experience death and have to provide for and reproduce themselves. Some readers will note in this story a clear resemblance with "the fall" as recounted in the book of Genesis. Indeed, people in Metangula often mixed in

Figure 2.1. Two women wash and sort the cassava they have just harvested. Photo by the author.

elements of the biblical creation story, such that the first man and woman were named Adam and Hawa (Arabic for Eve), and a snake told them to light the fire.[5] Regardless of apparent or veritable syncretism with Christian tradition, the story had a distinct interpretation in Metangula. Specifically, there was special weight placed on the postlapsarian transference of responsibility for provisioning oneself and others from God to fellow human beings. To be human in a postlapsarian world, in other words, came to be synonymous with labor. I will return again to the creation myth in chapter 4.

The prevalence of hardworking diligence for the Nyanja and related lakeshore populations has been noted since explorers first came through the region and recorded local behaviors in writing. David Livingstone, previously introduced as the Scottish explorer credited as being the first foreigner to set eyes on Lake Niassa, described the Mang'anja people he encountered living on the banks of the lake's only outlet, the Tchiri River, as "an industrial race." His observation was based on the varied arts and extensive cultivation he witnessed there (Livingstone and Livingstone 1865, 110). On a later sojourn he added that fishermen lounging along the lakeshore during the day gave him an initial impression of laziness, "but, on a little better acquaintance . . . it is found that these forenoon sleepers have been hard at work the greater part of the night," fishing by moonlight (Livingstone and Livingstone 1865, 375). Livingstone additionally remarked in his personal journal that both Mang'anja men and women were "exceedingly industrious" (Waller 1874, 95). These written accounts of the Mang'anja and other Maravi peoples also detail the devastation, terror, and inhumanity wrought by human trafficking in the Lake Niassa region. Livingstone and other foreign explorers during the mid- to late nineteenth century paint a dismal picture of life near the lake—the land was depopulated, villages were abandoned, and the paths were littered with bodies of those who fell at the direct hands of slave raiders or indirectly through starvation wrought by fear and lack of manpower to work the fields. Despite the slave trade being abolished in Portuguese territories in 1836, slave raids are recorded on the eastern shore of Lake Niassa clear through 1895 (R. Howard 1904, 19; Stuart 1974, 108), with captives shipped primarily to the Ottoman Empire (Beachey 1976), various French islands, and Brazil (Good 2004; Hafkin 1973).

When Livingstone returned to England, he proposed that a mission society be formed to stop the East African slave trade by "civilizing" the Lake Niassa region through Christianity and commerce. The Universities' Mission to Central Africa (UMCA) formed in response, and by August 1861 the fledgling group had settled in the village of Magomero in present-day southern Malawi. The mission foundered, and within two years, five of the fourteen original mission staff had passed away, five went home invalided, and the remaining four retired. In 1863 the UMCA abandoned the Lake Niassa region and transferred to Tanzania. It was not until 1885 that the UMCA set up another mission at Lake Niassa. This time they selected for their headquarters Likoma, the island of seven square miles just a stone's throw from Mozambique. From this location the church's sailing vessels plied the coast, proselytizing among the Nyanja inhabitants and into the hills among the Yaawo, their coal-powered ships inspiring a nickname of "the steamer parish." Long-standing UMCA presence on the island of Likoma and the neighboring island of Chizumulu and the missionaries' alliance with the British colonial government over that of the Portuguese are likely what led to British sovereignty over the landmasses (Anderson-Morshead 1897; Stuart 1974; L. White 1987).

The Likoma mission station was personified for many years by William Percival Johnson, who lived aboard the steamer ships for weeks at a time, traveling from village to village establishing and visiting schools and churches (Good 2004; Mills 1933). Johnson had been the first from the mission to reach the eastern lakeshore (in 1882 along with Charles Janson, who died soon after arrival and is buried in the village of Chia), and he did the work to develop community relations in the area. His ostensible placating of slave raiders won him the trust of local people, and the drought that followed his departure and ended with the arrival of other UMCA staff helped to inspire a spiritual following.[6] Johnson took up permanent residence on Likoma in 1886 and remained in the region until his death in 1928. When not directly proselytizing, Johnson tirelessly worked on translating the Bible into Chinyanja, several times accidentally lighting his beard on fire working by candlelight (Mills 1933). The mission, in fact, insisted on religious work and education in local tongues (Paul 1975). This, among other things (like the UMCA's Anglican allegiance), led to clashes with the Portuguese colonial government, which was deeply entwined with the Roman Catholic church and worked hard to minimize Mozambican access to formal schooling. In introducing literacy in any language to a large swath of lakeshore residents, the UMCA is notable for offering educational opportunities that were virtually unparalleled in colonial-era Mozambique.[7]

Staff of the UMCA, later renamed Diocese of Nyasaland (Tengatenga 2010), made comments about the local population that are comparable to Livingstone's. They noted, for example, that despite the land's infertility its inhabitants were "an industrious people" (Anderson-Morshead 1897, 171). Johnson himself recorded that adults encouraged girls to marry only boys who could materially provide for them, making hard work necessary in order for a man to enter into marriage. Boys were encouraged to begin working around age seven, and they were chided if they passed the day too close to home. When he married, a man conventionally resided with his in-laws for a "trial period" of several years' bride service, during which time he proved his ability and willingness to care for his wife by farming and building houses (W. Johnson 1969 [1922], 84, 74). Concurrent ethnographic reporting about neighboring populations supports the idea of a broad, regional propensity for vigorous engagement in the laborious tasks through which life unfolded. Anthropologist António Rita-Ferreira noted, for example, that among the Chewa in Tete Province "inactive husbands are repudiated and summarily replaced" (1966, 175). A. G. O. Hodgson found the same was true in central Malawi, where a woman could divorce her husband if he failed to feed and clothe her, do his share of the work, or pay her taxes. A husband likewise could divorce his wife if she persistently neglected to cook, bring water, or perform "her other work" (1933, 139–40). Hodgson's characterization of women's work is similar to that recorded by Rita-Ferreira. But, despite the distinction of male and female labor, Rita-Ferreira qualified, both were similar in that they were "completed to assure the survival of the social group" (1966, 176). In other words, gender complementarity in labor crafted and sustained interdependence.

Comments penned about local peoples by Portuguese government officials are of similar tenor to those of Livingstone, the UMCA, and colonial-era anthropologists. An early twentieth-century administrative handbook for the region describes the Nyanja as "an industrious people, assiduous in cultivating crops" (Naval Intelligence Division 1969 [1920]), for example. A comparable text notes that "among the Mang'anja everybody works, men and women, elders and children" and suggests that they are an "active and hard-working race" (Coutinho 1931 [1893], 52–53). But such historical accounts by colonialists are sparse. Portugal's presence in Mozambique—though it began with trading settlements along the coast as early as the fifteenth century—was minimal prior to the 1884–85 Berlin Conference, in which European powers decisively carved up the continent of Africa. Faced with an ultimatum of developing the land or losing their claims, Portuguese imperial occupation intensified, if sometimes indirectly. What are today the Niassa and Cabo Delgado Provinces, for example, were placed under command of the privately run Nyassa Chartered Company (known in Portuguese as Companhia do Nyassa) from 1893 to 1929. Even then, however, there were few foreigners stationed in the region (Vail 1976).

The first official colonial administrator to set up headquarters along the Niassa lakeshore (José Hyginade Jesus Nolasco) did not arrive until 1900. An archived summary by an appalled Reverend C. B. Eyre (1902) suggests that Nolasco forced the population at Messumba, just north of Metangula, to pull down their houses and build him a fort in their stead. Unsatisfactory work resulted in beatings, sometimes to death in the recordings of Deacon Augustine Ambali (1916, 54–56). In my discussions with elders in the Lago District, their recollection of the behavior of Portuguese government officials echoed such accounts. They recalled foreign men walking around demanding things from people, calling them "dogs" or just "blacks," and indiscriminately beating people for any act that could be interpreted as insubordination. Several elders mimicked with relish the arrogant swagger of the Portuguese colonialists, chest out, an evaluative overturned lower lip, and head alternately swiveling left and right in tandem with the sway of fisted arms. The most constant complaint, however, was simply that the Portuguese officials seemed to think they were better than everyone else and demanded a reverence and respectability deemed by local residents to be undeserved due to their harmful actions and policies.

The observations about "industriousness" recounted in this section come largely from individuals concerned with exploiting local resources (colonialists) and spreading a spiritual message meant to control the mind as well as the body (missionaries). These contexts are likely to have colored writers' attention to both sedulousness and indolence. Still, concordance among these recordings and the fact that such a wide range of individuals were so impressed with the pervasiveness of indigenous laboring that they felt the need to remark on the condition suggest some basis to the idea of a long-standing, cultivated work ethic among peoples of the Lake Niassa region. I bring in these primary sources not to suggest that the Maravi are of one personality or character, nor to imply that their culture has remained static since time immemorial or even since the nineteenth and twentieth centuries. The point of these citations is to suggest that there has been some continuity over time in the *importance* of working to contribute to the social good or at least appearing as if one is doing so. This indicates that the practice of conspicuous labor is deeply rooted, even where its manifestations and perhaps its meanings have changed such that, in Metangula in the early twenty-first century, continuous and productive, *vitamina*-fueled labor was an essential act of humanity.

Plan Making and Intelligence

Being and becoming human in Metangula thus necessitated participation, and more specifically labor. But these things also required *njeru*. This word roughly translates into English as "intelligence," though with a meaning far broader than mental acuity and abstract knowledge. *Njeru* was also a matter of wisdom, or the moral capacity to do the right thing and the will to enact it. *Njeru*, in other words, required mental known-how to engage in a variety of productive tasks— to keep track of expenditures, plant and harvest at the right times, and so forth. An individual would gradually accumulate this type of knowledge over time, through both formal and informal learning, and many sought out new opportunities to accumulate firsthand experiences with which to speak and act knowledgeably about the world.[8] I often overheard adults comment that children were showing signs of nascent *njeru* when they did things that demonstrated curiosity about the world around them, like turning the radio knob to hear and silence the broadcast, and when they began to engage in imaginary play, for example using scraps of wood as cars and maize cobs as soccer players. Adults also gave children tasks to complete so that they would increase their capacities to carry out work and otherwise "learn to do things." But it was when a child began to anticipate such requests and answer them, without having to be asked, that they had truly begun to develop the *njeru* of principled sentience. This second aspect of *njeru* is perhaps best described as having a conscience-driven will to do the right thing, and more specifically to engage in the work required to nourish rather than to deplete relational interdependencies, and the forethought to do so. It was this second form of *njeru* that encouraged acting on the first in order to enhance vitality and reduce suffering.[9]

Unlike *njeru* of knowledge, the *njeru* of motivation and morality was present from birth, though it could not be acted upon at an early age because a child lacked enough of the first type of intelligence to understand it. It also derived from a separate source. Specifically, while acquaintances associated the first form of *njeru* with the brain, many (though not all, and notably few who had spent a significant portion of their formative years in Malawi) asserted that the second form of *njeru* derived from *vungu* (sing. *chungu*; also *chiungu/viungu*)—worms that resided in the head of all animals and for humans served as a spiritual conduit for motivation and moral thought. The concept of morality and planning as dependent on cerebral grubs is seldom mentioned in regional literature, and I was able to find only a handful of references to organic, internal, worm-based moral conscience. For example, Geissler and Prince (2010, 167) cited A. B. C. Ocholla-Ayayo (1976, 52–56) to suggest the Luo understood their heads to be inhabited by maggots influenced by the moon and somehow related to vital force, Henri Junod (1912, 1:431) mentioned in passing his observation that people in southern Mozambique complained of illness caused by a worm when it wandered from its normal placement in the head, and Arne Steinforth (2009, 139) wrote in a footnote that one traditional healer in southern Malawi told him that intelligence, mental health, and proper social behavior were determined by a small worm (*kachimbozi*) in the brain.

In a casual conversation with friend and Malawian linguist Experencia Madalitso Jalasi, I mentioned that people in Metangula told me they had worms in their brains. She dismissed the idea as some sort of rural nonsense she had never heard of. But Jalasi's tone changed when her husband, who was sitting nearby, reminded her that growing up in southern Malawi they sometimes spoke of *vimbozi* (worms; sing. *chimbozi*) in a person's head as a kind of internal voice telling them what to do and not to do. Jalasi acquiesced and added that people would say that someone acting strangely had malfunctioning *vimbozi*. Further, if an individual had a premonition of impending danger, such as not getting on a bus that then went on to crash, they would credit survival to worms in their head. These comments suggest that, as in Metangula, morality, planning, guardianship, and mental health were each components of the cerebral worm concept that Jalasi and her husband grew up with. But the reference to worms was just an expression, she insisted, which was why she did not initially make a connection between *vimbozi* and the *vungu* I described. In Malawi, she said, they did not *actually* believe that larva took up residence in the head (personal communication, 19 March 2011).

I first came across the concept of *vungu* in a conversation with a market vendor as we playfully haggled over the price of a radio. He said that my bargaining tactics (of suggesting a very low price) were wielded as if without *vungu* (seemingly in my own brain, though possibly also in his). After this first introduction to the subject, I began to notice discussion of *vungu* all around me. The day that followed, for example, Clara told me that *vungu* were the reason that your ear hurts when you get water in it (*vungu* do not like water). A few weeks later, when a speeding driver refused to listen to my pleas that he slow down, the other passengers blamed his behavior on inebriation, which had impaired his *vungu* functioning. Likewise, while lecturing me on the ravages of drug use, Florinda gave as example the atrocious acts of violence committed by soldiers during war. "Smoking is how the soldiers could kill people and cut out their unborn babies," she rationalized, in reference to the horrific practices undertaken during a sixteen-year "civil war" between Mozambique's Frelimo-ruled government and foreign-backed Resistência Nacional Moçambicana, Mozambican National Resistance (RENAMO) guerilla forces. Marijuana, like alcohol, paralyzed *vungu*, causing them to malfunction.[10] Another day soon thereafter, Filomena stopped her eight-year-old stepdaughter from leaving the yard by asking, "Who do you expect will finish preparing lunch if you leave? What is the matter with you? Are your *vungu* not moving around?"

Key to *vungu* functioning, in fact, was *vungu* movement, as this was how they communicated moral knowledge and motivational impetus to their human host. *Vungu* moved within the brain, stretching this way and that, pressing on specific locations to send their messages. Judite explained this with the analogy of fingers strumming a guitar. "When a guitar is played properly, the music that comes out is beautiful and people can dance to it." A young child could not yet interpret these messages or "dance to the music" because their brain was still developing, and they had not yet amassed the experience to know how to respond. It was, as such, that a child would be easily forgiven for transgressions such as public nakedness, begging, or relieving themselves around the house. But older children and adults, Judite explained, were expected to be able to "dance" to the moral and forward-thinking thoughts inspired by properly moving *vungu*. If there was no movement of *vungu*, on the other hand, or sporadic or erratic movement, there would be no "music," only noise, and regardless of age there would be no *njeru*. Judite pointed to Glória, a five-year-old girl with cerebral palsy lying several feet away on a soiled reed mat, her head just below the small block of soft foam it had slipped from in a recent fit of movement. Glória spent her days on her back, staring at the sky or the ceiling, laughing for no apparent reason, and then crying and violently protesting when being fed. "She does not know good from bad and cannot react properly to anything," her grandmother offered, "because Glória was born with *vungu* that just sit there, watching."

In fact, I came across several disabilities associated with *vungu*. While people in Metangula generally labeled individuals with intellectual disabilities as "crazy" (*wamisala*), other terms distinguished handicaps caused by malfunctioning *vungu* (including *wozereze[te]ka*, *wopunguzika*, and *wochilekwa*) from those caused by cerebral impairment (for example, *kuzungulira mutu*, *kuvundula mutu*, *wopepera*, and *wololomwa*).[11] Those suffering a brain-related deficiency behaved in a manner that might be described elsewhere as "slow" or mental retardation. These individuals could be assigned tasks or may even define their own agenda and would be able to plan to complete those tasks, if at a measured pace and with much instruction. Several such persons were well known in Metangula. For example, Andre, a young man who daily wandered from house to house, where he sat and observed what people were doing, answered basic questions and completed small tasks asked of him by his hosts. Andre had further become convinced, after watching a televangelist program, that he could cure people with the touch of his hand and chanting, which people frequently requested him to do. Though he was clearly different and required a lot of guidance, people considered Andre to be a productive member of society, which was evidence that his *vungu* were intact. It was his brain that was not functioning as that of others' did.

Those with insufficient or malfunctioning *vungu*, on the other hand, could not be expected to contemplate or complete anything of consequence. Ana, a young woman, was one such person in Metangula. Like Andre, Ana daily wandered from yard to yard, but when she arrived she just sat and stared at her hosts, danced to existent or nonexistent music, demanded food, or insisted on something repeatedly—in my interactions with her, most often that she had no shoes on or that she wanted hair product from the market. Her mother literally tied Ana's *capulana* around her waist each morning, with a knot, rather than just wrapping it around her and tucking it in like other women did, because Ana could not be counted on to adjust the cloth throughout the day when it came loose. Ana's utterances were barely intelligible, and her gait was one of sporadic fits and starts rather than fluid motion. She had given birth to two children and was aware of this fact, but she did nothing to care or provide for her offspring. Unlike Andre, whose brain was faulted for his intellectual disability, acquaintances told me that Ana's condition resulted from her having "too few" or idle *vungu* in her head, such that she did not contribute to society. Her brain, on the other hand, worked fine.

To further explain the distinction between the sort of intelligence provided by *vungu* and by the brain, Judite offered the hypothetical example of a woman thinking with her brain that her family was hungry. The brain would recognize and define the situation based on prior knowledge—I am hungry because I have no food; I must get food. The *vungu*, on the other hand, would inspire appropriate solutions—for example, that she go to the market and buy something to cook for lunch. But *vungu* also acted as a sort of moral conscience. For example, if the woman had then proceeded to go to the market with the intention to steal, because she had no money to buy the food, the *vungu* would move about, this way and that, such that she would realize this action to be dishonest. While not precisely in dialogue with their host, *vungu* in this way reacted to thoughts in the brain to provide the impetus for moral decision-making. *Vungu* were, then, distinct from their human host, symbiotic and with their own lives.

Acquaintances explained the impetus for *vungu* to twist and turn to impart wisdom as stemming from their serving as a conduit for "the ancestors."[12] Across much of Africa south of the Sahara, those who have passed away often serve an important role in the lives of those still living, constituting a single social world in which the actions of one (living or dead) impact the other (Kopytoff 1971). The ancestors protect those who still walk the earth through bringing forth rain, ensuring social harmony, and otherwise shielding them from illness, death, and other forms of calamity. In turn, those alive in physical form support the dead by remembering them and by showing them respect through rituals, offerings, avoiding conflict, and following appropriate moral codes based on interdependence, caring, and responsibilities. Without such actions, the ancestors may withdraw protections or otherwise punish the living and, over time, cease to have any capacity to act at all (Bagnol 2017).

In Metangula, the dead were referred to as *mizimu*, as they are in Malawi, where ethnographers have extensively studied indigenous cosmology. Among the Chewa, Brian Morris (2000) confirms the premise of a singular moral community shared by the living and the dead, the latter of which may withdraw support or enable misfortune if they are upset. Morris stresses that the spirits are conceived among the Chewa to be a part of this world, rather than occupying their own, and that the dead transform into spirits through proper burial rites. Communication between the living and the dead, he notes, often takes place in the form of dreams or the appearance of animals. J. W. M. van Breugel's (2001) attention to *mizimu* in Malawi likewise meshes with that which I observed in Metangula—where ancestors were associated with the wind, peace, and shadows, and individual spirits were spoken to directly at their graves or at the base of a tree, particularly in tumultuous times to ask for guidance and assistance with good fortune.

With this description of the relationship between the living and the dead, and *mizimu* in possession of wisdom and interested in moral conduct, it is notable that the imagery Judite provided for *vungu* guidance as like "strumming of a guitar" bears intriguing resemblance to that put forth by Weidtmann (2019a) about drumming as a form of communication, through which the musician adapts his playing based on the movements of dancers and the general atmosphere, and the dancers respond and move in time with the changing beat. He cites a Luba folktale (discussed in Bimwenyi-Kweshi 1982) in which a man requests a profession from God, who provides him with a drum. God then ties a string between the drum and the man's heart. By playing the drum, the musician could bring the wisdom of God to fellow humans by allowing them to feel, resounding through their bodies, the depth and responsibility of being bound to the past and to the future. This imagery helps us to imagine the wriggling of *vungu* as not imparting direct advice about moral action so much as they played out internal rhythms to inspire a response in the form of movements, or actions, appropriate for the "beat."

While I was never able to find anyone who could elaborate more than Judite had on the manner in which *vungu* and ancestors communicated with one another and with living individuals, there was widespread agreement among acquaintances that there were actual, physical worms crawling around in their heads. And it was not only humans who had *vungu*—most living things did, though each species' *vungu* had different potentials. Filomena, for instance, recounted constantly coming across *vungu* when she was married to a man who raised and slaughtered cows, and she gave me a detailed account of also seeing *vungu* crawl out of a dead sheep's ear. Curiosity led me to the Metangula market where I paid thirty meticais for a goat head (usually used as *ndiwo*, not science experiment), and then I asked the seller to cut it open for me; I wanted to see the *vungu*. While he found this an incredibly strange request, the promise that he could afterward have the goat head for his own cooking pot prompted him to humor me, and he began hacking away with his machete to split the head in two. Once he had exposed the brain, he began searching for the *vungu* with his fingers. He reached into the folds of tissue and into the nasal cavity and the ear canal, but he failed to find *vungu*. There are *vungu*, he assured me; the goat head I had bought was just too small a specimen—it was a young goat, and its *vungu* were not yet big enough to see. Reluctantly, and at the vendor's insistence, I paid another seller fifty meticais for a larger goat head, and with the same promise of *ndiwo*, he eagerly began splitting the head and searching within the cranium. This time, one live larva was extracted. Victorious, the second vendor ran around the market, showing the fish vendors and the soap vendors and the salt vendors his feat. I had to chase after him to get a good glance at the *vungu* myself. The grub crawled around his hand, showing definite life to the crowd of onlookers and looking nothing like I had ever seen.

What happened in the market that day was not the product of sleight of hand. What the butcher removed from the goat head would be classed biologically as botfly larva, which complete prepupal development burrowed into the tissue of goats or other ruminants, who inhale the grubs while rummaging through grasses.[13] The warmth and nutrition of the host body enable the grubs to survive. Infection with botfly larva is termed myiasis, and one study found up to 70 percent of sheep and goats in South Africa afflicted with the condition (Horak 2005). While botflies are medically documented as having been extracted from human nasal cavities, tear ducts, scrota, and brains, such cases are seemingly rare. Still, nearly everyone I talked to in Metangula was convinced of the presence of *vungu* within human crania and of their importance for enabling humans to plan and reason with a moral compass to enact labor that nourished relational interdependencies.

While cerebral-dwelling grubs as integral for intelligence may be somewhat regionally anomalous, a focus on principled sentience as essential, definitional even, of humanity is not. Abbé Alexis Kagame (1976), the first African scholar to refer to Ubuntu in writing, places special emphasis on intelligence and will in his conceptions of African persons (cited in Mojola 2019, 24). Philosophers like Masolo (2019a) have followed suit, though disavowing Kagame's claims of intelligence justifying the ethnic superiority of some over others. Masolo uses the term "capacity for reason" rather than "intelligence," and he emphasizes that it is through such abilities that individuals can be entrusted with the responsibility to deliberate and to make choices. For Raul Ruiz de Asúa Altuna, the importance of intelligence is also its marking of distinction between humans and animals. While many African populations traditionally acknowledge all animals' possession of cognitive faculty, other species are not attributed rational thought and the ability to plan. "To be human is to be intelligent," writes Altuna. "Humanity is life with intelligence" (2006, 252). These points on decision-making and human-animal relations will be further explored in chapters 3 and 4.

Capitalism and Compassion

Energy to labor (through *vitamina*) and the intelligence to plan and act in a principled manner (through *njeru*) thus together enabled humans to operate as economic beings in Metangula, and so to produce the objects and the relations that constituted humanity. In the past, much of this labor was funneled into activities related to sustenance—like farming, fishing, and hunting, along with gathering useful materials from the natural environment like firewood, water, clay, grasses, bamboo, fruits, and medicine. In the twenty-first century these products and forms of productivity continued to be part of (a) nourishing life. However, they were supplemented with work in the form of waged employment, petty trade, and day labor. Indeed, life in Metangula in the twenty-first century, as with life in most places around the world, was enmeshed in the market economy. And paying for the clothing, food stuffs, construction materials, transportation fares, communication costs, and school fees that had become an integral part of life in Metangula required cash.

Monetization was slow in coming to the eastern lakeshore. The UMCA's Anglican theology placed virtue in an ascetic lifestyle that did not include "frivolous" material goods.[14] Unlike other mission stations, the UMCA offered few opportunities for converts to receive training in trade skills or to find employment with the church. Lakeshore residents were instead encouraged to maintain a subsistence lifestyle rooted in horticulture and simplicity. Congregants were specifically discouraged from participating in migrant labor to places like Zambia (then Northern Rhodesia), Zimbabwe (then Southern Rhodesia), and South Africa, through which cash could be earned by working in diamond, coal, copper, tin, and gold mines, along with other opportunities for cash wages. Migrant labor was thought to encourage gambling and the spread of both sexually transmitted diseases and tuberculosis. Especially central to missionary interests, migrant labor could instigate "backsliding" in faith, in part because of distance from the church, but also because both the laborers and their stationary wives might be tempted to abandon monogamous ideals and perhaps marriage altogether. UMCA mission staff kept close tabs on church members, purportedly denying the Eucharist where a congregant married a non-Christian, entered into a polygamous relationship, or engaged in extramarital sexual relations (Good 2004).

To minimize the value of currency, UMCA missionaries for more than twenty years bartered for the goods they needed for their own everyday sustenance. They began using cash in such transactions only after 1910, when the colonial government of Mozambique began demanding that each family pay a "hut tax." This forcefully introduced a need for currency into the lives of congregants (Good 2004, 111). Still, the church could not support widespread employment. Some families fled to avoid hut tax payments, while others sent a representative to find employment as a migrant laborer (Neil-Tomlinson 1977). The word used for money in Metangula—*kopili*—especially among the older generation, in fact derives from this era, many of the men finding work in "copper" mines. The younger generation in Metangula in the twenty-first century, as I encountered them, were more apt to use the Chinyanja/Chichewa word *ndalama*, and their use of currency went far beyond the payment of government taxes. Money was necessary to buy food for those without the interest, skill, labor, or land to produce it themselves. Money also bought clothing, insulated serving dishes, construction materials and the hired labor to build a home with cement walls and a corrugated iron sheeting roof, an electrical current, a television, and a cell phone.

How did people earn cash? Opportunities for migrant labor were largely stymied by regional instability, xenophobia, language barriers, legal restrictions, and a labor surplus. Day jobs within Metangula were sporadic and intensive, most often associated with home building or farming. Technology enabled additional entrepreneurial hustles, including the organization of informal backyard cinemas, pirating digital content, or serving as the photographer for special events. Some had (or feigned) skills that enabled moneymaking as carpenters, electricians, welders, drivers, and other such occupations almost exclusively available to men. Women were successful in maintaining businesses that sold processed foods like fried dough (*bolos*), samosas, flavored ice (*gelo*), cornbread (*chigumu*), and banana bread (*chikonda moyo*), as well as the alcoholic beverages *kabanga* and *kacholima*. Crucially, preparing each of these foodstuffs could be done at home, during and amid a woman's other caretaking responsibilities. Some individuals also earned money by selling products that they gathered from the land (men: stones, bamboo; women: grasses, firewood) or fashioned from them (men: rope, wooden planks, wooden cooking implements, canoes, baskets, grain storage bins, pigeon coops, bricks, charcoal; women: clay pots). Others roasted (*zowotcha*), dried (*zowuma*), or flash boiled (*zofutcha*) fish, increasing their longevity for transport to inland locations. And some operated as small-scale traders in manufactured products. Even those with little money for initial investment in stock or with the need for a quick small-scale turnaround could earn a little cash by setting up a table outside the market at night to vend nonperishable or inexpensive necessities that were sure to sell—like candles, candies, cookies, body and laundry soaps, salt, tea leaves, and sugar.

That people were interested in and operating with money in the twenty-first century should not be taken as equitable with the adoption of capitalism whole cloth. A capitalist market system is defined by profit-driven transactions engineered for private individuals to take advantage of differentials between supply and demand for their own, boundless accumulation. Making money was certainly among the goals of traders and laborers in Metangula. However, there were other ambitions and objectives in their financial transactions as well, namely to labor in a manner that was life-enhancing, rather than life-depleting—the principle of participation as driving market exchange (at least, on the surface). In the Metangula market, vendors sometimes offered products below a profit margin or free of charge in order to ensure that a customer could leave with what they came for. One day, for example, I witnessed Sonia provide an elderly woman with two heaping handfuls of salt at no charge. She explained simply, "The woman has no money, but why should she suffer without salt?" But I also saw Sonia several months later ignore a different woman's prodding woes that she had no salt with which to cook at a funeral commemoration ceremony (*sadaka*). "I have nothing to give today," Sonia declared, with the justification of slow sales. She was eventually cajoled into giving the beggar one cup of salt. However, when pouring it into a small, flimsy plastic bag, the handle broke. The salt spilled onto the ground, rendering it unusable. Sonia seamlessly procured another, larger bag and put *two* cups of salt inside of it before sending the woman on her way. I asked Sonia about her change of heart and her doubled generosity. The bag breaking, she said, was an indication that her initial denial of the woman's request had been wrong. She laughed as she offered this explanation, and I am not sure whether the levity in her response reflected sarcasm or nervousness. Her actions, however, indicate that she felt the need to conspicuously demonstrate that she was not out to profit at the expense of others' suffering.

Feelings of distress at witnessing others' adversity were encompassed in the Chinyanja word *lisungu*, best translated into English as "compassion," but also used to denote more specifically self-abnegation, sympathy, forgiveness, empathy, and sorrow.[15] Enacting *lisungu* underlay not only market relations, but human relations broadly. Martha, an older woman with impaired mobility, suggested, for example, that a person like herself without the physical capacity to farm or to do piecework was dependent on the *lisungu* of others to survive. A younger woman sitting beside Martha confirmed that a person should feel *lisungu* when they come across anyone who is suffering (*wolaga*). She gave the examples of encountering a person who had eaten *ntchima* made from bran flour (*gaga*) or who was carrying a very burdensome head load. But personally witnessing suffering was not necessary to feel compassion. "Even when you hear on the radio that someone you have never met has died," the young woman continued, "you feel *lisungu*." Others with whom I discussed *lisungu* gave examples like a woman who worries when her children are sick, and a brother who cares for his sister when she becomes divorced from her husband.

Direct intervention to end suffering was not necessary to show *lisungu*. Sympathy alone could be enough in certain circumstances. For example, I was once chatting with Clara, who recently started reroofing her home with tarpaulin and grasses. Such projects required impeccable timing—the grasses are sufficiently dry just as the destructive *mwera* (southern) winds begin to pick up. A person wanted to wait to start the process of reroofing until the winds had died down, lest their efforts be foiled. But this could come at a high cost: wait too long and the rainy season would arrive, and the grasses would no longer be viable for roofing. Clara had begun too early, and winds had destroyed her partially assembled roof the previous night. She pointed to the gaping holes in the tarpaulin covering the portion that had been under construction. Perhaps because Clara was her usual jovial self when explaining the predicament, my first reaction was to laugh. When she expressed concern that she had lost too much grass and would not be able to repair the roof, she became more somber. She had a physical handicap and asthma, which prevented her from collecting grasses. I suggested that she move her sleeping quarters to the opposite side of the house with an intact roof or that she ask a friend to collect more grasses for her. When we were later conversing about emotion and she explained the importance of *lisungu*, I apologized that I had failed to show compassion when I laughed at her roof predicament. But she corrected me: by giving her ideas on how to remedy the situation, I had recognized the gravity of her suffering and thus had properly expressed and so extended my sympathy.

That the person(s) for whom compassion was felt had to be perceived as *suffering* solidified for me the day I witnessed a goat break free from the ropes tying it to the roof of a car owned by a Metangula elite. His paid driver was speeding down the road from Lichinga to Metangula, and the goat happened to fall to the ground just in front of the stalled minibus in which I sat. I watched villagers slowly creep toward the wounded animal and then, in a rush, grab it and run, no doubt to celebrate their windfall by butchering, distributing, and consuming the meat. Later that night I told the story of the fallen goat to anyone who would listen (as it was rare that I had such juicy, firsthand gossip to share without damaging my reputation as a trusted confidant), each time completing the story with a lament of "*Lisungu!*" as people were apt to do when telling of someone else's suffering. I was surprised when the exclamation fell flat, again and again. Finally Judite, with a look of compassion herself, explained to me that *lisungu* was not the appropriate sentiment for such an event because the loss of a goat would in no way cause the elite owner to suffer. Surely, he could just buy another one. Similarly, a vendor who inflated prices for a tourist was justified in doing so because all foreigners were (perceived to be) wealthy. A higher price would therefore not cause a tourist distress, despair, pain, or suffering. This legitimized making a higher profit. The same logic was also sometimes applied to the purchases of government employees and other members of the local elite, several of whom told me they sent minor family members or employees to do shopping in their stead in the hope of finding a better deal with the anti-price-gouging principles of *lisungu* at play.

Lisungu was important not only in life, but also in death. People vaguely defined and imprecisely located the dwelling place of spirits, referring to it variously as *kumwamba* (on top), *mphepo* (wind), *mtendere* (peace), and *sawabo* (from *sawab*, Arabic for the reward a person gets from doing a good deed, and Swahili for fortune). Notably, I never heard the Portuguese or Arabic words for "heaven" (*céu* and *aljana*) used. Individuals aspired for themselves and their family members to enter into this realm as spirits, such that they could provide guidance, oversight, advice, and advocacy for relatives still living on earth. Becoming an ancestor was, however, not guaranteed. While acquaintances were unable or uninterested in articulating precise guidelines for this transformation, many stated that the most important criterion for becoming a spirit was *lisungu*. Mustafa, the oldest man in the neighborhood of Micuio, for example, one day spoke lovingly of his daughter-in-law who lived in a home beside his own, rather than joining her husband in Lichinga, in order to care for him. After describing all that she did for him and a great-grandchild with epilepsy, he summarized, "She has *lisungu*." I asked if the daughter-in-law would become a spirit when she died. "Same thing [*mwemo*]," he responded. Personhood itself, in life and in death, was determined in large part by hard work rooted in compassion to relieve suffering and to otherwise nourish, rather than diminish, the lives of others.

Islamic and Christian denominations in Metangula both, in fact, defined as sinful any act that harmed or otherwise failed to show compassion "toward your friends," which should include, at a minimum, all human beings.[16] Theologically driven or not, individuals *did* sometimes seemingly strategize to appear more

Figure 2.2. Mustafa, surrounded by family in Micuio. Photo by the author.

compassionate than they really were. Such was perhaps the reason that when I asked one market vendor why he had lowered the price for a cup of beans from seven and a half meticais to seven, he loudly declared his *lisungu* as motive. The price of beans had recently increased, and he was feeling sorry for the people who could not afford the purchase. As I chatted with him further, I occupied my hands by mindlessly sorting out from his stock the beans that had been nibbled by weevils. After several minutes, I looked down and realized the large quantity I had removed. He eyed my recognition that he was selling an inferior product, grimaced, and quickly brushed the beans I had removed back in with the others. "Compassion" in this case was a cover for his attempt to profit at the expense of unsuspecting customers, who would have to discard a large portion of their purchase and thus would suffer from, rather than find relief through, their purchase. Meanwhile, the vendor could divest from spoiled stock. This was not labor; it was exploitation. And, the vendor was clearly embarrassed. Transforming people into money was morally suspect. It was, instead, through forward thinking and hard work that a person could and should seek profit while maintaining their stake in the multifaceted moral project of interdependence.

While the lure of profit made the marketplace what it was, benefiting through processes that hindered rather than enhanced and that separated rather than united was not only shameful, but also, ultimately, unprofitable. These realities were embedded in widely circulated stories recounting the financial downfall of merchants operating without compunction. One such story had to do with Marco, who sold maize at high prices amid a food shortage in the year 2002. Rather than taking pity on those who were suffering by restricting his earnings to a small profit, he had gouged his customers and profited handsomely. He made enough money to purchase a car, an exceedingly rare luxury in Metangula at that time. But, and here is the kicker, the car soon malfunctioned and became a useless heap of metal in his front yard. When I asked for an explanation of this series of events, people explained to me in various ways that when someone profits while others suffer, "money cannot last [grasp]" (*sinagwire ndalama*).

There was another story that I had more personal experience with because it related to someone I knew personally—Julio Mercader, an archaeologist specializing in Stone Age archaeology, whom I worked alongside for several field seasons in the Lago and neighboring Sanga Districts. In the story first told to me by Jose, a self-proclaimed "love doctor" about whom I will have more to say soon, Mercader was a merchant (coincidentally, the meaning of "Mercader" in Portuguese). And rather than seeking out evidence of Hominin lifeways through phytolith analysis from ancient tools and faunal remains, he came to Mozambique to steal human bones. These he shipped home to Spain to be ground up and used to manufacture plates. While this project made the merchant rich, it also disrupted the spirits whose bones were displaced. As such, the merchant's fortune only led to ruin—each time he returned for more bones he had a new car, because the previous one had malfunctioned, and he was forced to purchase yet another vehicle for his nefarious efforts. Eventually, the man ran out of money and stopped coming to Mozambique. Indeed, the Spanish archaeologist suffered car troubles, he would tell you because of the rough roads, poor car servicing options in Niassa, and set after set of faulty used tires. And he did stop coming to Mozambique (his grant ended, and the politics of conducting research in the region were getting excessive). The tale, clear to me as fiction, though based on actual events, had become locally useful as a reminder of the importance of maintaining relations with both the living and the dead and the inevitable downfall that comes with disrupting social connections for personal gains through commercial exchange.

Regardless of how much of the "gift logic" prioritizing relationships over revenues in Metangula's marketplace was real versus rhetoric, much effort was made to engage customers in mutual dependencies rather than one-way transactions. The importance of these market-based relationships was made especially apparent to me one day when I inadvertently began selling tomatoes. I was chatting with one of the vendors, Sara, and she left me in charge when she had to step away. Uncomfortable enacting with someone else's stock the proper etiquette of including a "gift" (*basera*) with the transactions of frequent customers, friends, and those making large purchases, I simply gave each customer the tomatoes they had paid for. Sara thus found the amount of money I collected remarkable for the number of tomatoes gone when she returned (I had also sold quite a few tomatoes, due to the novelty of my vending). And although the windfall seemed to privately elate Sara, those to whom I sold tomatoes later confided that they had taken offense when I failed to give them extras as a gift. As if to clear her own name, Sara came to my house later that evening with an enormous bag of tomatoes. A gift for my work, she told me. And proof to others that she herself did not profit from my miscalculated miserliness.

Cooperation and mutual aid also characterized vendors' relations with each other. There were rarely price wars or overt competition for sales between vendors in Metangula's market, and prevailing practices otherwise ensured that each vendor had a fair shot at making a sale. When vendors were absent from their booths in order to attend a funeral, for example, neighboring sellers always took over transactions on their behalf. Though they were selling the exact same products at the exact same prices in the exact same locale, it would not have been proper behavior to deny the absent vendors their chance to sell goods when unable to be present for pro-social reasons. In one case, I observed only one of four salt sellers at the market (the other three absent for a funeral), but all four tables were open for business, with the one vendor simply rotating between them as customers arrived. While this ethic was not maintained for the larger business owners, there were still few efforts at price wars or competitive market practices among them. Where multiple vendors offered the same product, it was almost always sold at the same price by everyone. The one exception was a Portuguese man who operated the only store on the Sanjala hill. When he had something for sale in the store (shelves were just as often empty as not), the prices often varied radically from those in the marketplace. I personally patronized the place regardless, drawn in by the fact that the employee there always gave out change in the form of chocolate bonbons. Others seemed inclined to come in because it was the only place in town to purchase toilet paper. But the store did not seem to have the same regular patronage as the vendors who valued the customers as much as their financial transactions.

Scholars including Aristotle, Thomas Aquinas, and Karl Marx have warned for generations that money meddles with and muddies sociality (Parry and Bloch 1989). But Africanists have also long noted strategies to mitigate the creation of social distance and the crafting of impersonal relationships that tend to arise with market exchange. There is, for example, widespread segregation of money according to the means through which it was earned (Hutchinson 1992) as well as restrictions or mandates on funds garnered through illicit or predatory means (Shipton 1989) or without sweat (Ferguson 2006). African markets likewise do not always fully embrace capitalist priorities, strategies, and moral orientations. Mary Njeri Kinyanjui (2019) explores what she calls the resultant "utu-ubuntu" model of business relations, where the marketplace is valued for its capacity to sustain networks that perpetuate relationality. These principles, she argues, are widespread in the "African metropolis"—resilient urban spaces that insist on humanist solidarity and equitable and sustainable urban development. The notion of "utu-ubuntu" resonates with the ethnographic observations of Tuulikki Pietilä (2007) who documents how Tanzanian market vendors manipulated and experimented with moral ideals for mutuality as an explicit strategy for building both profits *and* relations. They spoke of themselves as "mothers" and "farmers" rather than traders, capitalized on kinship obligations to lure customers, and spoke of the need to feed their children to justify the very activity of making money. But, at the same time, Pietilä notes, they manipulated measuring containers to cheat customers, stacked fruits and vegetables in a manner that was deceiving, and employed a host of additional tactics simultaneously clever and beguiling. Rather than seeing the moral economy as antithetical to the market economy or completely separate spheres of "gift" and "commodity" logics (Gregory 1982), Pietilä argues that the language of mutuality can be used to convert profit-driven transactions into something that is at the same time relational. In other words, participation in monetary transactions does not necessarily equate with adherence to capitalist logics and moral orientations, but it also does not negate them. And often more important than intentions are appearances and outcomes.

Conclusion

From a biomedical perspective, the question of why people eat has a simple answer: to stay alive. In Metangula, however, people did not conceive of eating as a means to ensure life in the sense that it is opposed to death—for whether or not a person was alive was the domain of God. Food was, instead, a source of *vitamina* and vitality to perform the daily work of caring for self and for others—"caring" used here in the double sense of provisioning and also having compassion. With labor morally prioritized for capacitating relationality, we can look back to the importance of energy attainment (rather than, for example, flavor, calories, nutrients, or personal predilection) in food categorization, as outlined in chapter 1, as a reflection of productive labor as essential for humanity. In Metangula, *vitamina* was required for the daily work of care and dependence that was integral to being and becoming human. Hence, its centrality in local foodways.

The importance of economic pro-sociality for humanity should not be mistaken for unproblematic or automatic primacy in action. A person could choose to disregard moral imperative or to manipulate opportunities for gains making to achieve alternative ends. This was seen most notably in the marketplace vendor selling an inferior product at a "discount" through appeals to compassion for the plight of customers with a small budget. Likewise, perhaps, was how some young men spent their days gathered in the shade of a tree to share bottles of gin, justifying their behavior as a necessary action to maintain the networks that would lead to opportunities for day labor. As these situations allude, a "principle of participation" in Metangula does not indicate an erasure of the tensions between relational and egocentric sensibilities and desires. And *appearing* to act in ways deemed appropriate for humanity was, at times, enough to stave off the criticism that might otherwise lead to accusations of mal-intent. It is to such appearances and actions that I devote my attention in the next two chapters—considering how foodways are caught up in the project of asserting personhood through distinguishing oneself from witches and animals (chapter 3), and crafting belonging among, as well as showing consideration for, the well-being of others (chapter 4).

Notes

1. Edward Kanyike's phrasing of the "principle of participation" follows the work of Vincent Mulago (1969), not Lucien Lévy-Bruhl (1925) whose concept of "participation" was rooted in assumptions of primitivism (Mousalimas 1990).
2. See Aloo Osotsi Mojola (2019) for a detailed consideration of the etymology and meaning of Ubuntu.
3. Previous generations of scholars, particularly those associated with negritude, African socialism, and "ethnophilosophy," positioned African personhood as distinct in actively prioritizing the individual over the community. Later generations of scholars have modified this positioning, recognizing that both individual and society are integral to definitions of self everywhere (cf. Ogude 2018) and that models of personhood are perhaps more effectively conceived when squarely focused on the ontological conception of the person as embedded within or separable from society. By way of contrast to the prevalent African model considered here, many populations around the world conceive of society as a derivative product of the association of preformed individuals, who can leave said relations and be fundamentally the same persons as they were before. Individuals, then, are autonomous within society, and they come together more contractually than organically, with morality in these interactions governed by rights rather than obligations (which are a burden, rather than a source of strength). In such frameworks, society is often conceived to be in conflict with the individual, individuality, and in particular individualism (which is premised on freedom from constraints and social determinacy), rather than mutuality being perceived as integral to individual being through its requisite connection, caring, and responsibility. Without the intention of petrifying a strict dichotomy, implying frameworks that are rigid, completely at odds with one another, and followed without agency or debate, distinctions in fundamental orientations toward being as holistic or atomistic are palpable and with consequence for cultural beliefs and practices and broader engagements with everyday life.
4. For a broader discussion on the similarities and distinctions of African creation stories and other myths, see Alice Werner's *Myths and Legends of the Bantu* (2010 [1933]).
5. For a discussion on religious pluralism in the Lake Niassa region, see the work of Agustine Musopole (1984).

6. Charles Good (1991) contends that UMCA missionaries actually did very little to stop the slave trade.
7. Malyn Newitt cites only one government secondary school admitting individuals of African ancestry in 1930, and the school had only one African student at that time (2009 [1995], 440). The UMCA made secondary educational training available from 1900 at St. Michael's Teacher Training College in Cóbuè, enabling the diocese to staff the majority of its schools with native teachers. Medical training on Likoma was available as of 1912, providing trained African staff for the majority of its dispensaries as well (Good 2004, 326).
8. A similar point on accumulating knowledge through experience is raised by Edward Alpers (1969) for the Yaawo, Julie Archambault (2017) for the Tonga, and Didier N. Kaphagawani (1998) for the Chewa.
9. Didier N. Kaphagawani (1998) alternatively translates *njeru* (or, in Chichewa, *nzeru*) as "wisdom," which he argues is distinct from knowledge in Chichewa, though no separate word for knowledge exists. Colleague Experencia Madalitso Jalasi suggests that some in Malawi also mark the distinction as *nzeru za mkalasi* (book knowledge to solve technical problems) and *nzeru za umunthu* (human knowledge, the moral capacity to do the right thing), the two existing, expressed, and evaluated distinctly (personal communication, 5 January 2020).
10. In addition to *vungu* finding offense with the consumption of alcohol or drugs, ancestors (*mizimu*) did as well.
11. Steinforth (2009) recognized a similar division of the category *misala* (crazy) in southern Malawi, where *kuzerezeteka* was applied to persons showing signs of mental retardation, and *kuzungulira mutu* to persons prone to bouts of unprovoked violence and other unusual behaviors. *Vungu* did not, however, play a role in Steinforth's categorization.
12. On the inadequacies of the term "ancestors" to capture generational authority in association with growth and maturity, the distinction (or lack thereof) between the status of living and dead elders, and the continuous presence of the dead in the lives of the living in much of Africa, see the classic work of Igor Kopytoff (1971). While some Africanist scholars have preferred "living-dead" to refer to those who are deceased and still remembered (Mbiti 1970), in the present era this term has unfortunately become synonymous in the global north with zombies.
13. I am indebted to both Justin Sondergaärd and Gary Alpert for their assistance in scientifically identifying the *vungu* extracted from the goat's head.
14. The UMCA was High Anglican, with roots in the Oxford Movement of the Church of England, which aimed to reassert apostolic descent and emphasized the spiritual and vocational rather than the authoritative role of priests and of broader missionary work (Rennick 2003, 56–57). For further information on the theological orientation of the UMCA, see the work of Terence Ranger (1982a).
15. Several acquaintances suggested translation of *lisungu* into Portuguese as *sentir pena* (to feel pity, sorrow, compassion, mercy, commiseration, suffering, pain), into Chichewa as *chifun(d)o* (mercy, clemency, generosity, compassion), and into Chiyaawo as *c(h)anaasa*.
16. According to raw data from the 2007 national census, obtained directly from Instituto Nacional de Estatística (INE) in Maputo, about half (51 percent) of Metangula residents affiliated with one of two Islamic sects—Nasala or Africa Muslim. Nasala Muslims, also known locally as Shaziliya and internationally as Qadiriyya or Sufi, were much more tol-

erant of traditional beliefs and practices than Kadiyani Muslims, known locally by the English moniker "Africa Muslim" and elsewhere as Sukuti. The other half of Metangula residents identified with a Christian faith—Anglicanism (36 percent) the most prominent, followed by Catholicism (10 percent), and Pentecostalism (1 percent).

CHAPTER 3

Witches, Animals, and Humans

"Did you see how they were walking around without shirts on?" Pedro asked his wife, Judite. "And their language—who could understand that!? They do not even speak Portuguese, except one of them, and he can barely speak it." Pedro did an imitation of the way the visitors spoke among themselves, replete with "sh-" sounds to begin each new word—"shing, shong, shun." He paused for a moment, shaking his head in disbelief, then continued his rant, "They cannot laugh and chat with people. Their workers do not get weekends. And, did you hear that they are refusing to pay for mangoes!? They just enter into the grove and take them, like thieves." He took a drink of water and then for another moment became absorbed in his own thoughts. "No," he said in what seemed a conclusion to internal deliberations, "the Chinese are not people."

We had just returned from Michumwa, a town about six miles north of Metangula, slightly inland from the lake. Michumwa was Judite's hometown, and Pedro was from the lakeshore town of Chia. The two had met during the war years in the town of Chuanga and then moved together to Metangula when Pedro secured a job at the naval base. In his time there, Pedro had seen many foreigners—mainly Portuguese soldiers, but there had been others, too. Some suffered from "bad hearts," he reported, but "all had been people." This was unlike the five Chinese men living in Michumwa while overseeing the construction of a new school. Occupying a house near that of Judite's extended family, the behaviors of these five men had been the subject of intense critique over the course of a three-day remembrance ceremony (sadaka).

Judite retorted that of course the Chinese are people. "Are their bodies not the same as ours?" she asked Pedro. They proceeded to discuss more details about these Chinese, taking much time to contemplate the fact that these men did not hesitate to hit their employees, who had to ask for permission to use the bathroom and even to drink water and were forced to work in the hot sun from six in the morning until five at night without a break. "The Chinese are living in the past," Pedro said. "This is a democracy. But they are just acting like the days of colonialism." This sentiment echoed Judite's family's in Michumwa; over the weekend I had heard them referring to their neighbors not as os Chineses (Portuguese, "the Chinese") or akuchina (Chinyanja, "those *from China"*) but newani—*"the new ones." The label seemed as much a reference to their recent arrival as to the concept of replacing something of the same character that pre-existed them.*[1]

Pedro turned to me as if I were a source of authority and asked if it is true that the Chinese are cannibals. I said that while I did not know for sure, I supposed that they were not. "But, they do eat dogs," Judite offered, based on what she claimed to be personal observation. "And, they also eat a lot of potatoes." She specified that she had observed that the five Chinese men in Michumwa used a peeler rather than a knife to remove the potato skins and cut the potatoes into a sort of flour that they fried in something that did not resemble any oil that she was familiar with. Judite became quite animated, reporting that they also used water to boil a kind of bread, I assumed dumplings, and that they mixed together fish and goat. The family members present in the room with us found this combination to be quite curious. "After they cook everything," Judite continued, "they go inside to eat—each with his own plate, and not with a fork or even with their hands, but with wood[en chopsticks]." We sat in silence for several moments, taking in this firsthand accounting of Chinese foodways. "No," Pedro doubled down based on Judite's report. "They are surely not human."

This chapter is about foodways in Metangula as they relate to the broad moral project of being and becoming human persons—taking the central importance of mutuality as outlined in chapter 2 and examining its manifestations more closely in the alimentary realm introduced in chapter 1. In the opening vignette, it is the foodways of Chinese nationals, along with other behaviors, that led Pedro to question whether it could be possible that—despite their physical form—five men in Michumwa were actually not persons. More commonly, it was behaviors through which an individual approximated an animal or a witch that had the potential to bring their humanity into question. If chapter 1, then, showed that the energy enabled through *vitamina* was a key ingredient in understanding what people ate, and chapter 2 demonstrated the relevance of vitality for the compassionate labor essential to human personhood, chapter 3 is about what persons were not—namely, witches and animals. These nonpersons were not cast as opposites of humanity, but rather as a mirror of very natural human tendencies like jealousy, selfishness, and solitude that people overcame by "imposing humaneness upon our humanness" (Masolo 2010, 155) to become persons.

In this chapter, I consider how people in Metangula distinguished themselves from nonpersons, focusing on alimentation as site for the demonstration of actions deemed appropriate for humanity and the avoidance of actions deemed inappropriate. I begin with a description of witches and witchcraft, emphasizing both as very real to the people of Metangula. I then hone in on witches in association with cannibalism, or the eating of human flesh, something presumed in Metangula to be quite tasty (satisfying), but also diabolical in signaling one's

Figure 3.1. Bare-chested Chinese men are surrounded by curious onlookers in Michumwa. Photo by the author.

prioritization of life-depleting over life-generating practices. In discussing cannibalism, it is not my intention to imply, legitimize, or in any other way support depictions of Africans as backward, brutish, or otherwise distinct in their humanity from any other people. In fact, in their relegation of flesh-eating to individuals who represent uncivilized behavior (witches), people in Metangula, and Africans more broadly, very much resemble other human populations around the world that employ cannibalism for drawing cultural boundaries and "Othering" (Said 1978) those they wish to conquer, civilize, and defame (Arens 1979). I round out the chapter by documenting and assessing a series of prohibitions against the eating of animals that resembled human beings in physical, emotional, and spiritual form, and I suggest that articulating and following these taboos and exhibiting repugnance at the thought of eating these animals were actions that contributed to distancing oneself from accusations of witchcraft. I also consider briefly the distinctions that people in Metangula drew between humans and animals. By interrogating the behaviors that people in Metangula emphasized as characteristic of animals, and of humans, much of which played out in the realm of food and foodways, I highlight additional ways in which everyday alimentary behaviors served as an arena for the cultivation, or failure, of humanity.

Witches and Witchcraft

Scholars have long noted witches and witchcraft as phenomena that are not merely believed in sub-Saharan Africa, but understood as fact. In other words, for many Africans, energy can be magically and maleficently manipulated to effect change or to control the course of events. It is important to note that witches in sub-Saharan Africa are not envisioned to be the long-nosed, wart-bearing, green-hued, pointy-hat-donning, broomstick-riding caricatures of cartoons and Halloween décor in the global north. Rather, witches look just like you and me. Though they may transfigure at opportune moments into animals or other forms, witches, for the most part, appear to be regular people in the community. What sets them apart is that they are hiding a deep secret—that their actions diminish rather than enhance relationality, often through diverting resources (material or metaphysical) for their own enrichment, enjoyment, sustenance, and hoarding. They are, in a word, destructive, rather than life-sustaining and generative. These actions are often invisible or otherwise hidden, and they take place at night.

That witches and witchcraft exist is so credible that questioning their factuality is, for many, beyond the scope of inquiry. This surety can be difficult for many who have been raised outside of the region to grasp. But it is important to recognize that witchcraft answers questions that science cannot (Evans-Pritchard 1976 [1937])—often moral and ethical, regarding the simultaneous attraction and danger in accumulations of wealth and power (Geschiere 1997). Also of note is that despite widespread exposure in Africa to science and world religions, the place of witchcraft in the social fabric of African life does not seem to be dissipating, and it may in fact be on the rise. It cannot, then, be considered an antiquated concept or otherwise a relic of the past, destined for disappearance. Witchcraft is, rather, a lived reality for many Africans, at times seemingly a response to changing political and economic arrangements and other contemporary realities (Ashforth 2005; Ciekawy and Geschiere 1998; Comaroff and Comaroff 1993; Moore and Sanders 2001; Shaw 2002), but also very much a realm for the negotiation and revitalization of "tradition" as locally envisaged (Sanders 2003).

Some scholars distinguish "witches" from "sorcerers," the difference being a matter of whether evil emerges from inner qualities a person may be unaware that they possess (witchcraft) or is enacted through incantations and tools (sorcery) (Middleton and Winter 2004 [1963]). In practical form, many Africans do not themselves distinguish between these categories. I think here, for example, of Patrick, my cultural guide and interpreter when I first began to work in Metangula. Patrick, who spoke English and Chichewa, was the only person in Metangula I ever heard use the term "sorcerer" (or its Portuguese equivalent, *feiticeiro*). But, for Patrick, the relevant distinction between a witch and a sorcerer was not how they enacted their maleficence, it was gender: a "sorcerer" was male, and a "witch" was female. In Chichewa/Chinyanja, there is a single term for witches and sorcerers—*afiti* (plural; singular, *mfiti*). In practice, *afiti* blur the lines between "witches" and "sorcerers" by combining elements of both. The occult actions of *afiti* in Metangula, for example, might involve the gathering of potent herbs and roots, reducing them to ash, and sprinkling the resultant *dawa* with mal-intent into food or onto structural thresholds or pathways in order to effect harm onto others. This falls into the academician's category of sorcery. However, *afiti* also acted on *natural* emotions and desires, like ill will, greed, jealousy, and the longing for power that are present in all humans.

Afiti can, in this way, be conceived of as not an antithesis of persons, but instead as a product of failed humanity—an embrace rather than a training and taming of callousness, insulation, selfishness, and destruction, each widely conceived in Africa to be socially and cosmologically ruinous for unraveling the intimacies that keep us connected to one another, and so whole (Beidelman 1993). The potential for operating as *afiti* was therefore inborn within us all (as is the prerequisite for witchcraft), even if its activation required tools and learned knowledge (as is the prerequisite for sorcery). I thus do not see application for a split between witchcraft and sorcery in Metangula, and in their collapse I seek to highlight witchcraft as not an opposite of human nature so much as it was a succumbing to deeply human desires for power, insulation, and greed. Witchcraft was thus not so much an antithesis of humanity as it was an integral part, if one that must be managed to deepen the mutuality upon which generative potentiality depends. I choose to use the term "witchcraft" here as a catch-all for occult action because it is the word preferred by regional scholars and many Africans themselves when dialoguing about the capacity for individuals to wield mystical powers to cause harm in the material world (Smith 2019, 68–69).

Like many African towns and cities, gossip regarding witchcraft was thick in Metangula. While unexplainable events and behaviors were sometimes blamed on "luck" or "God," it was hard to escape witchcraft and its causative roots in pathogenic emotions as alternative explanations. Illness was surely the effect of a neighbor's jealousy, an untimely death was the result of a greedy wife, and a child was misbehaving because his grandmother had indoctrinated him into the occult. All of these were forms of witchcraft (*ufiti*). There were several individuals in Metangula who were particularly feared as witches—for example, Sancho, an unassuming middle-aged man who was quite prosperous by local standards. The source of his earnings supposedly came from him killing his brother and burying the body near his business as an occult act of "medicine murder," enacted to enrich himself through siphoning the vitality of someone else (Murray and Sanders 2005; Ranger 2007; Vincent 2008). Although nobody had hard evidence that this had occurred, disappearance of the brother just as Sancho was beginning to earn his fortune was cause for suspicion. Similar to stories of Marco (the greedy flour seller), money that was earned through medicine murder "would not stick," and this was why Sancho's businesses were beginning to fail. His family was likely scared, many speculated, because they knew that Sancho would be motivated to kill again to renew his former wealth. Some avoided patronizing Sancho's businesses in a seeming bid to distance themselves from his reputation as a witch. For example, I invited Judite out for a drink one evening, and she chose the venue of a small restaurant in the market. When they did not have anything in stock, I suggested Sancho's bar instead, where there were always cold beverages and good music. Judite expressed an uncharacteristic hesitancy and asked at the small restaurant if we could purchase drinks from a vendor elsewhere in the market and then drink them where we were. She was told no, but we could imbibe in the restaurant's storeroom if we wished. She accepted this proposition, preferring to drink lukewarm beer in a musty closet over the risk of being seen enjoying herself publicly at an establishment owned by Sancho.

While Judite did not outright call Sancho a witch, her reluctance to be associated with the occult was clear in other actions—such as strongly encouraging that I not visit with Jose, the traditional healer billing himself as a "love doctor" and the only other person in Metangula beside Sancho that I consistently heard labeled as a witch. Judite's hyperawareness was perhaps because of her own status as an amateur healer. While she did not bill herself as a *sing'anga*, people in Metangula knew Judite to be adept at preparing concoctions that could cure headaches and minor breathing problems. The line between using such medicines to heal and to harm was thin, hence the single word *dawa* used to describe natural products with the power to restore and to disrupt, and those operating as a healer were often suspected of (also) being a witch. Judite's apprehensions about being linked with the occult seemed to heighten after the death of a well-respected veteran soldier, who several days before had come to her complaining of asthma. Judite, of course, provided medicine to help relieve the symptoms. When the man died, some people suspected that Judite had clandestinely passed him a poison rather than a cure. In the evening after the veteran's funeral, I overheard Judite nervously sharing these rumors with Pedro. The conversation helped me to make sense of her behavior at the crowded lakeshore cemetery earlier that day. Judite had been sitting in the front row of an overspill area behind the main proceedings of the Anglican graveside burial rites, a location that faced the majority of onlookers. In this very visible position she seemed to be making a show of her mourning, with the wailing and uncontrollable body spasms typically expected and enacted by close family in grief (which she was not, on either count). A witch, rumor had it, did not mourn the death of their victims. And they most certainly did not show up at the funeral.

While many people privately confessed to me their suspicions of neighbors' and other community members' practicing of sorcery, they were less likely to confront the accused than to cut the individual out of their social networks. Monica, for example, was convinced that an aunt had snuck into her home and burned her two-year-old daughter's feet because she was jealous of the girl's beauty, about which the aunt had always been commenting. Without evidence, though, Monica could not present the matter to her local neighborhood *nduna* or to Chief Chilombe for arbitration, and the only way to confirm that the aunt was to blame for her daughter's disfiguration would be to hear as much from a traditional healer. Local healers, however, were reluctant to reveal the perpetrators of sorcery, as the government had warned that they could be held responsible for clients' retaliation against the accused. If, on the other hand, Monica accused the aunt without a healer's evidence, she might be said to be a witch herself. Otherwise, how could she know that her aunt was a witch (as witches know their own)? Monica's only recourse was to ostracize her aunt and to encourage others to do the same—which, they did. Such exclusion is of course incredibly damaging where vitality is dependent on networks of mutuality.

Perceptions that a person is involved in witchcraft can also lead to physical harm, as periodically reported in news stories where the accused (often orphaned children, widowed women, and elders) have been stoned to death, set alight, or otherwise subjected to violence (Van der Meer 2013). There was only once that I personally witnessed the fervor that can erupt when an individual is directly accused of being a witch. It started when someone came across a stranger who was sleeping on the ground by the secondary school in the neighborhood

Figure 3.2. A man accused of being a witch, recovering from his ordeal. Photo by the author.

of Seli, alongside a jacket tied into a makeshift bag. Dried leaves, barks, and gourds peeked through the loose knots. A winnowing basket was also spotted nearby. Passersby concluded that the bundle's contents included *dawa*, and the man must therefore be a witch whose "airplane" (the winnowing basket) had run out of fuel and fallen from the sky. Such events were sometimes recounted on the radio waves that reached Metangula from Malawi, inclusive of interviews with the accused witch who admitted to their nighttime ride and the owner of the home onto which the witch had crash-landed. That day in Metangula, a crowd gathered around the sleeping man and a consensus was reached—this was most definitely a witch.

The man was hoisted up and carried to the home of the chief, where his bag was dropped. A crowd then paraded the man around town. Rumor spread fast, and soon hundreds of people, including me, appeared to see for themselves a live witch. The man was kicked, swatted at with tree branches, and verbally assaulted. He was barely conscious when the municipality lent its tractor for the final parade from Sanjala back to the chief's house. Here a red-eyed Chief Chilombe, wielding a saw in one hand and a metal pipe in the other, fended off the crowd as he took possession of their prisoner. When I appeared at the gate to his yard, Chilombe let me pass and showed me that within the man's rucksack he had encountered papers suggesting the accused's official AMETRAMO (Associação dos Médicos Tradicionais de Moçambique, Association of Mozambican Traditional Doctors) status. This meant he was a certified traditional healer. In practice, of course, this title did not negate the possibility of the man also being a witch. But there was at least a plausible explanation for the contents of his bag, and Chilombe was willing to give him the benefit of the doubt: the man's magic airplane had not crash-landed; he just happened to have collapsed (likely from being drunk, judging from temperament and breath) near a winnowing basket. Chilombe's pronouncement slowly spread to the crowd outside the gate, and everyone soon left the matter to go about their other business. Still, acquaintances recounted the story gleefully, for months afterward, as the time they apprehended a real witch right there in Metangula. Were the AMETRAMO papers not found by the chief, it is very possible that the crowd's rage toward those who inflict rather than work to relieve suffering could have resulted in greater physical harm for the accused.

Witches as Cannibals

People suggested to me that witchcraft was so rife in Metangula that it was best to engage in preventative measures before tragedy struck. Medicines buried around a property could keep a sorcerer from finding and entering a house to cause harm—they would see only water in place of a home. A locked door (which very few people had) could effect the same result, according to some. But it was especially important to protect a recently interred corpse from witches, for a member of the occult who was craving human flesh would murder their victim, wait out the funeral, and then rob the grave. It was as such that burial sites were physically guarded or protected with *dawa* in efforts to thwart this sort of theft, knowing that witches might be on the prowl. Residents of Metangula in fact posited witches to be avid and very physical consumers of human flesh. This is a common formulation across Africa, as it is for many world populations, though the specifics of who eats whom and to what ends vary (Whitehead and Wright 2004). In Africa, witches are often specified to consume the flesh, blood, and/or bodily organs of persons within their own communities, often family members (Arens 1979), and these acts are conceived to have the effect of transferring vitality or life force (and so longevity, luck, and riches) from the deceased to the consumer. Witchcraft scholar Peter Geschiere (2003) refers to the tendency of witches to seek victims among their own family members as the "dark side of kinship"—a betrayal to the family as a source of solidarity, trust, and support, but *not* a counterpoint, as witchcraft highlights the jealousy, aggression, and danger that are an inherent aspect of intimate relations. Where kinship is not central to witchcraft accusations, victims still seem to come from the same locality as the accused, such that it is mutuality, shared everyday life, and ruptured relations at the heart of the occult in Africa.

There is divergence, however, as to whether witches physically consume human flesh in a visible and worldly form or only in spiritual essence. On the side of anthropophagy as astral, where the victim shows no visible signs that they are being attacked, Rosalind Shaw (1997) writes, for example, of Sierra Leone, where witches suck an individual's blood and remove their heart. The victim continues to live, but because blood holds a person's life and the heart their intentions, they will only exist as the empty shell of their former self. J. W. M. van Breugel (2001) explains that in Malawi, on the other hand, witches physically consume human flesh, which can be observed in wounds that do not heal among the living and the disappearance or disturbance of corpses among the dead. In Metangula also, witches physically consumed the bodies of their victims. "Human flesh tastes sweet," people mentioned on multiple occasions when I recoiled at the thought of cannibalism. Not that they had any personal experience, they were quick to assure me, but rumor had it that those to whom human flesh was fed would find the experience of eating it to be pleasant. The flavor would be so enjoyable, in fact, that once a person tasted it, they would develop an insatiable craving and enlist the help of others to obtain more, eventually becoming a witch themselves and killing family members to obtain meat for sharing at cannibalistic feasts. This is how witches bolstered their ranks and secured a steady supply of human flesh and why the recruitment of children (who do not know any better than to eat unfamiliar meats) was so important. An adult, on the other hand, should know better than to eat a strange meat when it is offered. Ian Dicks reported that the Yaawo, in fact, performed a ceremony when installing a new chief that entailed presenting the candidate with an array of meats, one of which was human. The candidate's meal would be monitored, for a witch would not be able to resist human flesh. To elect such an individual as a chief would, of course, be unwise (personal communication, 25 March 2011).

I confirmed this interpretation of physical rather than astral cannibalism through many conversations in Metangula, but most memorably through an encounter facilitated by Florinda, a woman enrolled in the dietary survey and whom I visited from time to time to chat. I enjoyed hearing the stories that she told me and observing the dynamic between her and her daughter-in-law, Luana, whose husband was stationed at a military post in Cabo Delgado. Florinda once told me that long ago, in the days of her own childhood, Luana engaging in an extramarital affair would have caused her absent husband to be susceptible to injury via mystical force. To prove her fidelity, Luana would have been subject to regular urine analysis. Florinda was unable to articulate the operation of such a test. Still, through our conversations, Florinda was someone I pegged as somehow having a deep knowledge of the mysteries of the nonmaterial world.

One afternoon I sat in the backyard with Florinda and Luana, passing the day. They were sorting through cassava leaves, tossing the "red" ones to the ground and keeping the green ones to cook for dinner. I tried to help out, but they all looked green to me. "Why are people selling the red leaves mixed in with the green ones at the market if nobody wants to eat them?" I asked. "Money," Luana answered. "[They are] without any *lisungu*." I took the opportunity to ask something that had been on my mind—whether animals had *lisungu* (compassion). "Some do," Florinda said, "like a snake." She explained that a snake will sometimes go find and administer medicines to "its friends," while other animals just see a dying compatriot and keep moving. Snakes also will sometimes decide not to bite a human, again demonstrating compassion. I asked about children. "They develop *lisungu* when they are around the size of these ones," she said, pointing with her chin to the two children in the yard who looked to be about six or seven. "Once they start to develop intelligence, they develop *lisungu*. Before that they may see somebody in pain and just laugh or do nothing. But with *lisungu* they will say, 'Mama, are you wounded?'" I asked if all adults have *lisungu*. "Arianna," she responded, "an adult without *lisungu* is a witch." Thinking of her son, I asked how soldiers can manage to have *lisungu* when they routinely injure or even kill their enemies. She said that, indeed, soldiers lose their *lisungu* during war, but then they get it back when the war is over. "And during a war they only kill people," she was sure to specify. "They do not eat them like a witch does." I expressed surprise at her statement. "Yes, Arianna, witches do eat people," she affirmed. "I saw it in a video."

This last claim put an even clearer look of incredulity on my face. "Come," she said. "Let us watch." Taking me by the hand, one above and one below my own and cupped near her thigh, Florinda led me across the paved road to a neighbor's house. We sat on the veranda and exchanged pleasantries before Florinda explained that I wanted to see the recording of the witch. A broad smile came across the neighbor's face, and she led us into her mud and grass thatch home and sat us in front of a television and DVD player. She popped in what turned out to be a compilation of music videos by Moses Makawa, a Malawian singer. The neighbor pressed play and *Lithe* (It [the marriage] should be over), the first video, began. It depicted a man physically abusing his wife, interspersed with individuals and small groups of people slowly gyrating their hips to the rhythm of the song while standing in grass fields, in front of concrete homes, and at the entrance of fancy hotels. Florinda and her neighbor explained the plot of the video in a way that suggested they took the images to be documentary rather than dramatic performance. "Look, he is beating her!" they exclaimed and pointed. "Look at the blood!"

The song ended and the second video began, this one entitled *Umakwiya Chani* (Why are you upset?). It opened with a man sitting on the stoop of a house listening to and then kicking a radio where the announcer is heard praising Moses Makawa. The two women pointed at the TV screen on which the images played out, exclaiming excitedly, "That is the witch!" and "Look, watch, and you will see—he is a witch!" The same man was then shown jumping off the stoop and magically transforming into a very black-bodied monster with a white-masked face akin to a Scream franchise movie. The women squealed in what felt like something rooted in genuine terror and indicated that the man, now a monster, was the witch. The first verse began by outlining the artist's plea to not accuse him of witchcraft just because he sings songs exposing the evil acts of witches. His intention is to help, but he fears that witches will kill and consume him in order to stop his proselytizing:

Do not tarnish my image	*Usayipise mbiri yanga*
I do not practice witchcraft at night	*Sindimatamba*
I have never consumed a corpse	*Sindinasusepo maliro*
I do not know witchcraft	*Ufiti sindimadziwa*
Do not ask me many questions, I do not know anything	*Mafunsowa asakuchulukire palibe chomwe—ndidziwa ine*
When you practice witchcraft at night, do you see me?	*Monga mukamauluka phluuuu—Ineyo mumandionapo?*
Do not just be quiet—you should answer me, have I offended you?	*Musangoti pheeee—muzindiyankha apa ndakuchimwani—chiyani?*
I just wanted to inform you that I am not a member [not a witch]	*Ndimangokuuza kuti uziwe siine membala wamva*
But if you are upset, go and report	*Koma ngati ndakutenga mtima upite tenga ukazisiye*

Go and tell him that he has failed; he is tired of that	*Ukamuuze kuti walephera watopanazo zimenezo*
If you are disgusted, just close your ears	*Eee ndimakunyasadi basi uzingosekela makutu*
I will fetch a witch hunter to twist your ears!	*Ndizatenga namulondola akupotole mapilikanilo!*
What kind of a person are you; you continue practicing sorcery	*Nanga munthu osamva bwanji uzingopitilizabe kuchimwa*
All right, kill me	*Ndiye undiphe*
Consume me, be satisfied, I should stop offending you	*Unditafune mtima ukuphwe ndisamakunyase*

The video then cut to a group of coal-black-bodied men in front of a bloodied winnowing basket with meat in it. The women grew excited again, Florinda shouting, "See!? They are eating uncooked meat! They are eating humans!" Several of the men stood with raw meat hanging from their mouths, and another smiled with bloodied teeth. The song's chorus cut in, imploring people to realize that even though a person is smiling, they could still be a witch:

If you do not practice witchcraft, why are you offended?	*Ee-ee!! Ngati sumatamba nanga chimakunyasa ndi chani?*
If you are not a witch, why are you upset?	*Iii-ii! ngati siwokwima nanga umakwiya chani?*
He is a witch, he is a witch, do not be fooled with his smiles	*Ndi mfwiti, ndi mfwiti uyo, musamuone kusekelela*
He is a witch	*koma ufiti ulimo*
Uncle, brother—your mother's brother is an animal [witch]	*Amoyaye achimweneyi—Alongo wawo amayi anuwa ndichilombo*
If you keep smiling at him [are not careful], you will perish	*Mukati muziti manombeee nde mutha muwona*
He has his own tricks—you will perish	*Alinazo njira zake ameneyo ee mutha muwona*
When he listens to Makawa's songs, he scorns them in his heart	*Akamamvera nyimbo za Makawa amatukwana mumtima*
He does not have a real reason anyway	*Alibenso chifukwa chenicheni*
He has no explanation	*Amangoti kakasi*
Please, please, uncle	*Pepani, pepani Malume*
Please, I am on my knees [begging you]	*Pepani, ndagwira mwendo wanu*
I do not see you, you see me	*Ine sindimakuwonani mumandiona ndinu*

The original man-turned-witch was shown flying in a winnowing basket and then teaching a young boy to do the same. Two more verses followed in which Makawa indicated that the witches in his community were plotting to kill him because of his singing about the evils of witchcraft—to silence him. The witch in the video became a bird, flying about and cawing. Witches heard instead a call for attendance at a meeting in which Makawa's murder would be plotted so that his body could be consumed. Makawa then asserted that he would not be intimidated by these actions. He would continue to sing his songs, to warn people about witchcraft, and to praise Jesus:

There is witchcraft in this world; I have witnessed it!	*Ufiti ulipo paziko panondazipenya eee!*
I have invited trouble with the songs I have produced	*Nyimbo ndayimba zija! Ndangoziputila nkhondo eee.*
Calamities, atrocities	*Malaulo, msempho*
The witch hunting has put me in trouble	*Namulondola zandigwesa mmavuto*
It was quiet, the sun was shining!	*Kunali kunja kuli duu dzuwa likuwala Meee!*
I was quiet at the veranda composing songs	*Ndinali chete pakhonde mmutu mwanga nyimbo zikubwata*
A bird flew; they call it *mkhwezule*	*Panadusa mbalame ina poyichula amati mkhwezule*
It sadly shrieked around the whole village	*Inalira momvetsa chisoni kuzungulila mudzi onse*
It went pyeeee-pyeeee, then pyuuu-pyuuu	*Ikati pyeeee-pyeee kuzati pyuuu-pyuuu*
I was naïve I just thought it normal for birds	*Kusadziwa kanthu ndimangoti basi monga mbalame*
I did not know it was a person mobilizing for a meeting at night	*Osaziwa kuti anali munthu amamemeza msokhano wausiku*
They want to kill me, consume me	*Akafuna andiphe, anditafune*
I should stop rebuking them	*Ndisamawanyanse eee*
I will not stop rebuking you even if it disgusts you	*Sindisiyabe kukuzuzulani olo zizikunyasa*
When you listen, how do you feel?	*Ukamamva nanga umamva bwaa?*
Like you are dreaming	*Ngati ukulota*
If you cannot stand it, then just turn into an ant [disappear]!	*Ngati ndakuwonjeza ungosanduka ukhale nyerere!*

What offense have I committed that you come at night to threaten me?	*Nanga ndakuchimwanji kubwera usiku kumazandiwopseza?*
Has your business failed because of me?	*Kodi bisinesi yako yayimachifukwa cha ine?*
When you produce another witchcraft song, you will make me disappear!	*Ukangoyimbanso nyimbo yaufiti uzandisowetsa!*
Uncle, you are fooling yourself, you are not God; [God] is Jesus	*Mbuyanga mutonama, siinu Mulungu; Ndi mbuye Yesu*
When you stop witchcraft, I will also stop [rebuking you]	*Mukazasiya zokhwimakhwimazi nane ndizakusiyani*
If not, I will get a guitar and perform in front of you	*Apo bii ndizatenga gitala ndizayimbe mmaso mwanu*
What offense have I committed to deserve this?	*Ndalakwachiyani ineyo mfumu kuti muzinditero?*
I do not sleep in your house [such that I should be afraid] that you will beat me	*Sindimagona m'nyumba mwanu kuti muzandimenya*
Eye to eye	*Diso kulipa diso*
When you will stop, I will stop [rebuking you in songs]	*Mukazaleka nane ndizakulekani*

The video ended and Florinda looked at me with an "I told you so" sort of glimmer to her eye. I was without words. Having caught the gist of the song, but not the full meaning of the lyrics, and having not expected to actually see a DVD recording of a witch, I fumbled for a meaningful question. "But, how did they find witches to film?" I eventually asked. "How can we know!?" both women shouted simultaneously and then slapped their thighs and erupted into laughter.

From Florinda's neighbor's house I went next door to visit an elder woman named Joana. "Odi," I said at the side gate to announce my presence, and hearing a quick "eeh" from inside to welcome me, I walked through. I found Joana seated on her veranda, cutting up a dead duck. I told her about the video I had just watched. "They are not real witches," she reassured me. "It is just an example." That being the extent of what she seemed to have to say about the matter, I nodded toward the duck—meat was unusual in her homestead's diet. What was the special occasion? "The duck was just sick," Joana explained. She could tell, because it had not been taking care of its eggs. "So," she explained, "I decided to kill it." If the duck had died on its own, I had learned, it would be discarded rather than consumed, because in its stiffness it would look like a human cadaver. It is the connection between dead ducks, and other tabooed animal flesh, and cannibalism to which I now turn.

Anthropomorphic Anthropophagy

It is unusual to find a person, or a population, willing to eat everything that is physically edible. While there may exist loose food restrictions or individual repugnance and preference, strict limitations that *forbid* particular forms of consumption for a population or a subset of a population, with consequences for transgressors (whether social, spiritual, legal, or physical), are collectively known as "food taboos." Considering that most items tabooed in one society are permitted fare for many others, the question naturally arises as to why specific foods are implicated when they are, where they are, and by whom. Anthropologists offer a broad range of explanations. Structuralist analyses, for example, interpret food taboos as a product of cultural ideology, which organizes the world by assigning value to its physical components and forbids that which stands out as anomalous (Douglas 1980 [1966]). Materialist explanations privilege the practical results of taboos, such as environmental conservation or the avoidance of eating animals that are utilized for economic pursuits (Harris 1977). Others posit that belief systems and rituals simply offer powerful magico-religious motives for prohibiting certain fare (Simoons 1994). Each explanation in partnership with the others helps suggest an origin and explanation of food taboos that are deeply rooted in culture.

In Metangula, the desire to distance oneself from witchcraft and the association of witchcraft with the consumption of human flesh coalesced in a set of dietary taboos prohibiting not just cannibalism proper (humans eating other humans), but also the consumption of any animal that resembled a human—a sort of anthropomorphic anthropophagy, whereby eating any human-like animal was treated as a form of cannibalism. This was true not only for animals resembling humans physically, like primates or poultry that died without slaughter, but also animals like snakes, dogs, cats, lions, leopards, crocodiles, and hippopotami that resembled humans in less obvious ways. This listing is not exhaustive; there were other forms of tabooed and restricted flesh in Metangula. But this listing does encompass those animals most commonly mentioned when I inquired as to which animals were inedible, or *osati nyama* (not meat). And while I heard different reasons for banning the consumption of each of the animals I have listed above, the explanations all coalesced around one thing—the resemblance of the animals to persons—and thus consumption of these animals as something akin to cannibalism. Eating these animals or even pronouncing an interest in eating them was cause for suspicion that an individual lacked humanity.

Before I present the details of these flesh taboos, it is necessary to point out that, as with witches, acquaintances in Metangula positioned other animals as a sort of variant, rather than an opposite, of humanity—a "distorted mirror" but "a mirror nonetheless," as phrased by anthropologist Allen F. Roberts in his description of human-animal relations in Africa, broadly (1995, 16). Many readers are likely to be more comfortable conceiving of humans as separate from other animals (hereafter simply referenced, for clarity, as "animals") and identifying distinctions, rather than similarities, between ourselves and them. This tendency has roots in the seventeenth-century Enlightenment philosophy often discussed in association with René Descartes, who saw animals as something like unconscious automatons, ruled by passions and instincts rather than thought or reason, a position still popular across much of the global north (cf. Ingold 1994). But many African societies, as with those from other places around the world (Willis 1990), posit a continuum, rather than a separation, between ourselves and other species, meaning less interest in identifying distinctions between humans and animals and more attention to their similarities. Ethnographer and naturalist Brian Morris has written extensively about Maravi attitudes toward the interdependence of humans and animals and perceptions of their similarities in sociality, consciousness, and subjective agency (Morris 2000). While the ontological distinction is clear (animals are in no way seen *as* humans), the dividing line for Maravi populations, he argues, is not always sharp. Where humans are notably privileged, however, is in their divine favor in comparison to all other forms of life. Humans are placed in the heart of the cosmos, with other living beings having primary purpose in aiding our own species (Morris 1998). This is why, for the Maravi and many other sub-Saharan African populations (Altuna 2006, 63, 253–54), it is only humans who have spirits, ancestral oversight, and the potentiality for an afterlife. Humanity, it is worth noting, is also held up as unique in its mutuality. As a Chichewa proverb makes clear, "the one who is alone is an animal, two are human beings" (*kalikokha nkanyama ali awiri ndi anthu*; Kayange 2019, 19).

With this background, we can return to the subject of meat taboos based in uncomfortable semblance between animals and humans and better understand them as something akin to cannibalism. To begin perhaps with the most obvious of the resemblances, let us consider the two primate species in Metangula—baboon (*nkhwele*) and vervet monkey (*pusi*). When I asked acquaintances if they would eat either of these, their answer was always no. Many added the caveat that there were neighboring ethnic groups whose members did eat baboons and monkeys and that they had heard from such individuals that both animals were quite tasty to consume. When I pressed for additional insight into why the Nyanja, then, did not eat primates, I was most often told that it was because these species looked too similar to humans. As one woman explained, "The monkey's hand and the human hand are almost the same." Some even suggested the common origin of monkeys and humans as creating a familial bond. Unlike evolutionary theory, however, it was monkeys that descended from humans—their altered form a punishment from God for some unnamed transgression.

Being human, however, was about more than physical form, and so with being human-like. As put forth in chapter 2 regarding mutuality, generative labor, and compassion, being human was about comportment. Likewise, many with whom I spoke on the subject of primates also justified their aversion with mention of the species' behaviors that resembled a human's—for example a baboon checking to see if sweet potatoes were mature enough for harvest before pulling them from the ground or even forcing sexual relations on human women farming in their fields, both actions that a human might also perform. Filomena told me about an infant baboon she once found and raised as if it were a child. The animal responded to its name, drank from a cup, and sat with humans while they chatted, "just like a person," Filomena insisted. Each of these details contributed to an inventory of traits, in form and in conduct, that explained local aversion to eating primates as a matter of the species' uncomfortable similitude with both the human form and humanity.

The only other situation in which I recorded individuals avoiding the consumption of meat due to its physical resemblance with humans was where poultry had died naturally, rather than through slaughter. Such aversion is why Joana killed her sick duck, as noted above, so that the meat would still be edible. When I sought an explanation for this avoidance, some acquaintances cited Islamic proscription that declares it forbidden to eat any animal not ritually slaughtered with a swift, deep slit to the neck. Of note, though, it was only aversion to the consumption of poultry that had died without slaughter, not other locally raised livestock (such as cows or goats), that people spoke of in this way. And it is the flesh of poultry alone, among locally raised livestock, with the potential to resemble a dead humans' in color and consistency. Most acquaintances with whom I raised the question of unslaughtered animal meat brought up the fact that a bird dead from natural causes looked like a human cadaver and that such semblance made the meat unappetizing. Establishing oneself as comfortable consuming meat resembling a dead human body could be socially dangerous, in the same way that drinking at Sancho's bar, seeking love medicines from Jose, failing to make a show of being emotionally distraught at the funeral of an associate, or being a stranger passed out near a winnowing basket might implicate dealings with the occult.

Still, some people in Metangula did eat poultry that had died from natural causes. But they did it in private. When I noticed my own host family eating chicken three times in one month and without being offered any myself, for example, I asked Judite for an explanation. She replied with some embarrassment at my perception of exclusion; she had tried to keep it a secret that they were eating the chickens. She had not wanted to offend me by openly serving chicken that had died of Newcastle disease. The chicken, she said, looked like a dead human body. Serving it less clandestinely, I surmised, would place me in a socially awkward position and perhaps lead me to question the nefarious intentions of my hosts (were the rumors about indoctrinating others into the occult correct, and Judite was serving human flesh in an attempt to make family members, or even me, into a witch!?). Metangula was, at the time this incident took place, going through a seasonal bout of Newcastle disease, in which a large number of chickens always lost their lives, despite government efforts at inoculation and the isolation of infirm birds. With the devastating loss to their livestock, families like my hosts seemed willing to bend the rules, if quietly. Several acquaintances, like Joana, alternatively watched their sick birds closely and slaughtered them when their end seemed near to ensure that they would still be (culturally, and for some perhaps physiologically) edible.

Other tabooed species resembled humans not in form, but in sentiment. For example, recall that Florinda explained that people in Metangula do not eat the meat of snakes because of their empathy and solidarity with humans (snakes at times choosing not to attack us). Other acquaintances would add that humans have a reciprocal relation with domesticated dogs and cats. For example, a cat kills rats, and a dog offers protection in exchange for human care. Killing, let alone eating, such "friends" (as some called dogs and cats when discussing food taboos) was not the same as killing and consuming a human, but it was still improper behavior due to their incorporation into our social lives. More closely resembling cannibalism proper was eating animals with a penchant for consuming human flesh themselves—lions, leopards, crocodiles, and snakes, for example. During my time in Metangula, reports would sporadically reach town of persons gone missing near a river—a woman bathing, a child playing or washing dishes, and so forth. Accompanying the news was almost always the explanation of crocodiles, which were known to live in the mouths of the tributary rivers that feed into Lake Niassa. People likewise feared attacks by lions and leopards, and they encountered with uncomfortable frequency the black mamba, one of the world's deadliest snakes. To eat one of these species or others known to occasionally make a meal of humans was like eating the flesh of these animals' human victims too.

Still other animals (and, by some accounts, lightning) could contain within them a human spirit. Jose, the love doctor and rumored witch, suggested that in the past, a family head or a chief might use a special *dawa* to transform into a lion after death. In this new form they could help protect their family or community from enemies or deliver to them meat in the form of hunted game animals. But beginning around the time of "the war" (which was a vague term that meant somewhere between 1964 and 1992, inclusive of the war for independence from Portugal and the "civil war" that followed), sorcerers began transforming themselves into lions and other animals for illicit purposes, like attacking their enemies or otherwise causing harm.[2] "*Chira chinthu chili ndi nyengo yake*," Jose offered when I inquired about this sudden change. "Everything has its time." The time of persons raising lions had ended, and now it was only witches who engaged in human-lion transformation.

When I first visited Metangula in 2005, the town was in the midst of a human-lion scare, seemingly brought about by a development scheme through which a parcel of land was being cordoned off as forest reserves to surround luxury vacation homes being marketed to wealthy white South Africans. This meant sudden and difficult-to-explain limitations on farming activities, the gathering of plants used for traditional medicines, and simply walking familiar thoroughfares. Guards were stationed along well-trodden paths through the parcel of land to thwart foot traffic (ostensibly to preserve the miombo woodlands, but more likely to improve its curb appeal by making it devoid of human presence). But the plan backfired when rumors spread of human-lions attacking people who avoided the guards by passing through the bush. Someone set the parcel of land afire, making it easier to traverse the land while avoiding the paths. The developers, aghast, responded by hiring additional guards to station throughout the land, in the hope of preventing more fires. But the more guards that were hired, the higher the anxieties about human-lions seemed to rise, as did rumors of the guards as caught up in witchcraft, for why else would they be willing to protect the human-lions? The incident escalated to a point where Chief Chilombe made an announcement on the radio that those who were responsible for the human-lions had better get rid of them, as they would soon be found out and face consequences. Whether in response to the chief's warnings or the development scheme pulling out from the region soon thereafter, the issue quickly dissipated as land usage and foliage returned to normal.

That the animals that humans could become through transmogrification were tabooed fare is made particularly clear through the example of hippos. In the past, hippopotamus meat was not considered edible. This was at a time when individuals suffering from leprosy were rumored to transform into hippos at death—a connection likely spurned by the resemblance between a hippo's foot and the digit-less feet and hands of an individual with advanced leprosy. But while leprosy was widespread in the colonial era (Zamparoni 2017), it had been all but eradicated at the time of research. In a change from the past, people reported to me that while they were aware of the previously negative connotation of eating hippopotamus, it was now acceptable fare. I never witnessed anyone consuming hippo with my own eyes, so I cannot confirm that people actually did this. However, on the day that a dead, bloated hippo floated into one of Metangula's bays, I did see over one hundred people line the lakeshore with tools to butcher the animal in the hope of securing a portion to bring home. These individuals were not desperate for nourishment; they were just excited to capitalize on their neighborhood's windfall. At the end of the day, nobody did eat the hippopotamus. Government authorities declared that the animal was hazardous to consume, and to the dismay of the crowd that had gathered, the municipality tractor removed the carcass to be burned at a trash heap atop a nearby hill. That people were keen to receive a share and that they mused among themselves that the "possible contagion" excuse to destroy the carcass was a ruse to enable government higher-ups to split the meat among themselves because it was so delectable, however, suggests that taboo on consuming hippopotamus was indeed passé.

Figure 3.3. A dead, bloated hippo washes ashore. Photo by the author.

Beyond providing support for the idea that taboos on meat can be related to animal-human similitude, this anecdote also forcefully demonstrates that food taboos are neither timeless nor immutable. People *do* things with food prohibitions; they do not just follow them as a matter of habitus, tradition, or routine. In Metangula, anthropomorphic anthropophagy as tied up with human semblance suggests that the project of being and becoming human not only *manifested* in food taboos, but was intimately enacted and embodied through them. By resembling a witch in behaviors that suggested familiarity and comfort with eating meat that looked like a human, physically or socially, or that had the potential to contain a human spirit, an individual thus risked compromising their own humanity.

Eating Like a Human

The distinction between humanity and animals was likewise visible in the alimentary realm. Whenever I asked people in Metangula about the differences between humans and animals, in fact, respondents almost always answered in the form of a question related to food and that stressed humans' mutuality, industriousness, intelligence, or compassion: Do animals farm? Do animals cook? Do animals eat *ntchima*? Do animals have houses (where they share their meals)? The answer to each of these inquiries was intended to be no. Animals wake up and forage; they do not farm or otherwise plan to ensure food supplies and meals. They do not cook or prepare their food at home, but eat what they find on the spot as they find it, on the go and raw. And they most certainly do not eat *ntchima*. In these ways animals, like witches, lacked in attitudes and behaviors definitive of humanity. While examples of these things can, in fact, be found in the animal kingdom (e.g., a lion stalks its prey, sometimes for days; chimpanzees wait to eat certain nuts until fires have roasted them, and they distribute meat among kin and allies), the point of interest is that people in Metangula used these characteristics to distinguish themselves from the animal world, marking foraging, raw foods, and alimentary miserliness as unhuman, and by contrast foresight, formal meals, cooking, and the sharing of food as definitive of and thus proper for humanity. We might then expect some emphasis on these behaviors in local foodways as an arena for the establishment, monitoring, and regulation of humanity. Indeed, evidence is suggestive of these ends.

Take, for example, the issue of foraging. When preparing a dietary survey along with the two research assistants who would carry out the work and a short-lived project manager, we sat down together to brainstorm every possible edible food that our survey participants might tell us they had consumed the previous day (so that we could code responses, to increase accuracy). The team listed 214 distinct foods (we would later add 29 more), sharing tips with each other on how to prepare the more unusual items and debating the foods' *vitamina*. Of these, they categorized seven leafy greens as *ya tchire*—from the bush, or wild foods. Each of these seven greens had the potential to serve as a side dish. But in nearly twenty-two hundred homestead visits over the course of thirteen months, my research assistants recorded only twenty-two instances where household members consumed these bush foods (twenty-one *chimbongwe*, one *kaminga*)—that is, 0.01 percent of meals. Meanwhile, these same households consumed cultivated greens quite frequently, including rape and mustard leaves, chard, cabbage, and the edible foliage of cultigens like cassava and pumpkin. These plants collectively made up 21 percent of afternoon and evening side dishes recorded in the survey. I am not so naïve as to think that these data are a perfect representation of everything survey participants consumed—recall is imperfect, and demographers and survey participants manipulate data for a variety of reasons, including to improve the accuracy of results (Biruk 2018). But the fact that very few people were eating wild greens, or admitting to eating wild greens, when these foods were readily abundant and when many could use the caloric and nutritional contributions to their diets (and relief for their budgets) is significant. This situation left me asking what it was about gathering wild foods that was so offensive.

The root of disparage for wild foods was arguably not inherent inferiority in nutrition or flavor. Several acquaintances suggested that the leaves contained vitamins (though seemingly not *vitamina*), and some even let on that the leaves, intrinsically, tasted good when cooked properly with salt, tomato, oil, and onion or with baking soda. Thus, very much like they did regarding human flesh, people seemingly disparaged wild leaves for reasons that stood apart from gustation. In addition to being avoided due to their association with hardship (as discussed in chapter 1), the denigration of wild greens also seems to have to do with their accessibility through something other than hard work. Kathryn de Luna's (2016) linguistic and archaeological analysis of the history of food procurement in central Africa traces the emergence of the concept of "the bush" as a place for the carefully planned and ritually managed execution of expertise. The collection of wild foods in circumstances of desperation certainly does not meet such criteria. A person could take wild greens without skill, without cultivation, without effort, without—in a word—forethought. This indicated paucity in *njeru*, discussed in chapter 2 as the mental capacity and the moral impetus to nourish life, and a unique trait of humanity.

Similar preference for generative, moral, and forward thinking may have also been a part of local preference for making *ntchima* with refined maize flour (*ufa woyera*, literally "white flour") rather than un-soaked, refined maize flour (*celeste*) or unrefined maize flour (*ngaiwa*). Producing *ufa woyera* flour required multiple days, and therefore planning, to ensure the time with which to properly carry out its many steps: de-husking, shelling, milling to remove the bran pericarp (a process called *kukonyola*), soaking again, drying again, milling again, this time to grind the kernels into flour (a process called *kuthebula*), and drying for a final time. *Celeste* and *ngaiwa* maize flours, on the other hand, could be made in less than fifteen minutes if there was maize in the market, you had money in your pocket, and the line at the mill was short. *Celeste* was prepared by milling maize kernels first to remove the bran pericarp and then a second time immediately afterward to grind the kernels into flour. Finished. *Celeste* was thus a common grind when receiving unexpected guests, for whom flour had to be obtained quickly. The flour was also useful in other time crunches. In September of 2010, for example, my dietary survey recorded a spike in *celeste* consumption when a rumor spread on a Monday that electricity would be unavailable for a month beginning two days later. Lines at the mills swelled, with women eager to stock up on flour before the fated event (which never did occur). The whole-grain *ngaiwa* flour was made by skipping pericarp removal and going straight to grinding. The resultant less refined product was least popular of all, used to make *ntchima* at a ratio of 1:14 in comparison to *ufa woyera*. This was despite the fact that *ngaiwa* produced more flour than *ufa woyera* (and *celeste*) with the same amount of maize, and people often recognized the nutritional vitamin-based (though seemingly not *vitamina*-based) benefit of retaining the bran.[3]

In trying to better understand this hierarchy in flour preferences, I recorded a number of explanations. Some suggested, for example, that *ntchima* cooked with *ngaiwa* caused diarrhea and flatulence. Others told me that *ngaiwa* paired well with only a few side dishes (while *ufa woyera* could be eaten with anything). Critically, people reported that *ngaiwa* did not pair well with beans, the *ndiwo* side dish for 28 percent of *ntchima* meals recorded in my dietary survey. Grinding maize into *ngaiwa* thus made it less versatile, and so limited dietary variety (which could deplete *vitamina*, discussed in chapter 1). Some with whom I brought up the rejection of *ngaiwa* also mentioned its darker hue (a result of retaining the bran), making the flour visually unappetizing (in chapter 1, I also discussed the importance of visual appearance and appetite for *vitamina*).[4] While each of these factors may have played a role in underscoring the predominant preference for *ufa woyera*, it is notable that preparation of the refined flour also required the intelligence, foresight, and generative labor discussed in chapter 2 as integral to *njeru* and (so) humanity.

Regardless of the flour base, life without *ntchima* was virtually unimaginable in Metangula. A popular topic for the casual conversations in which I engaged was the fact that in my own country people did not eat *ntchima*. "What do you eat, then?" people would ask, utterly and completely perplexed. I would list common carbohydrate alternatives: rice, potatoes, bread, noodles, and so forth. During one such conversation a woman responded that she ate like this while in

Figure 3.4. A woman stirs the pot of *ntchima* she just removed from the cooking fire. Photo by the author.

South Africa on a church training excursion. "It was terrible," she said. "I was never satisfied." Foods like rice, potatoes, bread, and noodles are nice for festive occasions, people told me, but they do not leave a person feeling the same satisfaction of *ntchima*. "You must take flour home with you and teach the people of your country how to make *ntchima*," acquaintances implored more than once. When I responded that we do have flour in the United States and that I had made *ntchima* before for friends and family, who rejected it as inedible, my acquaintances were in shock (though not disbelief, as they knew my *ntchima* to be full of lumps and watery). While there was no living memory of famine in Metangula, people did remember devastating periods where flour was unavailable to make *ntchima*. When asked about these times of hunger (*njala*), many recalled the year 2002 when the rains came late, the harvest was delayed, and there was no maize available in the market (except for that sold at exorbitant prices by the unscrupulous Marco, mentioned in chapter 2). That same year a plague also decimated the cassava crop. Many recounted that in 2002 *ntchima* had been called "Bin Laden" because like the Al-Qaeda leader around this same time, it was very badly wanted but difficult to find.

For some semblance of normalcy, people in Metangula had made flour in 2002 from dried, pounded, unripe bananas, a base for *ntchima* also recorded in the region over a century ago (Johnston 1897, 436). They also cooked unripe banana and the wild-growing *mpama* root as *ntchima* substitutes. But none of these were preferred foods, and this made them unsatisfying. "People were thin and always hungry," one woman described. "Even though we were eating plenty of food, we were missing *ntchima*." I will have more to say on the disconnect between the amount of food consumed and a person's body size in chapter 5. For now, I want to highlight that despite the inconveniences of 2002, people were at least eating *something* that was cooked. Such was another of the distinctions pointed out to me when I asked the difference between humans and animals: humans used fire to prepare their foods, rather than consuming them raw. This important difference between cooked and uncooked foods was linguistically marked. The verb used to describe consumption of raw foods was *kutafuna* (to chew), as an animal does. *Kutafuna* was also used when a person was snacking on any food (often done alone, rather than as a social act). When describing the eating of cooked meals, though, my acquaintances used the verb *kudya* (to eat) instead. The *kutafuna* verb was also used in situations where foods were eaten on the go, and many times I overheard children being scolded that to eat while moving, as if grazing, was to behave like an animal. Eating while seated was proper human behavior and seemingly just as important a part of etiquette as washing hands before a meal. As often as I saw children's hands dunked into a basin of water and rubbed together to cleanse them before they were allowed to begin eating, I saw the same children pulled down to the ground and spoken to harshly by adults when they attempted to eat while standing.

The same goes for the sharing of foodstuffs. In Metangula, animals were posited as finding something to eat and then consuming it on the spot, rather than taking it to share with others. Should another animal come across them in their feasting a fight would likely ensue, with the more physically powerful or socially dominant animal winning the morsel. Within and across species, acquaintances

Figure 3.5. A child is handed a bread roll, and others immediately outstretch their hands for a portion. Photo by the author.

emphasized, animals never shared. And an animal would never take food to another animal unable to provision itself, such that even one's own offspring would be required (after weaning in the case of mammals) to sustain themselves independently. This indicated that animals lacked the compassion and mutuality of *lisungu*. Human persons, on the other hand, placed special emphasis on both provisioning and considering the welfare of others (see chapter 2). It was thus particularly important that a person neither hoard in a manner that would cause others to suffer, nor consume food in a way that could be considered selfish. It was, instead, proper behavior for human persons to invite (*karibu*, from Swahili) anyone present or passing to join when a meal was in progress. To do otherwise meant that a person was selfish (*chipili*) and animal-like. To always accept invitations to join meals in progress or to request inclusion where not explicitly asked to join would build a person a bad reputation as greedy and deceitful (*wotunduka*). But an invitee or hungry passerby was expected to join in the consumption of foodstuffs if they were hungry, even where there was no previous relationship with the host. Eating food on the go was thus inherently problematic, because spectators might feel the emotional torment of anomie and physical pain of hunger. Disregarding such a predicament for the sake of selfish consumption compromised humanity.

Conclusion

We can now return to the opening vignette of this chapter and to Pedro's jarring question—Are the Chinese human?—with a bit more contextual understanding. When I took Pedro's question to various acquaintances in Metangula, their answers varied. Some interpreted the inquiry seemingly in reference to biological species and concluded, like Pedro's wife Judite, that the Chinese of course were human, their behaviors just those of a "different type of people." Others, apparently more concerned with the question of personhood, like Pedro, denied that the Chinese could possibly be human—not only were their traditions strange, but the principles that underlaid them lacked basic human characteristics. How could the Chinese be human, in other words, if they were antisocial, selfish, and uncompassionate? Where evaluated only in form, their humanity could not be denied. But when considering the men's malicious and insular constitution, their status as human persons was debatable. People did not, of course, restrict their concerns over personhood to the Chinese men in Michumwa. They were also concerned with the humanity of neighbors, friends, and themselves. To exhibit behaviors that indicated an absence of basic human traits could result in wariness extended in the form of gossip (as in the case of Jose), lost business patronage (as in the case of Sancho), ostracism (as with Monica's aunt), or even physical harm (as with the drunk AMETRAMO-certified *sing'anga*).

The images of witches and the words of warning in Makawa's *Umakwiya Chani* music video are useful for understanding the positioning of witches along the shadowy fringes of humanity. People did not posit witches to be an *opposite* of humanity so much as they were the offensive embrace of deeply seated human tendencies to value individualism, greed, and other forms of insulation at the expense of growth and moving forward together through the transformative power of mutuality and togetherness. Witches valued relationships, yes, but only for the resources they enabled, rather than for the people they involved, and they lacked compassion for the suffering of others. This made them, ultimately, insular in orientation and callous in their constitution. Witches in these ways exemplified very familiar antisocial sentiments, such as envy, jealousy, spite, indignation, contempt, and selfishness. Witches lacked the capacity to overcome these natural predispositions because they were short on the intelligence for planning, the selfless motivation for hard work, the compassion for the suffering of others, and the drive to otherwise live according to a principle of participation.

A witch's moral orientation, like the consumption of human flesh, was posited to be personally *gratifying*. At the same time, however, it was destructive and therefore grotesque. These distinctions played out in the realm of alimentation, where particular ways of eating exemplified humanity, and others did not—including eating human-like animals. In this way people in Metangula conceived of anthropomorphous anthropophagy in a manner similar to that articulated by anthropologist Francis B. Nyamnjoh (2018), who used cannibalism to characterize the human condition—everyone everywhere always drawing on others for sustenance and at the same time constantly in danger of being "eaten" themselves. Such decoupling of cannibalism from the consumption of human flesh has immense potential to engage questions about what constitutes humanity (Englund 2018). In the case of Metangula, by including the avoidance of human-like flesh in cannibalism taboos, the question of what it is to be human was, in effect, answered with what is human. The body of *Homo sapiens* was not enough to assert or deny humanness, for both consumer and consumed.

Sympathetic food taboos are common and diverse (Bloch and Parry 1982; Sahlins 1976; Simoons 1994). Marshall Sahlins (1976) provides a particularly relevant analysis on the valuation of cuts of meat in the United States as inversely related to the integration of the source animal into American society. In combination with a preference for flesh over organs (the former representing the body and the latter the inner "self"), Sahlins concluded that there are aspects of American meat consumption that are driven by an implicit prohibition on cannibalism. In the United States, however, eating meats that remind people of themselves raises eyebrows as an oddity—it is not an outright taboo, and it does not compromise one's humanity. What I have proposed in this chapter is that the avoidance of cannibalism and a pseudo- or anthropomorphic cannibalism in Metangula were not just symbolic statements, gustatory preferences, or an assertion of benevolence to counter European misconceptions of primitivism. Following Alfred Gell (1979), these taboos did more than *express* the self—they also *constituted* the self; they were actual, practical ways in which individuals socially *became* human by showing disinterest in behaviors and orientations associated with the occult.

Other aspects of foodways described in this chapter centered on distinguishing humanity as something that separates us (if tenuously) from animals. Humans used foresight to plan meals and ration ingredients, while animals ate what they found on the spot. Humans cooked, whereas animals ate raw foods. Humans ate sitting down, and animals on the go. The ultimate distinction, however, was that humans shared their food with and provisioned others. Animals, by comparison, were nearly always greedy, selfish, and uncompassionate. Eating as if an animal indicated a failure in generative labor, compassion, and planning—traits through which humans distinguished themselves, as outlined in chapter 2. While acting as if an animal would not have the same set of dramatic repercussions as being suspected or accused of witchcraft, it did indicate a similar constitution, and thus concern. To err in proper alimentary behaviors was thus to potentially compromise one's humanity and face heightened suspicion of alterity. Again, by "alterity" I do not mean "opposite" so much as I do a sort of distorted mirror image—a reflection of the self, but reversed. Behaving as if a witch or an animal was, in this way, acting very much within the range of natural human behavior, though in ways that negated humanity. In the next chapter we will consider the role of taboos also in binding people together, living and dead, in a spirit of belonging and unity through both obligation and choice.

Notes

Transcription and translation of Moses Makawa's *Umakwiya Chani* was carried out by Experencia Madalitso Jalasi. Permission to print the lyrics to *Umawkiya Chani* for this publication was generously granted by Moses Makawa.

1. Small concentrations of Chinese nationals have lived in Mozambique since the colonial era, if not before (Zamparoni 2000), and Sino-Mozambican relations intensified well before the twenty-first century (Jansson and Kiala 2009). Still, in the early 2000s, Mozambique's Chinese population was not only significantly larger than it had ever been before, but it was penetrating into areas well beyond city centers. An outpouring of humanitarian aid meant that Chinese money and contractors were scattered across the countryside, and Mozambican students were travelling on scholarship to mainland China (Njal 2012). While it would be inappropriate to conclude that the working conditions for Africans in the employment of Chinese individuals and organizations are everywhere the same, scholars have noted conditions elsewhere in Mozambique very similar to those described for Michumwa (Nielsen 2012).
2. For further commentary on the wars in relation to human-lion transmogrification in northern Mozambique, see the work of Harry West (2005). A similar point of shape-shifting in relation to political upheaval and as a strategy of self-control during crisis is argued

by Michael Jackson (1990) based on data from Sierra Leone. Elizabeth Isichei (2002) also maps the emergence of rumored lion- and leopard-men in Africa in relation to violence and dislocation wrought by the slave trade and colonialism.
3. It is of note that the distinctions between these flour types can easily be lost on a foreign observer and the taste difference between the resultant *ntchima*s unperceived. People native to the region, however, recognized each flour for its unique taste, texture, and ideal pairings with various side dishes (*ndiwo*).
4. Negative perception of darker flours has been recorded elsewhere in the region (Chimwaza 1982, 70; Platt 1939, 198), and scholars, as well as development practitioners, have observed the rejection of vitamin-fortified, hued grains across the subcontinent (De Groote and Kimenju 2008; Muzhingi et al. 2008).

CHAPTER 4

Salt, Sex, and Fire

"Eh eh eh eh . . . Mayo ine, mayo ine . . ."[1] *The sobbing was audible as I approached Monica's house from the side gate. It was coming from an area of the yard fenced off as a shower and toilet. I stepped inside and sat quietly on the edge of the veranda of the main house, sensing that something was wrong but not knowing just what. A few moments later, Monica emerged from behind the grass-thatched bathroom walls with Diana at her side. Each of Diana's steps was slow and unsteady. Her left arm was draped over Monica's right shoulder and the rest of her body hunched forward, her right arm being pulled upward by Monica's left. The embrace distributed Diana's body weight between the two women. Monica looked up and met my gaze with a pained expression. We seemed to exchange silent words, me asking if I should leave, and her responding that it was only appropriate that I stay. I slid back to settle in, taking the bag from my shoulder and removing my sandals.*

Monica carefully guided Diana to the house opposite where I sat and into the room usually reserved for Agostinho, the minibus driver who utilized Monica's house as a hostel (others might argue as a brothel) when spending the night in Metangula. It would be inappropriate for Diana to sleep where she usually did, in the room next door, for that was where her baby boy had died only an hour earlier, the day after having been birthed at the health center. He laid there now, his tiny body cared for by Diana's mother, Filomena. The bedsheet strung across the doorway billowed back and forth, and I caught glimpses of Filomena grasping the baby's thin, stiff legs with one hand, lifting them slightly to wash his body with a damp cloth in the other hand. Filomena slowly lowered the boy's legs, then paused. She took hold of his legs again, lifted them, and then loosened her grasp to let the limbs fall to the floor with their own force. She repeated this several times, seemingly trying to will his body back to life with the jolt.

Diana let out another somber wail. Filomena moaned along with her from the adjacent room. When there was someone else to care for the boy's body, Filomena would enter into the room with Diana and comfort her by lying behind and embracing her. Meanwhile, neighbors ducked into the yard, and the internal veranda of Monica's house soon filled with women expressing their condolences. Men lined the external veranda outside of the fence. Monica emerged to greet both sets of guests in turn and to begin arrangements for the funeral, which would take place the next day. Early in the morning the women would gather again in the yard to comfort Diana, and the men outside to take the baby's body, wrapped in a white cloth, to bury.

For Diana, loss of the baby was devastating. Her first child, and a male child at that, was gone. The delivery had been another ordeal—over forty-eight hours of excruciating pain without even mild analgesics. The child was gone not a full twenty-four hours after his birth—a short life to be added to the statistical annals of infant mortality in the developing world. At the time, estimates suggest that seventy-eight infants under one year of age died per one thousand live births in Mozambique. By comparison, the number was seven deaths per one thousand live births in the United States, and just two in Iceland, the nation with the lowest infant mortality. Such numbers are used by the United Nations, among other international agencies and government bodies, as one indicator of a country's health. While Mozambique's infant mortality rate had been decreasing, in 2010 the country still ranked 154th out of 157 nations worldwide (United Nations Population Division n.d.).

From the moment of Diana's baby's birth, it had been clear that the child would not be alive for very long. While all babies were helpless—weak, or "cold," "watery," and "without salt" in local parlance—this one was especially so. His breath was short, and he had refused to breastfeed. Some would later come to blame the boy's constitution and fate on Diana's "husband" (serial sexual partner) Erasto, the father of the baby, who had "been too busy walking around" during the pregnancy. This phrasing could indicate that he was having sexual relations with another woman while Diana was pregnant, which can sour a pregnancy through an illness called *sanjiko*. But the symptomology did not quite add up. "Walking around" could also indicate that Erasto was not having sexual relations with Diana—a situation perceived to be dire, for repeated sexual relations during pregnancy were necessary for a healthy fetus (see chapter 5). Monica was quite vocal in her opinion that sexual relations had nothing to do with it. Though attributing the idea to others, in the weeks that followed the baby's death Monica frequently and freely suggested that fault for loss of Diana's baby rested squarely with her mother, Filomena, who had no shame in making public her disapproval of the informal marriage between her daughter and Erasto. Monica coyly offered that perhaps this was because Filomena was jealous that Diana preferred Monica's home over her own mother's. Whatever the case, Filomena's rebuking her daughter, Monica proffered, was to blame for the baby's death.

Regardless of how she lost the baby, Diana became ill because of the death with a symptomless affliction locally known as *nthaka*.[2] I first heard about *nthaka* several weeks after the baby's funeral. I entered Monica's compound that day near lunchtime. At such meals everyone in Monica's homestead usually ate together—women and children all taking from a common dish of *ntchima* and several plates of *ndiwo*. The exception was if Agostinho and his motley crew of hangers-on were there, or Monica's eldest son. On such occasion, a separate set of dishes for the man or men would be prepared. But this day there were no men, and it was Diana who ate a plate of boiled potatoes separately from the other women. When I asked why, Monica answered, "*Nthaka*." Her curt response suggested to me that either the answer to my question should have been obvious or my inquiry had been inappropriate—perhaps a combination of both. We went about the meal. Later, when it was just the two of us, Monica would explicate *nthaka* as imparting several restrictions on a woman when she lost a young child through death, miscarriage, or abortion. *Nthaka* required, for example, that a woman not place pots onto the cooking fire and that she not pour salt into the cooking pot. Indeed, while I was in the yard I had witnessed Diana call one of Monica's young nieces to add salt to the potatoes she was cooking. *Nthaka* also explained why Diana ate separately from the other women—to prevent spread of her illness. While symptomless for Diana herself, *nthaka* would manifest in others with a debilitating and potentially fatal cough. It was best to keep Diana separated from others at mealtime, as *nthaka* could pass through sharing food.

This chapter is in part about *nthaka*, but more broadly it is about the connections between alimentation and the interdependencies that are born out through a broader complex of everyday rituals called *mgosyo*. As with the previous chapter, I will use taboo as an entry point to consider the interweaving of food, morality, and mutuality. But whereas the previous chapter approached foodways as an arena for distancing humanity from witches and animals, in this chapter I concentrate on cooking and sharing meals as practices through which individuals intertwined their life with those of others. Specifically, my interest is in everyday alimentary rituals through which individuals asserted their belonging among and enacted their obligations to both the living and the dead. It was through these acts (among others), I contend, that they nourished humanity. I begin with a broad consideration of *mgosyo* as acts through which mutuality was actively and continuously revitalized. I continue with a deeper look at the centrality of coitus for understanding the labels of "hot" and "cold" in relation to *mgosyo* and at sex as it has been theorized more broadly in association with power and morality across sub-Saharan Africa. I draw out parallels between sexual relations, fire, and salt—each with transformative potential that can be both generative and destructive—and between the manufacture and manipulation of potash and *dawa* (substances that can serve pro-social ends, like restoring or assuring wellness, or antisocial ones, like causing sickness, death, or other forms of misfortune through witchcraft) to theorize the role of salt in cooking as more than a flavor enhancer. I round out the chapter by considering the contours of living with contingency in the twenty-first century and how *mgosyo* both reflected and anticipated, but was not enough to deal alone with, such precarity and change.

Mgosyo as Everyday Ritual

Nthaka was part of a broad category of misfortune called *mgosyo* that revolved around particular behaviors related to sexual relations and salt pouring. While never explained to me by acquaintances as succinctly as I am writing about it here, *mgosyo* essentially entailed following four rules: (1) anyone who was sexually active had to maintain physical distance from a newborn child—especially a baby who was the individual's own offspring and where that individual had recently engaged in adultery; (2) individuals were to practice sexual abstinence when they were concerned about events yet to unfold and that depended for their success on the goodwill and oversight of ancestors—for example, giving birth, funerals, and boys' and girls' initiation ceremonies; (3) an individual who was sexually active (especially a menstruating woman) had to call upon someone else to pour salt into food they were cooking; and (4) a woman who had recently experienced an abortion, miscarriage, or loss of infant needed to follow specific guidelines about pouring salt, cooking, and eating alone (these requirements, as discussed above, were collectively known as *nthaka*).

Attentiveness to *mgosyo* was important because missteps caused illness for third parties, most often children who had not yet reached sexual maturity, elders beyond their reproductive years, nursing mothers and their infants, pregnant women and their unborn fetuses, the infirm, and anyone else in a transformative or precarious state. While *mgosyo*-related illnesses could cause death, they more commonly led to debilitation through symptoms like bodily swelling and a deep chest cough, which could be relieved by seeking help from a traditional healer. Men also stood the possibility of developing a ruptured appendix, hernia, or distended testicles (*ntongomwera*), particularly where they ate food into which a woman experiencing uterine discharge (for reasons including menstruation, childbirth, lochia, miscarriage, or abortion) poured salt. Infants suffered a distinct set of *mgosyo* symptoms that centered on uncontrollable crying. Without receiving treatment, the baby's fontanel could fail to harden, or a depression could grow to divide the child's head or chest in two. It is worth noting that acquaintances equated the functions of an adult's chest with that of a baby's head—babies "breathed" with their fontanel (rather than with their lungs), justified with the ascent and descent of the forehead's soft spot when a baby inhales and exhales. According to anthropologist Matthew Schoffeleers (1968, 423), Maravi medicine broadly regards the (adult) chest and genitals as the locations at which illnesses caused by moral transgressions— we could include *mgosyo* here—tend to manifest. By way of contrast, he found that illnesses inflicted directly by spirits (such as ancestors) tended to emerge in the (non-infantile) head and legs, and illnesses caused by witchcraft in the stomach. The precise mechanisms through which *mgosyo* caused illness were a mystery to my acquaintances, though implications for disintegration of mutuality implicated ancestors, who throughout Africa are generally charged with oversight of moral conduct and unity among the living.

Many residents of Metangula actively followed *mgosyo* prescriptions. This was the case in my own host homestead, for example, where the majority of cooking was done by the wife of the eldest son of the heads of household. With regular monthly cycling, the sound of a child scampering through the yard would make Albertina look up from the pot of shimmering tomatoes, stewing leaves, or other *ndiwo* side-dish ingredients that she was preparing on a three-stone hearth or the charcoal burner. "Dinis," she would call out to the child, or Alice, Solange, Catia—any prepubescent child who happened to be passing through the yard would suffice. The child who had been called would then come to her side, and Albertina would uncover a wooden bowl or untie a knot in her *capulana*, whichever held the cooking salt that day. In a manner of routine, the child would place one hand above the cooking pot, accept the salt from Albertina, and overturn his or her palm to deposit the salt into the pot. Then the child left. There were often no words exchanged in these encounters; it was simply an expected and accepted part of life that someone other than Albertina was occasionally needed to pour the salt.

Figure 4.1. Albertina prepares lunch. Photo by the author.

Others protected against *mgosyo* through preventative measures. For example, acquaintances told me that near the end of a pregnancy many women would bury special medicinal plants at the thresholds of their home or yard.³ This would protect their unborn child from the sexually active individuals they were likely to encounter when birthed at the local health center or some other medical facility. It was also reportedly normal practice to protect a child postnatally through a ritual called *kumphika mwana* (cooking the child). This rite took place the morning that followed a couple's first sexual intercourse after their baby's birth. Among my acquaintances, the steps for *kumphika mwana* were generally agreed to be as follows: After coitus and before bathing, the woman and man placed designated wild plants into a pot of water, along with salt. Both parents then placed the pot onto fire, each holding one side. The mixture was allowed to heat and then slightly cool, and then both of them fed the child several spoonsful. The rest of the liquid was to be discarded or used to bathe the child.⁴ Many individuals explained *kumphika mwana* to me as "introducing a child to the world." Jose, the ill-reputed love doctor, went into more detail, suggesting that the ritual was necessary because "a baby becomes shocked when it comes into contact with sex." This was because coitus was "not something from the spirit realm." A baby, Jose went on to explain, was without sins—*woyera* (pure) and *wofewa* (vulnerable), knowing nothing except for that which is imparted by God. Children thus had to be readied for encounters with sexually active people through *kumphika mwana*, which "hardened" them and turned them from "angels" (Jose used the Arabic word *almalayika* here) into humans. It is perhaps for a similar reason that Brian Morris describes the equivalent ritual in Malawi as essential for imparting personhood upon a child (Morris 1998, 72).

Kumphika mwana enabled a baby to come into contact with sexually active persons and, throughout their childhood, to eat foods into which sexually active individuals (with the exception of women with active uterine discharge) poured salt, all without suffering from *mgosyo*. Protecting elders was not as easy of a task—medicines existed, but were difficult to come by. It was such that families often sent a prepubescent child to live with a grandparent who was too feeble to cook, so as to guarantee food into which salt had been poured by someone who was not sexually active. Elders, however, were also apt to complain about the behavior of "children these days," and specifically their early and secretive sexual exploits. These tirades may have been motivated in part by moral conservatism, but they also marked persistence or flare-ups in physical ailments like rheumatism, arthritis, and meningitis, which they blamed on *mgosyo* caused by a granddaughter-cook's licentious behavior. There were also no medicines to protect from *nthaka*. This meant strict diligence to protect those in one's own and neighboring households for the duration of the illness. The length of time for which the restrictions were observed, however, was inconsistently reported. When I inquired about Diana, for example, Monica explained to me that *nthaka* would continue for about two months, the typical length of post-birth uterine discharge (lochia). Conversations I would come to have with others suggested a different timeline—Filomena put forward, for example, that the restrictions on her daughter's cooking and eating would continue for a full year or until Diana bore another child. The timeline for *nthaka* recovery may have, in fact, been quite personal and related to the woman's desire to resume sexual relations, her partner's patience in waiting, or conclusions about the cause of her child's death.

Lack of unanimous agreement on this point might also reflect the broader significance of *mgosyo* as centered less in following specific rules than demonstrating respect for the moral principles behind those rules. Take, for instance, anecdotes provided by Fatima and Mustafa. Fatima, a middle-aged woman whom we will encounter again shortly in her preparation of *dawa* for her sister, confided in me that she had once contravened *mgosyo*. The story she told explained that she had fallen on hard times, and she was lacking food to provide for her family. When a neighbor had leftovers to share, Fatima eagerly took them despite the fact that the woman who cooked the food had *nthaka*. How else would she be able to feed her family? To Fatima's relief and to her surprise, she and her children remained in good health despite the fact that they should have become ill. Mustafa, a young man in the Micuio neighborhood, also mentioned to me that he had once disregarded *mgosyo*. He proceeded to explain that his grandfather had been hungry, and his sister, who usually did the cooking, was away from the house. Mustafa prepared his grandfather's meal, including pouring salt into the *ndiwo*. While this should have caused his grandfather to become ill (because Mustafa was sexually active, while his grandfather was not), the old man remained in good health. Both Fatima and Mustafa, then, contravened *mgosyo* in order to fulfill their obligations to care for others—precisely what seems to be the underpinning of *mgosyo*. The "taboo complex," then, is perhaps better conceptualized as a matter of "everyday rituals," or behaviors that express and revitalize moral ideals through their enaction (Ammerman 2007; McGuire 2008), imbuing quotidian and mundane routines with significance and power, and extending their meaning beyond the immediate present (Erdal and Borchgrevink 2017; Geissler and Prince 2010). The meaning of *mgosyo*, in this light, rested not with passively and routinely following specific customs or taboos, but in the opportunity *mogyso* afforded for actively and intentionally engaging with, and so reconstituting, mutuality, belonging, and moral frameworks for proper living. In this sense, *mgosyo* not only required but also enabled individuals to care for one another, as a commitment to be intentionally enacted rather than believed or obliged out of habit.

Mgosyo, then, prevented calamity in the form of illness, yes, but it also accomplished something more generative—shoring up interdependencies, and through them each individual's sense of being part of something greater than themselves. The writings of philosopher Niels Weidtmann (2019a; 2019b) are useful to draw upon here for his insistence on mutuality as more than the existence of social bonds. For Weidtmann, actions of mutuality have an affective quality, and their capacity for deepening and extending humanity relies on their continued engagement. The connections that bind us together, then, are to be performed and lived through everyday actions. This is precisely why I chose, in the first paragraph of this section, to articulate the rules of *mgosyo* as behaviors to enact, rather than tabooed actions to avoid. While I have written of *mgosyo* in terms of proscription in previous publications (Huhn 2017), I find it more productive to conceptualize *mgosyo* here in the realm of prescription, providing a heuristic device that enables us to think more clearly about *mgosyo* as a matter of decisive and deliberate actions aimed at accomplishing rather than merely averting.

The interdependencies that were revitalized through *mgosyo* were not only among the living; they were also with the dead. Patuma, the same traditional healer who helped me to work through the operating principles of *vitamina* (see chapter 1), hinted at this point through a series of examples. She started with herself: If she were menstruating and she poured salt into her husband's food, this would cause him to become ill. This would happen whether she poured the salt intentionally, or by accident. But, she went on to explain, if a woman arrived in Metangula from Portugal (or, I later clarified, another distant land) and she poured salt into food while she was menstruating, those consuming the fare would *not* become ill. This woman, in other words, was not bound by *mgosyo* in her own actions. The same woman would, however, become sick with *mgosyo* if she ate food into which a local woman who was menstruating had poured salt. The difference in the capacity to cause harm seems to have to do with allegiance to the land. Foreigners from overseas were unlikely to have the intention to permanently settle in Metangula (none had ever stayed so long, at least), thus absolving them of the need to follow *mgosyo*. All who intended prolonged residence, in which their lives became tied to the place itself (and so its ancestors) were, on the other hand, expected to follow *mgosyo*.

It was as such that the foreign woman from Portugal would, if she married and raised her children in Metangula, eventually become bound by *mgosyo* herself. Those who came to live permanently in Metangula from elsewhere in the region were also expected to follow Metangula's *mgosyo* upon their arrival, despite the fact that they might have different *mgosyo*-like restrictions where they were from. Elsewhere in northern Mozambique, for example, Francisco Lerma Martinez (2009) has documented the tradition of *mwiiko* among Makhuwa populations, and Ian Dicks (2012) described *ndaka* among Yaawo communities near the border with Mozambique in southern Malawi. Among other populations in Malawi, the label is often *mdulo*, with *kanyela* and *tsepmho* serving as additional variations (DeGabriele 1999; Drake 1976; Hodgson 1933; Kaspin 1996; Marwick 1965; Munthali 2002a; Rangeley 1948; van Breugel 2001; van den Borne 2005; J. Williamson 1956). In the broader region, one encounters *yila* among the Shangan, *makgoma* for the Shona, *kahungo* among the Tonga, *kweche* for the Luo, and *boswagadi* among Setswana populations (Geissler and Prince 2010; Ingstad, Bruuns, and Tlou 1997; Jacobson-Widding 1990; Mogensen 1997). This is but a sampling. The rules, restrictions, and illness manifestations vary in each case, but the underlying principle generally remains the same as that in Metangula: failure to follow rules, usually related directly or indirectly to sex or status as a sexually active person, results in illness and/or death for third parties, usually dependents of the transgressor.

Again, an immigrant to Metangula was expected to follow *mgosyo*, not the *mgosyo*-like complex where they were from. Mariana, a middle-aged woman from Metangula, inadvertently illustrated this point for me in recounting having had an abortion during her long-term residence in the Mozambican capital city of Maputo. Assuming presence of *mgosyo*-like prescriptions, she inquired of her neighbors as to the proper behaviors to follow. When they told her that there were no restrictions on women who have had an abortion, she continued pouring salt and eating with others, as normal, even though she would never think of doing this at home. While I cannot confirm the veracity of Mariana's reporting, what is crucial here is her justification of inaction with inquiry as an index of her moral constitution to care for others and her recognition of the importance of following the *mgosyo*-like prescriptions where she was living rather than where she was from. The same was true for Albertina, the daughter-in-law in my host household, who made great efforts to follow Metangula's *mgosyo* despite being herself of Makhuwa origins. She had migrated to Metangula with an uncle after her mother had died, and she married into a family that seemed wary of her presence. Judite silently judged Albertina with glances and facial expressions—she disagreed with her daughter-in-law's insistence on going to school while she had a nursing child at home, and the two women often butted heads over care of the homestead and especially treatment of Albertina's physically and mentally disabled daughter, Glória. When in a bad mood, Albertina would call the girl "a dog" and ignore her spasming limbs and head as they pounded against the concrete floor. Judite indirectly complained about Albertina, whispering for instance to her one-year-old son that he should move with his mother back to her hometown. Judite's husband, Pedro, would also sometimes comment about his food lacking oil, an insult to both Albertina's culinary skill and her economic resourcefulness. For these reasons, there was perhaps more at stake for Albertina following *mgosyo* than there was for some other women; by taking pains to follow *mgosyo*, Albertina was in effect asserting her integration into what were otherwise unsolidified relations. She was declaring her desire and her right to belong. And Judite took notice. In a meandering conversation one afternoon, she held up her daughter-in-law, despite any misgivings she had of Albertina, as exemplary of behaviors required by a person who marries into a Nyanja family. "She left her own *kamu* [people] to take this one," Judite noted. "Up to the point of following Nyanja *mgosyo*."

For both Mariana and Albertina, then, following local prescriptions was a way in which to intertwine their lives with those around them through assertions of belonging and mutuality with the living. But both were in effect equally showing reverence for and so crafting mutuality with the dead—ancestors of the place, tied to the land itself. It is useful here to consider Schoffeleers's (1992) observations that ancestors of autochthonous populations often retain spiritual control of the land in southern Africa, regardless of its present occupants, and even where their descendants have been politically marginalized. In showing respect for *mgosyo* or its equivalent, an individual was thus demonstrating reverence for the spiritual authority of the original occupants of the land. In this light, it is of interest that the word *mgosyo* itself comes not from Chinyanja, but from the Chiyaawo word *kukosya*, meaning "to care for and protect" (in Chinyanja *kupenyelera*), and the founding chief of Metangula settled in what had previously been Yaawo territory. It was also *nthaka* that seemed to inspire the most deference of the *mgosyo* prescriptions in Metangula, and the cognate *ndaka* is a name for the *mgosyo*-like illness complex among the Yaawo. The word *nthaka*, besides indicating illnesses caused by certain actions of women who have lost a fetus or infant, also means in Chinyanja "soil" or "land" (in Chichewa also commonly *dothi* or *dziko*). It is then possible that *mgosyo* as an everyday ritual-illness complex in Metangula was at least in part a matter of showing reverence for the mandate of Yaawo spirits among the ancestors whose purview it was to protect current occupants of the land.

In cycling back to chapter 2, then, the significance of *mgosyo* is to be found in the opportunities that it afforded for interdependence. As articulated by Michael Jackson in his assessment of life as a struggle between natural dispositions and acquired disciplines, "We need to augment, extend, enlarge, and complete our singular selves in order to be adequate for life—not simply to survive, but to exist" (2011, 93). Mutuality was a matter of entangling one's own life not only with that of others living in the same place, but also with the locality's dead. Weidtmann focuses on these relationships with ancestors and the spirit realm as integral for enabling an individual's recognition of their own life as both owed to and continuing forward the lives of others. This makes anyone's life not exclusively theirs, forging a sense of belonging to a historical lifeworld, and inextricably binding oneself to both the past and the future. These realizations and capacities are not achieved through the imagining of a fixed relationship with the dead or through rational analysis, but in *feelings* of embeddedness that can only come about through action. "Ubuntu," Weidtmann writes, and it is apt to substitute *mgosyo*, "is about experiencing the greater context or the underlying dimension being represented in the particular situation" (2019a, 152). *Mgosyo*, we can surmise using this logic, was, then, a practice through which individuals experienced and therefore renewed their belonging among others and fulfilled obligations to contribute to their wellness, and thus the continuation of life itself.

Heat as Responsibility

Mgosyo and similar everyday ritual-illness complexes in Africa are frequently couched in terms of "hot" and "cold," those who are "hot" or in some heated state typically causing harm to those who are "cold" or "cool" by failing to enact specific behaviors. The application and meaning of "hot" and "cold," however, vary culturally (Morris 2000). Among some African populations, for example, hot/cold seems to operate similar to the humoral traditions of Ayurvedic, Latin American, Chinese, and Greek medicine (Logan 1977; Manderson 1987), stressing equilibrium for the achievement and maintenance of health and well-being. In other cases, one pole (hot or cold) is prioritized in association with wellness and/or creative potentiality. In both situations, "heat" is attributed metaphysical powers as a causative agent, thus explaining *mgosyo*-like illnesses as the result of improper balance, ordering, or states of ritual temperature. Among Maravi populations, "hot" and "cold" have been observed to operate along similar lines—it is those who are hot who cause illness for those who are cold, or who otherwise enable ruinous consequences by performing actions that entail heat (or, more broadly, transformation or creative activity) while in a heated state themselves. But in accordance with several previous studies in the region (Drake 1976; Rita-Ferreira 1966), my observations suggest that in Metangula, the labels "hot" (*-funda*) and "cool" (*-zizira*) indicated little more than status as a sexually active or inactive person, and therefore one's capacity and so their responsibility to care for others. In this section I lay out the connection between sex, responsibilities, and heat so as to further support the positioning of *mgosyo* as an everyday, intentional practice for fulfilling obligations to care for the well-being of others and to secure unity with the spirit realm.

To accomplish this, we first begin with sexuality and establish that the act of sexual intercourse is not bound everywhere by the same connotations that it is in the global north. Specifically, the management of sexuality in places like the United States and Europe has a specific history linked to Victorian ideals, Freudian medicalization, the equation of childhood with innocence, ideals of romantic love and personal pleasure as the motivations of intimate relationships, and broader constructions of meaning in relation to repression and permissiveness (Caplan 1987). Sex and sexuality, then, like any other facet of human behavior, are culturally constructed, and we cannot and should not assume that differences between one's own understandings and those in some other place are a sign of primitivism, depravity, transgression, or innocence. Assumptions otherwise have been made in the past, often driven by ethnocentric or racist agendas to "other" brown bodies and so construct European and North American lives not only as distinct, but also as moral, liberated, civilized, or otherwise superior (Gilman 2010; Mohanty 1984; Vaughan 1991). The "way of seeing" that resulted still overshadows social science research on sex and sexuality in Africa (Ahlberg 1994; Arnfred 2004; Heald 1995).

While the trajectories of sexuality (or, more appropriately, sexualities) in Africa are yet to be historicized to the level they have been for Eurasia (but, see Arnfred 2004), studies of the present and the recent past suggest that sex on the African continent is often treated as a cornerstone of ethical reflections and practices. As articulated by anthropologist Suzette Heald (1995), this means not female chastity (the linchpin of sex as a point of morality in Eurasian models), but rather reticence toward and restrictions on sexuality as a part of broader patterns in proper decorum requiring respect and restraint in relation to processes with creative potential. While sex in Africa, or at least in much of east Africa Heald argues conservatively, is not conceived of as being "impure," the improper engagement of sex does risk disorder, danger, and misfortune, and thus sexuality requires being brought under social control. The power of sex, according to Heald, lies in the mingling of bodily substance through which two become one, potentially in the form of a child. Anthropologists Paul Wenzel Geissler and Ruth Jane Prince (2010) add crucial nuance to these ideas by bringing attention to the importance of *moments* of coming together (rather than perpetual merger) for maintaining processes of life. Sex, as such, like the everyday rituals of *mgosyo*, is positioned as an everyday act to be perpetually engaged with for experiencing and reconstituting mutuality.

With this preface, we can turn now to Metangula, where my acquaintances assumed that all individuals who were physically mature enough to labor and to have children were sexually active. Even the Catholic priest, many people told me, only *said* that he was abstinent. For him, or any other adult, to actually refrain from sexual relations would be preposterous. This was in part a reflection of the pleasures associated with sexual activity. But the importance of sex was also tied to health and energy in a manner very much akin to alimentation, requiring (in line with Geisser and Prince's analysis) regular engagement in sexual relations for wellness and vitality. Specifically, it was through sex that men and women exchanged sexual fluids (*ubazi*) that, like food, enabled *vitamina*. The *ubazi* of a man entered into a woman's body through her vaginal canal, and the *ubazi* of a woman entered into a man's body through his urethra. From there, it entered the bloodstream of the recipient, and just like food, it contributed to vitality. At the same time, sexual *vitamina* was distinct from food-based *vitamina*; no other substance could replace it. I once asked Monica why a sexually inactive woman could not just, say, eat a lot of tomatoes to ensure her energy and health. "Can a woman eat tomatoes with her vagina?" she responded. Nope.

It was because sexual fluids became *a part* of the recipient's blood that I often heard *ubazi* referred to as blood itself. Acquaintances intimated that a man's blood (in both senses of the term) was "stronger" than that of a woman. This was evidenced, for some, by men's superior physical strength. But most simply pointed to women's periodic loss of blood through menstruation, gestation, and childbirth, which made replenishment through *ubazi* especially important. If a woman did not have sex regularly (defined for me variously, but typically hovering around at least once per month), she would be weak because her blood was "moving alone" without "the blood" of a man. Indeed, seemingly whenever I was at Metangula's health center I would encounter women who told me that they were there because they felt weak, for which they anticipated a diagnosis of anemia. This would signal to both the medical technician and the woman being treated that she was lacking blood. For the patient, however, it might indicate that she was short on sexual *vitamina*.

When I expressed skepticism about this interpretation, women assured me that medical professionals asked women who showed signs of anemia if they "had a husband" (culturally implying a regular sexual partner) as part of the diagnostic process. They also reported that medical professionals instructed patients to have sex to address depleted blood stores, rather than giving these women medicine. While I could not find any member of the current medical staff who would confirm these rumors, the volunteers who gave lectures at the health center agreed that this *used to* be a part of advice offered in medical consultations for weak or anemic women. Among acquaintances, several maintained that they or their friends had experienced this form of interrogation and prognosis more recently. Regardless, similar perceptions were so strong in the provincial capital Lichinga that the Anglican diocese put together a brochure extolling the value of semen for sexual reproduction *only*, not female wellness (Rebecca Vander Meulen, personal communication, 11 February 2011).

Lack of sexual activity diminished male energy, as it did for a woman, but a man's inanition was unrelated to his blood's "moving independently" of that of the opposite sex. Acquaintances suggested that an abstinent man's blood would mix with his sperm and become foamy, and this consistency would make him weak. Men having "too much" sex (something like regular intercourse three or more times a day) were in equal danger of frailty. Again, however, this was unrelated to female *ubazi*. Rather, it was because these men ran out of their own *ubazi*, and new supplies had to be created from *vitamina* siphoned from their blood supply, which negatively prejudiced their vitality. Abstinence was one way that such a man could regain his strength. One male acquaintance in his thirties explained to me, for example, that he refrained from sex with his wife whenever he found that he was lacking the strength to collect bamboo or to make bricks or when he was clumsy on the job and continually wounding himself. Having few resources, he said, he did not have the luxury to simply eat well to regain strength when blood was redirected for sexual activity. He thus had to conserve what *vitamina* he had for other exploits.

If a man had a voracious sexual appetite, people suggested, another strategy for ensuring health was to consume foods that would directly increase his *ubazi*. I recorded raw cassava, sugarcane, peanuts, soaked rice (raw, shelled rice submerged in water for about fifteen minutes, softening it and making the water cloudy), and less frequently, coconut meat as foods that could increase a man's *ubazi*. Others noted coffee as an alternative *ubazi*-augmenting food when in the city (where the above-listed foods might be unavailable or too time-consuming to prepare). Following the Portuguese tradition, coffee drinkers in Mozambique often ordered a *galão*, a stein filled with one-quarter espresso (or, in Lichinga, more often instant Nescafé) and three-quarters milk, giving the drink a creamy color and consistency. To emphasize, these foods and drinks were not necessary to create sexual fluids, but they did directly add to them, improving a man's ability to sexually perform, not in quality but in quantity, without negatively prejudicing his blood and so his vitality. This was seemingly a popular desire. A frequent sight in the marketplace was men snacking on sugarcane, soaked rice was one of few foods I saw men preparing for themselves, and acquaintances often sent me home with a stalk of cassava and explicit instruction to deliver it to my husband.

While women also ate these *ubazi*-enhancing foods, it was less likely for them to do so to increase their sexual fluid output. This was for three reasons. One was that any excessive *ubazi* just leaked out of a woman's body, rather than storing internally as it does in a man's. Acquaintances pointed to regular female emission of vaginal secretions as evidence. Second, both women and men suggested that a

Figure 4.2. A group of young men snack on sugarcane before school. Photo by the author.

woman's sexual appetite was not as voracious as that of a man's. A woman could thus have sex once and be satisfied for long enough before having sex again that she could produce a new supply of *ubazi* without haste or depleting her blood supplies. Women sometimes complained to me that while they enjoyed sex, their husbands were going "to break" (*kuononga*) them with frequent demands for sexual activity, which they would be contented with at less frequent intervals. Finally, female *ubazi* was not an especially prized part of the (male) sexual experience. As elsewhere in Africa (Bagnol et al. 2015; Brown and Brown 2000), acquaintances indicated that men preferred "dry sex," and women took measures to both tighten their vaginas and to reduce their sexual secretions through use of astringent substances. With some embarrassment at discussing such things openly, women explained to me that they would mash leaves to soften them and then insert them into their vaginal canal to create the desired effects. Many adult woman I asked about the practice candidly acknowledged their participation and pointed to plants like *kobwe* beans, tomato, and several wild plants, all with leaves that could be harvested for such purposes. The preference for vaginal dryness is also perhaps why the effect of female *ubazi* on male health was culturally unelaborated, almost an afterthought or nod to the equality of the sexes rather than integral to physiology.

Like women (and certainly also some men), children ate *ubazi*-enhancing foods for the pleasure of doing so, not for the enhancement of sexual fluids. Acquaintances suggested that children did not yet produce sexual fluids, and they were not yet in need of receiving sexual fluids or sending them to the opposite sex for general health. Their "path" (*njira*), the trail by which *ubazi* was envisioned to enter the bloodstream, was "closed." Each individual's path "opened" with their first sexual encounter, henceforth making *ubazi* a necessary part of life because they had "become used to it" and so dependent on it. When I asked what would happen if someone never opened their path, remaining indefinitely abstinent, acquaintances pointed me to a physically disabled woman whom it was rumored had never had sex but was in perfectly good health. She "did not know what she was missing," they suggested in an explanatory rather than a taunting manner. In this way, she was physiologically like a child. I felt too awkward to ask the woman about this myself. But, some older women did tell me that their own paths had closed with menopause—since they no longer regularly lost their own blood, they were not in constant need of replacement through male *ubazi*, and since they no longer craved sexual activity, they experienced no emotional duress without it. There was no consensus among those I spoke with, male and female, on whether a man's path ever closed once it had opened, perhaps because it was unusual for men to live beyond their capacity for procreation. These distinctions, however, also pattern onto gendered paths of aging in matrilineal societies (like Maravi populations), through which women tend to become less reliant on men (and more reliant on adult sons) as they grow older, whereas the livelihoods of men remain tied to having a spouse and continued opportunities to procreate (Cliggett 2005).

In order to have the vitality that was necessary to labor and to care for others, then, adults needed not only to eat appropriate foods and to be sufficiently well in body and mind so that alimentation could impart *vitamina* (as discussed in chapter 1), but also to have the "blood" of someone other than themselves coursing through their veins, a state achieved only through sexual activity. This envisioned codependence of bodies exemplifies the cultural ideologies linking production and reproduction in Africa, along with the powerful bond that many African populations conceive to exist between regular sexual partners (Heald 1995). Necessity for another person's presence in order to be personally complete further speaks to the importance of mutuality—in a visceral sense, persons were literally composed and created through their encounters with and dependencies on other human beings.

But sex was also conflicted. While clearly positive for enabling vitality and mutuality, sex also had the potential for negative ramifications when engaged improperly, for example through *mgosyo*. Some readers will have picked up on the association of sex and harm also in chapter 2's discussion of the Maravi creation myth. Recall that the story begins with animals, humans, and God living together on earth. Humans disrupted this harmony by starting a fire that sent noxious smoke into the environment and caused both animals and God to flee. People in Metangula explicitly explained this fire as arising from the rubbing together of "a hard stick and a soft stick," which they were always sure to clarify as a metaphor for sexual activity. But unlike the biblical story of Eden, this first sexual act was not sinful for its violation of rules (Adam and Eve were told to "not eat the apple" from the tree of knowledge). Rather, sex was offensive because the smoke that resulted from the fire caused others (here, God and animals) to suffer. In response to this offense, God declared that humans would have to begin caring for themselves, rather than being reliant on God for their livelihoods. Humans would also thereafter be susceptible to death, rather than being immortal, thus necessitating reproduction for the continuation of life. Sex was therefore, from the outset, a definitive, if conflicted, part of being human and like fire with both generative and destructive potentiality.

By bringing in the Maravi creation story here I do not mean to imply that it is why *mgosyo* exists. I find the creation story relevant because it seemed to be embedded within and to embed socially relevant values related to sexual activity, heat, compassionate care, spiritual oversight, and humanity, all of which was similar to *mgosyo*. The creation myth provides a clear link between fire and sexual activity. This corresponds with labeling those who were sexually active as "hot." Likewise, those who were sexually abstinent in Metangula were "cool," a trait (together with wind, shade, and peace) broadly associated with ancestors. It is of interest, then, that *mgosyo* at times required abstinence (and so "coolness"), seemingly in the name of prelapsarian unity and reverence for the spirit realm. It was precisely in precarious situations with unpredictable outcomes in which people would most benefit from ancestral oversight—such as initiation rites (where participants were in limbo between one state and another), funerals (where an individual's spirit might go astray), and birth (an often dangerous event for mother and child)—where *mgosyo* required the cessation of sexual activity by concerned parties. In precolonial times, it was also a sexually inactive person who was sent to sprinkle flour at the base of a tree on behalf of a village or, in the case of some Maravi rain cults (not present, to my knowledge, in Metangula), to fictively marry and communicate the wants of a rain snake. In a more contemporary example, Reverend Felix Chingota (1998) noted that congregants in Malawian churches were reluctant to take the Eucharist, for participation in the Lord's Supper was conceived as requiring "coolness," and the majority were sexually active. Given these points of overlap, both the creation story and *mgosyo* can and should be useful for making sense of one another.

The creation myth also connects the sex act with taking responsibility for others' well-being, and *mgosyo* was one way in which those who were sexually active could, through preventing illness in dependents, carry out this mandate of humanity. In everyday rituals related to sexual activity and salt pouring, in other words, individuals had the opportunity to regularly and repeatedly prioritize, experience, and revitalize their obligations for care work. This included both the living, who were kept well, and the dead, who were shown respect through adherence to *mgosyo* (or at least the underlying principles) and provided oversight in return. In enacting interdependencies, individuals also confirmed the entwining of their own lives with those of others, past and present, deepening the multidimensionality of their humanity. This physically manifested by way of sexual *vitamina*, exchanged between bodies engaged in coitus and through which individuals both attained the vitality that was necessary to undertake the generative labor of caring for others and physically produced the next generation. "Heat," then, as a label indicating engagement in sexual activity, both necessitated and enabled responsibility for caring as an essential act of humanity.

Salt and Dawa

If there is, then, a connection between sex, responsibility, caring for others, affect, heat, and being and becoming human, which can help to make sense of the parameters of *mgosyo* as they operated in the beginning of the twenty-first century, the question remains: Why salt? As it turns out, the chemical compound of salt is symbolically privileged not only in Metangula, but in locations around the globe—wrapped up in a variety of meanings ranging from hospitality to class to holiness to evil (Parman 2002). Margaret Visser's (2005) pithy cross-cultural consideration posits that there are particular properties of salt that make it ripe for such cultural elaboration: salt can dissolve and then return to a solid state, it disappears and yet profoundly alters the foods to which it is added, it causes water to heat more quickly, and consuming salt is, in a way, eating the earth itself. Salt is also profoundly contradictory. Salt can preserve some things from rotting, for example, while corroding others. And while a little salt fertilizes the land, a lot can cause sterility. Thus, like fire and like sex in their Maravi formulations, salt is inherently conflicted. I cannot offer any definitive answers as to why the everyday ritual-illness complex of *mgosyo* implicated salt. I can propose, however, several related threads that together suggest that salt operated in Metangula in a way that was much more like *dawa*—powerful substances used by traditional healers to help and by witches to harm—than like food.

Let us first recall the quotidian and essential nature of salt in Metangula. As introduced in chapter 1, adding salt was an essential step in preparing tasty, and so *vitamina*-enabling, *ndiwo*. While salt is bitter or unpleasant tasting (*kuwawa*) on its own, it makes foods "sweet," or good tasting (*kukoma*), and acquaintances characterized meals prepared without salt as "watery," "poor tasting," and generally inedible. Monica one time mused that she would rather starve than eat food without salt, for saltless food was not palatable. Solange, one of the grandchildren of my host family, another time remarked that being fat was a terrible fate—because the doctors would tell you not to eat salt (see chapter 5). "Without salt," she mused one afternoon as we discussed the physical appearance of various characters in a Brazilian soap opera, some of whom were quite large bodied, "what is the point of eating?" On my part, it was sometimes difficult to believe the quantities of salt added to the meals that were cooked and served in Metangula. I would truthfully tell people that the salt they used in a week would last me a year at home in my own kitchen, which they inevitably thought was a joke.

Not only did salt make food tasty, salt consumption was essential for corporeal function. Whereas biomedicine posits salt as essential for its role in regulating extracellular fluid, transmitting nerve impulses, and contracting muscles, in Metangula salt was specifically tied to functioning of the gallbladder (*ndulu*), human development, and strength. The gallbladder was an essential contributor to the process of digestion—emitting a "yellow liquid" (which biomedicine would label as bile) into the stomach, which enabled foods to break down. This made the gallbladder central to well-being, Jose even calling it *presidente do corpo* (president of the body).[5] He explained that this was because without a functioning gallbladder, food would just sit in the stomach, making a person lose their appetite. Failure to eat would then lead to lack of energy and vitality. It was as such that "the body strengthens with salt," as I recorded hearing in multiple conversations, along with "salt causes the body to grow." A body without salt was likened to *ndiwo* in the same condition—because both were watery and without "power" (*mphavu*).

Some also cited salt as imperative because it was necessary for producing sweat, which only humans do (reasoned, as I heard it, because animals do not smell like human sweat). This distinction was why animals could be deceased for several days without stinking, while human cadavers required repetitive bathing until the time of burial; it was salt that caused the stench of human death. Others suggested that we pour salt into our food because to eat unsalted food was to behave like animals, which eat foods like grasses, trees, and other things that are bitter and unpalatable for human consumption. At home, Judite pointed out that salt was different in comparison to other substances because it *really* enters into our blood. "It liquefies [or melts, *kusungunuka*]," she said, "allowing it to enter our whole body." To support her claims, she pointed out that we ourselves taste like salt, and our urine smells like salt, rather than smelling and tasting like, say, *ntchima*. In these ways, salt was a privileged substance because that which is consumed so viscerally and thoroughly becomes a part of us.

Before rock salt (and later table salt) was available along the lakeshore, people seasoned their food and enacted *mgosyo* with a salty liquid called *matcheza*.[6] Not technically "salt" (sodium chloride), but a water-soluble potassium carbonate (potash), *matcheza* can be produced by collecting plant matter and burning it to ashes. Hot water is then strained through the ashes, and the resultant liquid poured into whatever is being cooked to add a salty flavor.[7] While not widely used at the time of my research, the process of making *matcheza* was still known in Metangula, at least among middle-aged and older adults, who regularly made and used *matcheza* as recently as the 1980s, a decade also known as "the time of Samora" (*nyengo ya* Samora). The reference was to Samora Machel, Mozambique's first president, who was driven by socialist policy-making and oversaw the country during its brutal, sixteen-year "civil war" (1977–92). These factors, among others, made household essentials often difficult to come by. People reported to me that during the time of Samora they used maize bran as body soap, tree bark as laundry detergent, and *matcheza* as salt. Many also endured life-altering sacrifices, such as loss of land and family members.

Diana's mother, Filomena, once demonstrated for me the process of making *matcheza*, doing it to produce a specific type known as *vidule*, which was explained to me as akin to baking soda more than salt in its culinary properties and was still used in some households to season fish and green leafy *ndiwo* (side dishes), as well as *malimbachala* (pounded, boiled orchid root). In her backyard, I watched Filomena burn cassava stems (the stalks of *matiwi* trees and vines would also work, she told me), place the ashes into a winnowing basket, and pour hot water through them to produce a liquid culinary additive that strained into a pot below. While documenting this process was important in itself, watching Filomena make *vidule* sparked for me a realization that reducing a plant to ash to make *matcheza* very much resembled the manufacture of *dawa*, another category of substances with transformative capacities that, like salt, could be helpful or harmful.

Figure 4.3. Filomena pours water through ash to produce *vidule*. Photo by the author.

To detail and extend these parallels, let us return briefly to Fatima, the woman with several young children at home who cautiously experimented with *mgosyo* when she had nothing with which to feed her family. One breezy morning Fatima graciously invited me to join her and her sister on the back veranda, where she was boiling a pot of cultivated *chipeta* roots (she was sure to distinguish them from the visually similar but wild-growing *mpama* roots, which would be an embarrassment to eat oneself, but especially to offer a guest). I accepted a cup of tea while awaiting what would be my second breakfast and started making small talk with Fatima's sister, Regina. Meanwhile, Fatima removed the aluminum pot of roots from the fire when they were sufficiently soft and replaced it with a small clay pot where she began to stir and singe dry leaves. When I asked what she was making, thinking it was a type of *ndiwo* I had not yet come across, she replied simply, "*Nsipuko*"—love medicine. This is how I learned that Jose was not the only "love doctor" in town.

Knowing how to prepare *dawa* was not something that Fatima had previously mentioned. She did not like to talk about it openly, she would later come to tell me, because she was not in it to make money. She just wanted to help family and friends when she saw that they were in need. That is why her sister was there that morning, in fact; the *nsipuko* that Fatima was making was for Regina. Fatima had learned how to make *nsipuko* from their grandmother, and she now had periodic visions that told her which plants she could collect and manipulate to produce the *dawa* that would enable her to act as a "helper of God" to promote, as she phrased it in Portuguese, "the fidelity and longevity of love." Though those who made *dawa* for pro-social or medicinal purposes were often suspected of making it for nefarious reasons too, Fatima was sure to clarify that she did not and that she most certainly did not use *dawa* to kill people. This seemed like a bid to distance herself from Jose, who was widely reputed to provision medicines for killing and other forms of malfeasance. I asked Fatima if it was not also something destructive to tamper with love. She insisted *nsipuko* was a helpful form of *dawa*, as there was no intention to cause anyone harm and because it drew people closer together.

The *dawa* that Fatima was making that morning was meant for what Allison Goebel (2002) calls "husband-taming." The ashes she produced had the potential for magical action when applied directly to a woman's body atop small parallel cuts on her forehead, chest, and abdomen. The medicine would take effect when she engaged in sexual relations with her partner, following which she would have the unique ability to sexually arouse him. While the act of sexual activation was, in my recordings, unique to *nsipuko*, there were many types of *dawa* that could be produced by burning or singeing plant matter that was then applied to or incorporated within the body for effect. Judite, for example, burned roots to produce a potash that she provided to friends and family to relieve headaches and minor breathing problems, as recounted in chapter 3. While there were surely other techniques for *dawa* manufacture that I did not directly witness, the burning of plant matter as a technique to produce both *matcheza* and *dawa* made me curious. I started to wonder if the simultaneous generative and destructive potentialities of *matcheza* (and in the twenty-first century also salt, as a widespread replacement for potash) indicated some kinship between these substances and *dawa*.

Many people in Metangula, in fact, spoke about salt as if it were *dawa*. Salt played an important role in the aforementioned *kumphika mwana* (cook the child) ceremony, for example, which some referenced alternatively as *kumphika dawa la mwana* (cook the child's medicine). The ritual introduced an infant to the existence of sexual relations, but it also made the body more powerful through the introduction of salt (and before salt was widely available, *matcheza*), without which a baby remained "watery" (*wamadjimadji*). But salt, like *dawa*, also had the capacity to serve as a vehicle for harm. Filomena once told me, for example, that salt "transmits illnesses that are caused by people" (*nchele umatengera uthenda wa munthu*), meaning through moral transgression, as opposed to those illnesses that were natural, or instigated by God. Salt also resembled *dawa* in its capacity to protect, in certain instances, from witchcraft—for example, by storing salt with money so that it could not be stolen or by pouring salt water in one's ear to protect from verbal incantations. Salt, and before salt *matcheza*, thus served a variety of roles similar to *dawa*, inclusive of those that were generative and destructive.

The parallels between *matcheza* and *dawa* drew closer together for me that afternoon with Fatima when she told me about another love medicine, *ntamiko*, meant for a woman to keep her husband faithful by preventing him from "walking around." A person who spent too much time circulating through town was surely looking for a(nother) spouse or relationship, and *ntamiko* would stop this behavior. *Ntamiko* was produced like *nsipuko* (and *matcheza*), through burning plant material to ash. But *ntamiko* had a different application process. Fatima explained that a woman would pour *ntamiko* into her spouse's tea or food, reciting her own name as she did so. Once her partner consumed the affected drink or meal, he would come to find himself satisfied just staying around the home. *Ntamiko* was in high demand in Metangula, Fatima told me, but its manufacture was not widely known. I learned this directly when I started joking with friends that my culture-shocked husband rarely left the house because I knew how to make *ntamiko*. I soon found myself with a steady stream of visitors asking if I could provide them with some for their husbands too. Several became particularly nasty toward me when I revealed my incompetence as a *sing'anga*, for they believed that I was just being selfish.

While Fatima knew of *ntamiko* only by name, her description piqued my interest not only for its resemblance (like *nsipuko*) to *matcheza* in its manufacture, but also in the importance placed on pouring to effect particular aims. Recall that for the *mgosyo* everyday ritual-illness complex, it was also pouring salt (not *touching* it) through which results transpired. I decided to take up the point of pouring with the elderly Mustafa, coyly "double-checking" that in the past people would pray by *placing* (*kuika*) flour at the base of a *msolo* tree (*Pseudolachnostylis maprouneifolia*), deliberately avoiding the verb of "pour" (*kuthira*) that he had used in association with such action when talking to me about the past. With a sense of annoyance at my failure to understand and remember things, Mustafa immediately corrected me. He emphasized that it was necessary to "pour" the flour, resulting in a small pile at the base of a tree, not to place the flour there. He imitated the action by pretending to scoop into his right hand a fistful of flour and then, with the back of his hand parallel to the ground, rubbing his thumb quickly, back and forth, against his index and middle fingers to sprinkle it onto the ground. "How else," he asked of pouring, "would your words be heard?" While *dawa* could also be operationalized in other ways, the act of pouring was clearly privileged in directing spiritual forces and (so) effecting results.[8]

The category of *matcheza*, then, is reminiscent of *dawa* in its manufacture (burning plant material to ash), potentiality for enaction through its downward discharge (pouring), and mercurial potentiality (to both generate and destroy mutuality). And it is plausible that *mgosyo* restrictions on pouring (but not touching) *matcheza*, and later salt, were a subset of broader norms for the proper handling of multidimensional substances with the capacity to direct metaphysical forces. I am not saying that *matcheza* was *dawa*, but comparison of these two categories of substances helps to contextualize their positioning, along with sex and fire, at a crossroads of generative and destructive forces at which individuals enacted conscious and active choices about the nature of their relationships with others, and so their humanity. One can triangulate the data but never truly know why salt was central to *mgosyo* in the twenty-first century.[9] Regardless, salt in Metangula was clearly more than simple culinary seasoning.

Contingencies and Contradictions

In addition to deepening our engagement with *mgosyo* via *matcheza* and salt, the consideration of *dawa* makes clearer that everyday processes, behaviors, relations, and substances in Africa have long contained possibilities for both generativity and destruction. These circumstances cannot be controlled or permanently overcome. They are, then, lived with, navigated, and temporarily ordered. Caroline H. Bledsoe (2002) puts forth that the sense of vulnerability and uncertainty that results from such conditions is an enduring theme across the African subcontinent. In her ethnography of fertility and aging in the Gambia, she outlines how individuals (in her work, women) did not just sit back, passively awaiting the unknown. Rather, they assessed the present, reflected on the past, and calibrated a trajectory by anticipating the most likely outcomes to propel them forward. Such engagement, action, and agency in designing and enacting creative response provided predictability, possibility, and meaning in the mitigation of contingency and misfortune, enabling individuals to maintain a sense of possibility for revision, growth, and becoming in an imagined future.

The conditions of humanity in Africa (and arguably everywhere) have, as such, long existed as ambiguous and indeterminate, though they have only recently begun to get widespread attention as such. Bledsoe's work, along with that of Susan Reynolds Whyte (1997), preceded the rise of scholarly interest in concepts like insecurity, ambivalence, opacity, pretense, and indeterminacy in the early 2000s, what Jacques de Villiers (2019) has dubbed the "uncertain turn" in African studies. This outpouring of research has focused on the destabilizing forces of "modernity"—such as mass migration, climate change, epidemics, warfare, and neoliberalism, compounded by the legacies of colonialism and postcolonialism, corruption, nepotism, and bad governance—and their impacts on ways of knowing and being in Africa (Cooper and Pratten 2015; Goldstone and Obarrio 2017; Haram and Yamba 2009; Vibeke, Jenkins, and Jessen 2005). And much of this work, while recognizing the constraints that exist on individual actions, has devoted extensive attention to the generative potentiality of uncertainty. The indeterminate nature of the future, in other words, while it can compound anxieties, inspire despair, and introduce doubts, can at the same time motivate creativity and hope and otherwise instigate socially productive action. The same approach characterizes research on "waithood," an elongation of the period in which individuals remain categorized as youth, unable (through various destabilizing forces of modernity) to obtain the resources or achieve the statuses associated with adulthood. These hurdles are a source of despondency for some, but they have also been engaged to forge new forms of identity and existence (Gilbert 2018; Honwana 2012; J. Johnson 2018; Versfeld 2012).

In the experience of and response to "modernity" in Africa, then, there are some elements that are deeply familiar from earlier times—namely, living in a world of uncertainties, hardships, and limitations, and approaching life with creativity, action, and hope. But there is also something new: global macro-forces that operate under logics that are impervious to ancestral interference and that make mutuality more difficult to achieve. These are structures and strictures like capitalism, neoliberalism, failed states, global pandemics, and massive economic inequalities. As carefully documented in Frederick Klaits's (2010) assessments of the changing nature of care in Botswana, mounting obligations that require money while lacking resources mean that unification and mutuality are difficult to achieve; there is simply never enough to meet everyone's needs. James Ferguson (2006) also writes passionately about the need for Africanist scholars to acknowledge the fact that opportunities of globalization are not evenly distributed. Many in Africa are in fact not set free by modernization, but bricked in by it.

Indeed, in Metangula increased exposure (in kind and intensity) to a world of possibilities was allowing new imaginings of the contours that life might take. At the same time, however, much of this new world required money, and this was hard to come by. Joseph Hanlon and Teresa Smart (2008) in fact estimate half of Mozambique's rural residents to be just as poor or poorer in 2008 than they were when the "civil war" ended in 1992, despite continuous and rapid improvements in macroeconomic indicators of wealth. At the time of my fieldwork unemployment was rampant in Metangula, as it was elsewhere in Mozambique (and across the continent of Africa). Prices of food staples were also spiraling out of control, and pledged micro-finance loans were seemingly impossible to qualify for. Sure, there were concrete houses with corrugated iron roofs rising up among the sea of mud brick and grass thatch, electricity that brought to life televisions that flickered with images of lifestyles from distant lands, and two recently erected cell phone towers that offered the possibility of communication with extended family and friends. But increased exposure (in kind and intensity) to a world of possibilities amid the conditions of late capitalism (everything commodified and consumable, amid widespread inequalities) also meant that many in Metangula found themselves for the first time characterizing their lives with words like poverty, feelings like marginalization, and incapacities to nourish humanity.

The transition I am describing is neatly encapsulated in the popularity of a song that I repeatedly heard sung during my first two visits to Metangula, in 2005 and 2006. The song had been composed (or, more likely if following regional patterns, adapted) to commemorate the end of the "civil war" in 1992. The words were, in short form:

In other countries (x3)	*Alipo mayiko ena* (x3)
They say that	*Anena kuti*
In Mozambique	*Ku Mozambiki*
We are poor	*Tasauka*
Do poor people ride airplanes? No	*Kodi osauka amakwela ndege? Ayi*
Do they wear shoes? No	*Amavala nsopato? Ayi*
Do they wear watches? No	*Amavala wotchi? Ayi*
In other countries	*Mayiko ena*
They do not know that	*Siakugiwa*
In Mozambique	*Ku Mozambiki*
There is peace	*Kuli mtendere*

In these lyrics is a rejection of the idea that the people of Mozambique are poor—by any standard. Not only do the people of Mozambique use technology and dress smartly (the specifics were changed out variously when different women sang the song but were always along these lines), as reflective of standards of monetary wealth and global citizenship, but they also—and perhaps more importantly—were living in peace. It was a political song, with themes similar to other postcolonial nationalist tunes, which included challenging colonial imaginings of Mozambicans as inferior (Meneses 2018). But it was also a song that was deeply embedded in local notions of wellness as achievable only in concert with mutuality, unity, and spiritual oversight. The song was ubiquitous at gatherings of Organização das Mulheres Moçambicanas (Organization of Mozambican Women, OMM). Watching barefoot women wearing clothes purchased from a secondhand market and worn to rags, who had seldom ridden in a car let alone an airplane, swaying side to side in unison, prolonging the song by repeating verses, joyously singing these lyrics proclaiming equity in the world, had struck me then as ironic. But the women were proud of their country, and its valor; their happiness, and so their wealth and wellness, were intimately tied to pacific tranquility.

Several years later, during research for the present volume in 2010 and 2011, I was sometimes encouraged at OMM meetings to take my turn leading the group in song. Without a vast repertoire of Chinyanja melodies to draw from, I often resorted to the above song, which I had recorded and translated years prior. But when I sang it, the women seemed to join me only half-heartedly, and often they would trail off before the end. I also never heard them sing the tune without my imploring them to do so. The song, it seemed, had fallen out of favor. Perhaps the simple result of changing taste, I could not help but sense that the women had at some level begun to feel that although there were Mozambicans traveling the world, with feet not hardened by a lifetime of barefoot traversing of rough terrain, and who told time by means other than the position of the sun, they and their families were, for the most part, not among the privileged few. While the women of OMM and the broader population of Metangula did indeed have peace, then, was this enough to proclaim that they were not as poor as others perceived them to be? Perhaps. Or maybe "peace" and its associated implications of ancestral oversight simply no longer characterized how they felt that they were living.

This brings us back to *mgosyo*, the efficacy of which I put forth in this chapter was dependent less on following specific rules than on enacting obligations of mutuality, through which belonging among the living and the dead revitalized and deepened humanity. But was this even possible anymore? This is not to suggest that people gave up hope in a nihilistic throwing in of the *capulana*. Indeed, acquaintances in Metangula were engaged in profound efforts to direct their lives forward through attending school, starting small businesses, healing sick bodies, and entwining their lives with others through social and physical reproduction. But the contradictions and conditions of life in the twenty-first century did mean that the nature of vulnerability had compounded in ways the spirit realm was not positioned to address. Thus, it should not be surprising that when I asked acquaintances about the relevance of *mgosyo* in the twenty-first century, I heard a variety of opinions. Some thought *mgosyo* was a relic of the past, dead with the ancestors. Others, seemingly persuaded by the tenets of Pentecostalism or reformist Islamic positioning, declared *mgosyo* to be the work of evil spirits, or *haram* (forbidden, in Arabic). Most of my acquaintances, however, explained that *mgosyo* continued to function as it "always" had. But, many lamented, there were fewer people adhering to *mygosyo* than there had been in the past. Individuals were no longer living together, in mutuality. As one elder acquaintance put it, they were "no longer of the same heart." As a result, ancestors were losing their capacities for protections. Increased misfortune could therefore be expected. Without a collective purpose, then, and amid massive wealth inequalities, the efficacy of *mgosyo* was waning—not for lack of belief or practice, it seemed, but due to a decline in unity.

It is important to note, however, that *mgosyo* was also not envisioned by my acquaintances to be a timeless relic from the past. Indeed, they suggested that it had been reconfigured over time as threats to well-being changed. When I asked elder acquaintances about the disappearance of prescriptions that in the past had regulated, for example, closing doors, stepping over pumpkin and tomato vines, and the firing of pottery, many simply shrugged their shoulders and offered something to the effect of "Those in the past, they were of a different *kamu*." A *kamu* is a group of people, as in an ethnicity, a generation, or an era. Asha, a great-great-grandmother living in Micuio, explained the relevance and implications of this generational structuring for *mgosyo* with an alimentary analogy: a person eats a meal, and by the time they defecate their food has completely changed in form, such that it is unrecognizable as that with which they began. Food that is ingested and the resulting excrement that is egested, in other words, are of the same substance. However, they are fundamentally different. This, Asha explained, was like *kamu*: as time passed, each generation became something other than that of its predecessors, with its own concerns and strategies for achieving wellness, wholeness, and unity. To emphasize this generational transformation, grandparents of grandparents sometimes referred to their great-great-grandchildren and subsequent generations as "feces grandchildren" (*vijukulu mavi*). The kin relationship between a feces grandchild and their great-great-grandparent was negligible because they were of separate *kamu*. The world, in between, was expected to change. And while failing to follow the *mgosyo* of one's own *kamu* was an infraction, disregarding the *mgosyo* of a different *kamu* was both accepted and expected if the situations they were meant to address were no longer relevant or the practices were no longer effective. Because there was no relationship between

Figure 4.4. Asha, surrounded by several generations of her grandchildren and "feces grandchildren." Photo by the author.

the two generations, there was no breach of respect and authority, and so no offense.

Thus where requirements for and threats to wellness shifted over time, social and moral values would contextually adapt. With all of the changes wrought by colonialism, war, democracy, and globalization, and with the spreading grip of neoliberal capitalism that had taken hold between the time of a previous *kamu* and the present, some would agree with Metangula's great-great-grandparents that what was left in the opening decades of the twenty-first century was little more than *mavi* (feces): something completely transformed and nauseating. But the remnants of generational change can also be the precise fertilizer that enables the next era to flourish and to negotiate humanity in their own, new world. Elsewhere in Africa authors note, for example, the extension of *mgosyo*-like complexes to address epidemics in malnutrition (Flax 2015) and sexually transmitted diseases (Mogensen 1997; Peters, Walker, and Kambewa 2008; van den Borne 2005; Wolf 2001). In Metangula, as with many peri-urban towns in Africa, times were changing amid new distributions of wealth, markers of morality, and possibilities for compassionate care. Rather than passively following the traditions of the past, it was up to a new *kamu* to determine if and how *mgosyo* would be reconfigured to address emergent pursuits of and threats to well-being in the twenty-first century. While a response to modernity and structured by modernity, shifts in the relevance of *mgosyo* thus did not seem to be about modernity itself. They were, instead, about continued efforts to nourish life amid the uncertain conditions that defined humanity.

Conclusion

Death, it is sometimes said, is the only certainty in life. This chapter opened with the loss of a baby boy and his mother's profound despondency. While the prevalence of infant mortality in places like Metangula means that a child's dying is in no way extraordinary, such matters are still deeply impactful for individual lives. When I met up with Diana in 2017, she showed me photos of the two children she had birthed since I left in 2011. The girl and boy, then two and five years old, were living in Nampula with their father. Diana explained that she bought airtime for her cell phone when she could afford it and would call them to ensure they did not forget her. While I spoke with Filomena, Diana fetched her phone from a neighbor's house, where it had been charging. She came back, and dialed the number. "*Alô! Alô?*" (hello, hello), she shouted into the phone; it was on speaker. She spoke in Portuguese because the children had grown up without learning Chinyanja. The connection crackled, and the children's grandmother's voice could be faintly heard encouraging them to speak. But the airtime quickly expended, a series of beeps informing us that the line had been cut. Diana looked chagrined as she switched off the phone to preserve the charge for future calls. She missed her children, she said, and she thought of them often—just as she still thought of the baby that she had lost. "That," she said, "is what hurts the most, in my heart." She excused herself then and went into the house.

Life is full of uncertainties. But this assurance does not make them any easier to cope with. Managing misfortune, envisioning possibility amid contingency, and navigating the life course have long been entwined with mutuality in Africa (Cooper and Pratten 2015). It is not that creative collaborations and deepened investments in social relations alleviate uncertainties; new vulnerabilities also arise when your well-being is dependent on the actions of others, particularly where sociality underlies all aspects of life, inclusive of physical growth, development, and decline (Bledsoe 2002). Rather, engaging in mutuality provides agency and possibilities for action. "Life," Jackson writes of the Kuranko in Sierra Leone, but with words that have broad resonance, "is not a problem to be solved, but a journey embarked upon." And that life "must always be lived within limits." The distinction, Jackson suggests, between the past and the present is not that people struggle; it is the kinds of limits that people struggle against (Jackson 2011, 168). In coping, there is nothing new. And through engagement and mutuality, now as in the past, persons continue to deepen and nourish their humanity.

This chapter has considered *mgosyo* as a set of everyday rituals through which interdependencies were nourished through obligations, and individual belonging to a particular place deepened and revitalized. By calling someone to pour salt into the *ndiwo* or by eating alone in the wake of a lost infant, individuals crafted their place in the world, and in society. The obligation to do so was imparted upon humanity at the dawn of their separation from divinity, a moment marked by the invention of fire and the origin of sexuality. Both heat and sex were, as such, profoundly ambivalent: full of creative potentiality toward both generative and destructive ends. This was, it is important to recall, also the condition of humanity itself, as discussed in chapter 3. In the present chapter, salt also showed itself to have potential for both enhancing and destroying life. In this way, and also in its manufacture through burnt plant material (as *matcheza*), and its effectivity through pouring, it was very much like *dawa*. I have suggested that these similarities help us to understand the place of salt within *mgosyo*, but they also enhance analysis of the complex as a form of communication with the spirit realm.

The relationship between the living and the dead, though still conceived to be important in Metangula, was less clearly able to deal with the conditions of the twenty-first century than it was with the contingencies of the past. Specifically, the challenges posed by late capitalism were difficult to manipulate and overcome through supplication, ritual, and mutuality. But *mgosyo* was also not a static set of rituals; it was a dynamic site for navigating the fulfilment of social roles and the adoption of values commensurate with becoming human persons. Its contours had changed before, and they very well could again. Its future, then, will depend on how things like "peace" and "nourishment," and thus what is constitutive of humanity, come to be defined and evaluated as the twenty-first century rolls on. In the next chapter I provide one glimpse into the intersection of globalization and cultural knowledge of wellness as tied up with interdependence and shared substance, leaving the kitchen to focus on the hospital as site of biomedical nutrition intervention efforts.

Notes

1. The phrase *mayo ine* is used to express both physical and emotional pain. When I asked for a translation, people told me that it meant "mother [take] me" (*mayo* sounding very much like *mayi*, "mother," when spoken aloud). But I could not pin down a precise English translation.
2. I have previously written about this affliction using the name *ntaka* (Huhn 2012; 2017). To align my spelling in the present volume with Chichewa orthography, I have reflected the aspirated "t" in the spelling *nthaka*.
3. On the symbolism of doorways, see Brad Weiss (1996) and Malcolm Ruel (1997).
4. Ceremonies resembling *kumphika mwana* are described as *kuthenga mwana* or *kutuluka mwana* in Malawi. See publications such as J. W. M. van Breugel (2001), Matthew Schoffeleers (1968), and Alister Munthali (2002a) for the comparative case.
5. It is of note for clarity, due to anatomical proximity to the gallbladder, that the liver has been commented on, directly or in passing, as related to emotion and reason for a variety of African populations. Examples include David Parkin (1985), who discusses the liver (and also the heart, kidney, and eye) among the Girama; René Devisch (1990, 129), who writes of the liver as containing perturbed or antisocial feelings among the Yaka; and Edward Kanyike (2004, 54), who pinpoints the liver as a seat of morality among the Chewa. Raul Ruiz de Asúa Altuna suggests a widespread African understanding of life as concentrated in blood and the "most powerful" organs, inclusive of the heart, genitals, and liver (Altuna 2006, 59). But my acquaintances in Metangula were very clear with me that, in discussing the *ndulu*, they were referring to the gallbladder alone.
6. I have previously written about *matcheza* as *mancheza* (Huhn 2012; 2017). I have made the change here to align my spelling in the present volume with Chichewa orthography. The word *matcheza* is likely derived from the verb *kutcheza*, meaning "to strain," as in the action through which the substance is produced by pouring hot water over ash.
7. For a detailed analysis of the historical usage of potashes among the Chewa, where they are more frequently called *vidulo*, see the work of Jessie Williamson (1956). Note that *mdulo* is the name of a *mgosyo*-like everyday ritual-illness complex among the Chewa and that contravening the complex is sometimes spoken of as "cutting" (*kudula*) the individual, who becomes ill as a result.
8. Signe Arnfred (2007) makes a similar point elsewhere in northern Mozambique when she suggests that the pouring of finely ground millet flour was used as a "pencil" for communications with the ancestors.
9. Other researchers have alternatively posited that the power of salt among Maravi populations has to do with tripartite color symbolism (Schoffeleers 1968, 207–8; van Breugel 2001, 50; Welling 1999)—red, white, and black in symbolic relationship, just as articu-

lated by Victor Turner (1967) in his classic assessment of African ritual. Lack of data from Metangula to explicitly point to color underlying the meaning of *mgosyo* makes it difficult for me to find satisfaction with this line of analysis, though it is possible that such symbolism was so esoteric as to be unremarkable.

CHAPTER 5

Weight, Nutrition, and Body Size

Elisa came into the Salimo compound through the side gate, wrapped in a red and purple capulana *cloth. She exchanged a few words with Monica and said hello to me, then quickly excused herself, apologizing for the haste. She had been bathing in the lake, in preparation for taking two-year-old Andrea to the hospital, she explained. "Is she sick?" I asked as Elisa headed for the bamboo door of her two-room home. "She is always sick," Elisa replied. "Since she was born, Andrea has had an illness in her body." With that, Elisa disappeared into the house to get dressed.*

Andrea meanwhile sat quietly, as she usually did. Someone had placed a small plastic plate of boiled potatoes in her lap. She lightly grasped a metal spoon but did not eat with it, resting her hand instead on the ground where she sat. The girl was slight of body, which was common among children in Metangula, but she was also unusually quiet. The anomaly of Andrea's placidness was amplified by the personality of her age-mate Alia, Monica's daughter, who was boisterous, adventurous, and independent. Andrea's gaze shifted to Elisa when she emerged from the house, dressed in her best clothes. She moved to get up and join her mother on the veranda, upsetting her plate of potatoes and spilling its contents into the dirt. "She has been constantly sick, which has made her weak," Monica offered to explain Andrea's feebleness and her disinterest in eating. "Elisa even stopped breastfeeding her early, fearing that her milk was what was causing the problem or making it worse." I turned to Elisa, who was tying a cloth around her hair. She nodded to confirm the reporting of her actions. I asked Elisa when she stopped breastfeeding Andrea. She responded very specifically: one year and seven months. "What did they say at the hospital?" I asked. "Two years," Elisa responded, repeating the length of time that the doctor, nurses, and health posters implored women to breastfeed. I clarified my question as an inquiry into Andrea's health. "They did not give her any medicine," Elisa replied. "I do not know why."

Elisa picked up Andrea by her armpit and swung the child around and onto her back. Elisa stood bent at the waist, with Andrea balanced motionless atop, and wrapped her into a capulana *sling. Monica explained that yesterday the girl turned two, and Elisa took her to be weighed at the hospital as part of a monthly routine of* child wellness checkups. Because Andrea had a low weight, they sent Elisa for a consultation with the nurse, who sent her to the doctor, who asked that Andrea be taken for análise [analysis], a Portuguese-language gloss for blood tests. Today Elisa was going back for the results and to receive counseling. "They will tell her to mix oil and peanuts and usipa fish into the child's food," Monica said. I asked why, if they already knew that this would help Andrea to get better, they did not already do it. "We do not have the means," she said. "But we could mix in beans when we have them." I chose not to bring up the fact that they also usually had oil, peanuts, and usipa fish in the compound. I would later come to recognize that in the eyes of Monica and Elisa, and many other people in Metangula, it did not matter what Andrea ate. So long as she was ill, Andrea would not be able to garner vitamina from eating.

I asked Elisa if I could tag along for the consultation and she consented, and so we arrived together at the health center around 7:30 in the morning. We positioned ourselves on the cold, concrete u-shaped bench and waited along with several dozen others for the one doctor servicing all of Lago District, an area of about 2,500 square miles. Once the service desk opened at 8:00 a.m., patients were invited one by one into the office; the rest of us slid down the bench a spot to the right to maintain the order in which we had arrived. While waiting, I glanced through Andrea's health card and saw that she had been pretty regularly weighed for the past two years—once each month, as the health center recommended. But Andrea had not gained weight for the past five months, corresponding with Elisa's reported cessation of breastfeeding the girl. The previous day's visit, Andrea's second birthday, had been the first time the child had slipped under the "normal" weight-for-age curve. This is what had triggered the health center's interventions.

When it was finally Andrea's turn, we entered the office and the doctor looked through the results of two blood tests, one of which was for HIV. Providing no explanation of what the tests had measured or what exactly they had revealed, she declared Andrea to be disease-free. The doctor then lectured Elisa in Portuguese, "The problem here is one of nutrition. Either the child is not eating, or you are not providing her with food." She proceeded to write out two prescriptions for Andrea and told Elisa to "take them to 'the fat one' [a gordinha]," pointing to the office of the health center's nutritional counselor, Beatriz. "Listen carefully to everything she has to say," the doctor ordered, and then she dismissed us. We moved to do as instructed and waited outside the nutritionist's office while Beatriz came and went, attending to various business. In the lull, I asked Elisa for her take on things. "The doctor just said Andrea was lacking vitamina and so she has no strength," she said. "This is why they provided her with the red pills." By "red pills" Elisa was referencing the prescription in her hand for iron tablets. While she could not read the paper, she knew from the experiences of others with underweight children what to expect. "And now," she added, echoing what had been said at home, "I will be told to mix things into Andrea's food—things with vitamina like oil, peanuts, and Sobo,"[1] She looked at me directly and spoke with a tone of exacerbation. "I know these things," she emphasized, "but conditions prevent me *from following the advice." I took her words, at the time, as an expression of lacking financial means to provide Andrea with a nutritious diet. Later I would reassess them as a reflection of broader constraints.*

When Beatriz finally invited us into her office, she ordered for Andrea to be measured so that her present weight for height could be calculated and the resultant number found on a chart indicating malnutrition level. Andrea's measurements did not fall into the chronic portion of the standardized curve. Because of this, Beatriz explained, Andrea would not need to be kept at the hospital and "fed milk." In the place of forced supplemental feeding, Beatriz gave Elisa a week's supply of Plumpy'Nut, a high-protein peanut paste with five hundred calories per three-ounce serving, and she instructed Elisa to give Andrea one package per day, mixing it with porridge if rejected plain. Elisa was also to bring the girl back in two weeks to have her weighed again. We were dismissed, went to fill the prescription for the red pills, and then trudged down the hill to start making lunch, as it was already close to noon.

Over the next few days, Andrea showed little interest in consuming the Plumpy'Nut, alone or mixed with porridge. This prompted Elisa to disregard the instruction she had received at the hospital, and she allowed Monica's daughter Alia to eat the peanut paste instead. While appreciating the vitamina *(or perhaps vitamin?) content in the nutritional supplement, Elisa did not conceive of the food as a medicine that would cure Andrea of the illness she was so obviously suffering, as evidenced by her weight. The supplement could not increase Andrea's vitamina without the mother's first taking measures to cure the underlying cause of blood loss. Andrea was, as such, unfailingly made to swallow the iron pills she had been prescribed. Her mother explained to me that, unlike the peanut paste, the medicine had curative powers. Food, on its own, would accomplish nothing to alleviate sickness.*

Malnutrition is a problem on the African subcontinent, where undernutrition (not getting enough to eat) affects approximately 20 percent of the population. This number has held steady for several decades despite international, national, and local intervention efforts (FAO, IFAD, UNICEF, WFP, and WHO 2018). While undernutrition leads to death only in extreme cases (it is rare for a person to die directly from starvation), the condition increases susceptibility to infectious and potentially deadly diseases, like polio, tuberculosis, and malaria, and can impinge upon cognitive development. Calorie deficiency, along with specific nutrient insufficiencies such as with protein and micronutrient intake (e.g., iron, iodine), can thus have a dramatic effect on health and the capacity of nations to improve the human condition of their citizenry. In Mozambique, statistics suggest that malnutrition impacts approximately 30 percent of the population and that child stunting is also high (FAO, IFAD, UNICEF, WFP, and WHO 2018, 117, 151). Recent events have also proved Mozambique to be particularly prone to food insecurity brought on by climate change, inclusive of drought conditions and cyclones of increased intensity and frequency. Raw data on malnutrition in

Metangula, obtained directly from the local health center, were available only for children aged five and under. While these data are unofficial, they suggest rampant undernutrition. For example, while 82 percent of children between zero and sixty months were in the normal range of weight-for-height in 2010, almost half of the children (46.4 percent) measured low in height-for-age, a proxy for long-term inadequate nutrition.

Childhood undernutrition, as such, can be considered prevalent in Metangula at the time of research. But overnutrition was also evident; 2 percent of children were overweight for their age in 2010, and 8 percent were overweight for their height. While the health center did not have a comparable data set for adults, I personally collected the weight and height of 325 of the 351 individuals aged fifteen and over in my dietary survey. This allowed me to calculate their BMI (body mass index), a common (if less than ideal) measure of dietary adequacy. Of these participants, 7 percent were clinically underweight (BMI less than or equal to 18.5), and 13 percent were overweight (BMI greater than 25 but less than 30). Four individuals were clinically obese (BMI greater than or equal to 30). This left 79 percent of the adult sample population falling in the normal weight-for-height range. These numbers are in line with provincial statistics for childbearing women (De Matteis 2006, 98), the only such comparable data I was able to find for populations in Niassa.

The simultaneous presence of undernutrition and overnutrition in countries undergoing rapid economic transition falls into expected patterns defined by Barry M. Popkin as the "nutrition transition." Undernutrition as a sign of lingering poverty and overnutrition as an indicator of emergent wealth coexist in much of the developing world. The situation has raised alarms for creating a "double burden" of disease—both those associated with undernutrition, as outlined above, and those that come about through overnutrition, like increased risk of developing type 2 diabetes, cardiovascular disease, hypertension, stroke, and certain cancers, among other health risks. Consuming significantly more calories than are expended or a diet high in refined carbohydrates, fats, and sugars can also alter enzyme levels, cause tissue abnormalities, and lead to organ malfunction (Caballero and Popkin 2002; Popkin 1998; Popkin, Adair, and Ng 2012). Rates of overweight and obesity are increasing in Africa, Latin America, and other areas of the global south at rapid rates (Popkin 2015). In several cases, countries in the "developing world" have even surpassed their counterparts in the global north. For example, data from the World Health Organization estimates that 27.8 percent of the population of Great Britain was obese in 2016, while in South Africa it was 28.3 percent. That same year, approximately 10.6 percent of Africans aged eighteen and older were clinically obese, and 31 percent overweight.[2]

The rise of obesity in Africa and other developing areas of the world has been linked to a combination of increased empty calories (refined carbohydrates, added sweeteners, edible oils, and animal-source foods), growth of the food service sector, decreased physical activity (related to changes in technology), urbanization, and mass media access, among other related factors. This rationale relies on familiar ideas: the number and type of calories we eat and the amount of physical activity we engage in impact both the size of our bodies (largeness) and our physical weight (heaviness). Growing larger then makes us susceptible to negative health consequences. But scholars are increasingly noting that the association of larger bodies with poor health may be overblown (Burgard 2009; Gaesser 2002), a case of biomedicine naturalizing culturally and historically couched values like self-control and regimentation as essential for morality and productivity, and medicalizing a natural diversity of human body shapes and sizes. In other words, scientists trained in the biomedical tradition may be primed to look for and to find correlations between high weight and poor health because these connections culturally make sense—largeness, heaviness, and weight-gain connote individual failure (laziness, gluttony, and broader inabilities in self-control), while weight stability or loss, along with a slimmer figure and low weight, indicate self-mastery, success, and overall health (Farrell 2011; Saguy and Almeling 2008). Fat Studies scholar Deborah Lupton (2018) suggests this positioning reflects cultural knowledge stemming from Judeo-Christian ethics that position the body as God's temple, and thus fat and unhealthy bodies as signs of moral corruptness, grafted onto nineteenth-century notions of body-as-machine that established the baseline for the science of diet and nutrition.

As the biomedical positioning of fat as unhealthy spreads and large bodies are increasingly stigmatized around the world (Brewis et al. 2011), the case of Metangula presents a different way of understanding the body in relation to weight, size, diet, and wellness. I have hinted at these distinctions in the vignette above, where I recounted my experiences participating in taking two-year-old Andrea for nutritional counseling. I elaborate this physiology below, explicating the differences between a biomedical approach yoking diet, weight, body size, and health in a particular fashion (eat more food, gain more weight, grow larger, and decrease in health) on the one hand and their fuzzier connections in Metangula on the other. I begin with a focus on weight as it was perceived in Metangula to be an indicator, rather than an instigator, of health. Weight also generally linked to health in a direction opposite to biomedical formulation (so, larger bodies correlating with better health). Weight loss thus indicated poor health, which could be remedied only through medicines, not diet. I use nutritional programming offered at the health center and through the local Catholic church as a focal point for discussion and to make clear how such interventions can so easily flounder. Next, I address local perceptions of body size as a range that is unique to each individual, making absolute measures like "fat" and "thin" inadequate for evaluation. Finally, I come back to sexual *vitamina*, introduced in chapter 4, and discuss the perceived impact of sexual activity on body size and fetal development, and so (potentially) on sexual health. The chapter thus presents a model for making sense of what we eat in relation to who we are that is distinct from biomedical understandings and documents how foodways can interface in unexpected and deeply embodied ways with public health.

Weighing In

Most individuals in Metangula, at the time of research, had absolutely no idea how much they weighed. In fact, given that the only scale in town capable of weighing more than several pounds of meat was located at the health center, and it was only children who were regularly weighed there, inability to conjure a guess as to one's weight could be said of practically every adult. Weight was something of an abstract concept without a scale, and knowledge of one's weight had no history of practical use in Metangula. But it was with much interest that my dietary survey participants stepped onto the scale when I asked them to—I was concerned with calculating their BMI to look for correlations between diet and wealth (Popkin's work on the developing world suggested these would tie together). Dietary survey participants, and the many others who stopped me on the street asking for me to weigh them, reacted to the opportunity with such enthusiasm that I was taken aback. Common responses to stepping on the scale included smiles, cheers, and laughter. Any weight was met favorably, with some individuals surprised to learn that they weighed anything at all—they literally expected to be weightless. It was not just in Metangula that I observed this enthusiasm at weighing and at having a weight. At a health fair that I attended in Lichinga (the capital of Niassa Province), I saw the same phenomenon play out—people waited in line for hours to have their turn to step onto a scale, receiving a scrap of paper with their weight written out as if it was a cherished gift. I was dumbfounded.

Beyond the novelty of being weighed, I came to understand the enthusiasm with which many individuals approached stepping onto a scale in Metangula (and perhaps further afield) as the product of a link between weight and wellness. Having weight, and especially a high weight and increased weight, in other words, indicated health. This is supported through consideration of the Chinyanja/Chichewa verb *kulemera*, which means "to be heavy" (as in "a heavy person," *wolemera*) and "to have weight" (as in *lilemera tres kilos*, "it weighs three kilograms"), but also "to be rich" (as in "a wealthy person," also *wolemera*) or "valuable." In a place where wealth has long been evaluated in terms of health, fertility, tranquility, and mutuality, rather than material possessions, a person whose life was enmeshed with those of others was both "rich" and "weighty." This is how the chief of a village, upon whom continued positive relations with the spirit realm depended (Schoffeleers 1968; van Breugel 2001), could always be described as *wolemera*, both rich and heavy, despite possible abject poverty or emaciation.

A person was well where they were heavy, and heavy where they were well. And because wellness was not a product of what a person ate, but rather the garnering of *vitamina*, which fluctuated in response to experience and context and manifested in quantity and quality of blood (see chapter 1), a person's weight was a proxy for their life circumstance more than it was for their diet. It was, as such, that those who stepped onto my scale sometimes treated the device as if it were measuring subjective, internal states or general health. One woman in the dietary survey, for example, shouted joyously when her weight in kilograms came up in the mid-fifties (around one hundred and twenty pounds). "Then I do not have AIDS!?" she declared, figuring that she could not weigh so much if she carried the HIV virus. I corrected her logic to the best of my ability, but she was far from convinced. At another house, a survey participant called me over and requested to step on the scale again, having done so two days previous. She explained that she wanted to see if she had lost weight while sick with a cold in the interim. When the scale suggested that she had gained half a kilogram (one pound) since her last weighing, she concluded that this must have meant she was better, such that her efforts to gain back lost *vitamina* (she had drunk beer that morning) had been successful.

It is important to recognize that there is a distinction here with biomedical formulations. In biomedicine, weight (as a measure of gravitational pull) is the result of diet and exercise and an inverse determinant of health (more weight meaning less health, beyond a base minimum). In Metangula, weight related to health in the opposite direction, such that more weight meant greater health (generally; exceptions will be discussed below). Also, weight was only an indicator of health, rather than its determinant—something like a symptom rather than a cause. And the relationship between weight and food had more to do with the context of eating (whether an individual was feeling well and was eating satisfying and pleasurable meals in contexts that did not induce pain) than the nutritional content of an individual's diet. Wellness enabled the garnering of *vitamina*, which impacted the quantity and character of an individual's blood and increased their weight. Illness, which reduced quality and quantity of blood, likewise manifested in lost weight, which could not be regained until the underlying siphon of wellness was eliminated.

This brings us back to the case of two-year-old Andrea, with which we began the present chapter. After she returned with her mother from nutritional counseling at the hospital, Andrea was unfailingly made to swallow the iron pills she had been prescribed. This was because her mother saw them as potentially curative for a sickness that was causing her daughter to lose weight. Without ridding Andrea of the illness, the child would not be able to gain weight. This was regardless of her diet, because her body could not garner *vitamina* where it was not well. As such, while Elisa offered Andrea the Plumpy'Nut as she was instructed to do at the hospital, when her child rejected the dietary supplement it was not cause for worry. Feeding Andrea Plumpy'Nut while she was still ill was out of order, because it could not begin to rebuild her blood stores through *vitamina* until she was already well. The proper response to weight loss was medicine, not food. Within Metangula, in fact, the most common response to my asking permission to weigh survey participants, besides the elation described above, was something to the effect of "And if you see that I have low weight, then you will give me medicine?"

The answer was no, but the logic is understandable. This was, after all, what often happened at the local health center. Nurses encouraged mothers to bring their young children to the hospital once per month in order to evaluate the progress of their growth—just as Elisa had brought Andrea, sparking the nutritional intervention. Assistants to Beatriz plotted weight and height in each child's medical record so that the mother could evaluate her child's growth in relation to median percentiles. But these standardized curves were of little interest to most mothers. When I asked women why they had come to the baby weighing station, they most often responded, "To know if my child gained weight" or "To know if my child is healthy." The responses are virtually interchangeable because a child gained weight when well and in good health, and lost weight when ill. Where a child lost weight from one visit to the next, the medical technician asked the mother why. The consistent response in my observations was "The child has been sick." While illness does in biomedical terms often cause weight reduction through appetite suppression and loss of fluids through vomiting and diarrhea, these women seemed to be answering what seemed to them an impersonal (and perhaps patronizing) factual inquiry: the cause of weight loss was ill-being. It was thus to know a child's weight, and so their health status, and to receive medication to address illness in the case of weight loss revealed by the scale that these women came to the health center.

That children brought for general medical consultations were also required to be weighed before being seen by a nurse, doctor, or other medical technician unintentionally perpetuated the assumption that weight was a direct barometer of health that guided professional medical care. After a child was weighed at their monthly screening, hospital staff sometimes also provided them a liquid dose of vitamin A or a mebendazole (anti-worm) tablet. These medicines were supposed to be administered at six-month intervals as a preventative health measure, but the sporadic attendance of many mothers at the baby weighing station and their particular attendance when a child was ill meant that technicians often provided medicine when a child had lost weight. When I asked mothers for their understanding of why they were provided these medications, most responded that the weighing process had shown her child to be ill (*kudwala*), or lacking blood (generally glossed with the term "anemia"). As I experienced when weighing people myself, and in the case of Andrea, expectation had developed that lost or low weight would be met with the provision of medicine to treat the underlying illness. Once recovered, an individual would be able to shore up blood supplies per usual through standard routes of pleasurable and satisfying alimentation, successes at which could be measurable through weight gain.

Nutritional Education

All of this meant that public health campaigns to improve general wellness through nutritional interventions were somewhat fraught, with messages promoting dietary change as a route to increased weight and improved health often received in unintended ways. By way of example I return to the work of Beatriz, the nutritional counselor who met with Elisa about Andrea's low weight. Beatriz's work to improve nutrition in the Lago District was not restricted to weighing babies and providing peanut paste and iron tablets for malnourished children. Her agenda also included cooking demonstrations to inform the masses about the benefits of a balanced diet for general health, improving the health of malnourished children, and caring for the ill. Specifically, she set her sights on teaching people how to cook enriched porridges and soups—common entry points for nutritional education, touted by seemingly every major funder, NGO, and individual do-gooder involved in public health in the region. While Beatriz planned many soup and porridge demonstrations during my time in Metangula, I only saw one event actually come to fruition—other times they were canceled for lack of funds, personnel, or transportation. Cooking at the one event that did transpire was done by Beatriz herself, along with three volunteers from the NGO Estamos and me.

"Porridge and soup are especially good for persons who are feeling sick," Rosa, one of the volunteers, told me that morning as we prepared the ingredients. "Often such individuals lack an appetite." You could also give sick persons juice or Sobo, she continued, but soup or porridge are better, "because you can add a lot of things to them." The porridge (*phala*) we cooked that day had oil, for instance (one could instead add peanuts, Beatriz later clarified), green leafy vegetables (ours were mustard greens), and sugar added to the flour and water base. You could also add banana, Rosa interjected, but she had forgotten to buy them in the market that morning. Beatriz, originally from Nampula, called the concoction *phala la magulu*, very proud of herself for the three Chinyanja words she strung together in a row. The word *magulu* means "groups," making the label *phala la magulu* something akin to "multi-ingredient porridge." This was different from the standard porridge people cooked, into which they added nothing other than salt or sugar to the water and flour base. The *magulu* for Beatriz were food groups like lipids, carbohydrates, proteins, vegetables, and fruits, along with their associated micronutrients. Their combination, according to biomedical models, would promote balanced nutrition and therefore health, and in the case of malnourished children and the infirm it would enable weight gain.

At 10:00 a.m., after two hours of preparation, the porridge and a bean soup (into which we had added mustard greens, rice, and oil) were ready to be served. Beatriz called over the women who had gathered at the baby weighing station since before 8:00 a.m. Beatriz spoke in Portuguese and Rosa translated into Chinyanja, the short phrasings and slowed pace of their delivery allowing me to record Beatriz's introduction to the event almost in full. "We are not here to play around, but to talk about health," she began, followed by a message seemingly aimed directly at what she perceived to be misconceptions about the connections between weight and illness. "At the hospital we weigh children to know if they are growing," she explained. "If their weight does not increase, or if it deceases, this is not normal. It means that something is wrong. *Not necessarily because they are sick*, but because they are lacking something in their body." The emphasis is original. She continued with the topic at hand and a bid to reduce the number of mothers who arrived at the hospital with malnourished children seeking medicinal interventions. "Today we want to teach you that if you cook a specific porridge, your child will grow. There is no need to come to the hospital to receive vitamins—all you need to do is mix things in! You have these ingredients in your home—just mix them together and they can help, like medicines, to get rid of diseases and to increase weight."

Figure 5.1. Women attend a nutrition-education seminar at the health center. Photo by the author.

Beatriz then switched gears to speak specifically about soup. "Anyone can arrange a cup of rice to enable them to make bean soup. The greens in the soup help combat diseases. The beans also have their work. The beans must be pounded and then pressed through a sieve to make them into soup porridge. When this is complete, add a small amount of rice and, if you have them, add tomato and onion, and then a small amount of greens. This is to be done at the very end, or they will lose their vitamins." The group of women listened attentively. Beatriz, via Rosa, continued, "The resultant soup has all the vitamins a child needs. *Every ingredient* has work in the body. If a child is missing *one thing*, they do not have vitamins in their body." Beatriz then quizzed the audience, asking how many "food groups" were present in the soup. The women responded in unison, "Four." Beatriz commended them, then listed the four ingredients—beans, greens, rice, and oil. She suggested that the soup "helps with any illness," because "with vitamins in the body we cannot get ill." While I concentrated on recording Beatriz's words for the most part, I did note that Rosa translated this last directive into Chinyanja by shifting the stated role of vitamins as protective or preventative to one more akin to *vitamina* as a determinant of health: "Some people think that we eat only to get full, but everything we eat has a job in the body, and those foods with *vitamina* make us healthy." The volunteers then distributed the soup in plastic cups and bowls for each audience member to try herself and to feed her child or children.

Those consuming the soup did so in virtual silence, respectful but also very clearly uninterested in prolonging the event. Cups collected, some of those in the audience began to gather their belongings and to leave, assuming the lecture was over and that Beatriz might finally arrive at her morning post and weigh their babies. But instead, Beatriz implored them to stay and to hear about porridge, which she pointed out also had four "groups"—flour, peanuts, greens, and sugar. When it seemed many of the women were no longer paying attention, she scolded them, saying that they were "not just here to eat, but to learn how to make the porridge at home." Like the soup, the health-provisioning properties of the porridge were touted, here in terms of combatting anemia: "Some are lacking blood, but if you make this porridge at home you will no longer lack blood. Just add one spoonful of sugar, one spoonful of peanuts, and some greens. *You do not need* any oil. This food is like milk and will make your bones grow well, and cause babies to get fat. Without vitamins, a baby cannot get fat." With this, Beatriz and her helpers distributed the porridge (which the volunteers had actually prepared with oil instead of peanuts, unbeknownst to Beatriz) for the women and their children's tasting. As they finished, the women washed their hands and went to wait at the baby weighing station. It now being 10:30 a.m., there was quite a backlog.

Beatriz's messages, along with the porridge and soup, were easily digested by these women, corralled to serve as her audience. I could not help but note, however, that the same language used by Beatriz to tout the benefits of bean soup and enriched porridge—couched in terms of variety, appetite, blood, vitamins, health, and weight—clustered in both biomedical and local cultural knowledges of physiology and nutrition. For Beatriz, eating enriched porridge and bean soup ensured the micronutrients that supported good health. Though the combination of ingredients was somewhat novel, the women accepted her rationale that representing multiple "groups" in a single meal increased the foods' nutritional value. This was not because the ingredients represented fats, proteins, fruits, vegetables, and carbohydrates, as Beatriz understood it. Porridge and bean soup had *vitamina*, participants at the cooking demonstration verbally rationalized when I asked for their understanding, because by including so many groups (*magulu*) or kinds (*mitundu*) of foods, the dishes would be appetizing to a wider range of people—if a person was not fond of beans, maybe they would be partial to rice, onions, tomatoes, peanuts, or greens. With appetite and variety a key to blood-based vitality (see chapter 1), foods with diverse ingredients were thus more likely to have *vitamina*. It was such that Beatriz's health programming seemed to support and further, rather than to reconfigure or upend, local foodways. An overt clash in these interpretations did not emerge, for nobody perceived one to be present; the information made sense to Beatriz and to the women in the audience, if for very different reasons. Beatriz's message, then, was lost in translation—not because Rosa's services were faulty, but because the distinct physiologies shared the same terminology. To an unsuspecting health worker, local talk about *vitamina* might even give the impression that their audience wholly accepted biomedical messaging.

While simplistic, and perhaps not effective in influencing dietary change, Beatriz's cooking demonstrations were far from patronizing, and they had more local relevance than a directly expository approach. A series of nutrition classes held in 2005 in Chuanga (just north of Metangula) by an American missionary with the Catholic church, for example, focused on technical explanations of dietary concepts, like the principle of dividing foods by their nutritional properties. His makeshift translator, the only woman in attendance who had linguistic capacities in both Portuguese and Chinyanja, struggled (in my observations) to explain the content of the missionary's presentation to the others. Outright confusion erupted at one point when she translated his suggestion that they feed their children more "rats' tails" (a mistranslation of the Portuguese *carboidratos*, "carbohydrates," heard by the translator as *caudas de ratos*). The mistake was as much linguistic as cultural. Despite the accuracy in the missionary's statement that undernutrition is driven in Africa largely by inadequate caloric intake, hence the nutritional benefit of eating more carbohydrates, categorizing foods based on their chemical composition and molecular structure did not have the same local resonance as relating them to energy, strength, health, blood, weight, vitamins, variety, and appetite.

Beatriz's approach also seemed more culturally sensitive than a project run by the Catholic church in 2009, this time employing a team of Brazilian nuns to cook enriched porridge and bean soup across the Lago District under the impression that it was only because people were unaware of how to make these foods that they were not the diet of choice. While I did not witness this project firsthand like I had the American missionary's, when I ran into one of the nuns and we got to talking about my research, she excitedly asked me to come to her home to learn more about her own work. When I arrived the next afternoon, Sister Lucha invited me into the living room of the home she had been sharing with the other nuns for the last eight years. Two of her fellow sisters sat on the couch watching the news on a channel broadcast from Brazil. The fourth, a gaunt and elder woman, was wandering at shuffled pace around the property, per usual. Lucha asked the other two nuns to move over and invited me to sit down, then quickly popped into the VCR a recording of the final cooking demonstration that the team undertook, this one at the village of Liziunga.

The video opened with several women pounding bananas, then quickly cut to two others cooking bean soup. Two women stood around a giant pot, singing songs and stirring the contents. Lucha explained that in each village they selected ten women to train in bean soup and enriched porridge making. There were many shots of a crowd looking on longingly, and the nuns patting children on their heads. The ingredients for the soup and porridge were shown laid out in bowls on a *capulana*-covered table. The video then cut to what Lucha explained was the "theatrical component." The actors spoke Chiyaawo, which I do not, so I did not catch the dialogue. Lucha explained that the play was meant to demonstrate the importance of each child eating from their own plate. In the video, three of the actors sat down to share one plate of food, and a fourth could not find a spot that would grant him access to the dish. He complained and began fighting with the other three. The crowd appeared to be paying attention, but I cannot imagine their interpretation—at least in my experience, I have never seen something remotely close to a scene like this unfold at mealtime, regardless of how many plates or people there were. When the play was complete, the next shot was of the cooks and the nuns handing out soup to children in the audience. Some ran home to get a bowl or cup when the church ran out. Most of the children ate with their fingers. A shot of mothers feeding their young babies prompted Lucha to explain to me that she told these mothers that doing as such was wrong, as the babies were too young for solid foods. Indeed, the next shots were of these same women wiping the soup from their babies' mouths. Footage of children eating continued for another ten minutes.

When the video concluded, Lucha detailed the extent of the nuns' efforts: trainings, cooking demonstrations, and theatrical performances in each of the villages in Lago that had, at the time, a health post (or, in Metangula, a health center). I asked the women what they thought had been the result of this massive,

Figure 5.2. A group of men share a meal, each taking from a common dish. Photo by the author.

yearlong effort. Lucha, who seemed to be most comfortable in the role of spokeswoman for the group, answered without hesitation that people in Lago were no doubt now regularly cooking enriched porridge and bean soup. Unfortunately, she offered, she lacked funds to formally evaluate the program's effectiveness. In my own yearlong dietary survey in Metangula—one of the nuns' training and cooking demonstration sites, and also where Beatriz delivered lessons in preparing the same foods—there were no reported instances of the consumption of bean soup in the year for which data were collected and only a handful of recordings (nineteen) of porridge enriched with peanuts. This represents less than 1 percent of porridge meals recorded. In no instance were the nuns' recommended ground fish, greens, or bananas added in.

Beatriz, the health center nutritionist, seemed more realistic about the sometimes futile nature of her nutrition education activism. "I tell them every time, 'Eat these foods. They are the ones that are healthy.' I say the same thing each time. But few people ever incorporate these foods into their regular diet," she told me one afternoon a few weeks after Andrea's consultation. "The problem is not ignorance." In my discussions about *vitamina* in Metangula, people indeed clearly recognized that bean soup and enriched porridge were good for the sick, as their liquidity made them easy to digest and their diversity in ingredients made them palatable. And it was important that everyone, even those who were sick, ate something. They did not, however, feel that they had the means to always feed these foods to those who were infirm, and they saw no reason to make these foods standard fare for the healthy, who could find satisfaction and pleasure (and thus *vitamina*) in other dishes just as easily. Even when I asked the Estamos volunteers who translated and cooked for the health center's demonstration, and Beatriz herself, if they regularly prepared bean soup or enriched porridge at home, each said no, citing the expense of procuring so many ingredients, the lengthy preparation time, lack of a sieve (to press the beans through when making soup), and a general preference for bread and tea for breakfast, and *ntchima* and *ndiwo* for lunch and dinner.

Larg(er) and Small(er) Bodies

One day I walked into Beatriz's office to collect the blank child health card she had promised to provide, so that I could bring it home with me for reference. This was her gift to me, in exchange for my having entered childhood nutrition data into an Excel spreadsheet for her. I happened to have the scale for weighing dietary survey participants with me, and she asked if I might allow her to weigh herself. I removed the scale from my bag, placed it on the ground, and stepped on and off of it several times for recalibration. When I indicated that the scale was ready, Beatriz took off her shoes and gingerly stepped up: 74 kilograms (163 pounds). She said that she knew her height was 1.53 meters (5 feet) and proceeded to pull out a calculator to determine her BMI by dividing her weight by her height squared. With a BMI of thirty-one, the health center nutritionist—*a gordinha*—was officially obese. She was in shock.

Africans are often credited with showing an aesthetic preference for fuller bodies, while giving the slender figure sought after by many in the global north a negative evaluation (Gremillion 2005). Though these predilections may be shifting (Draper, Davidowitz, and Goedecke 2016), my acquaintances in Metangula generally spoke of larger bodies favorably and treated smaller bodies with concern. Of note, however, being larg*er* was different from being large, and being small*er* was different from being small. This was because each individual's body had its own potential range of dimensions, some wider and some narrower (in both size and range). It was generally being larger, meaning at the higher end of an individual's personal size potential, that was valued positively in Metangula and being smaller, or at the lower end of the potential range, that was disconcerting. These relative evaluations are distinct from the absolute states of fat and thin. What is more, the size of an individual's body could fluctuate independent of their weight and diet, such that two individuals could look the same size or eat the same diet but have significantly different heft. While such understandings of physiology and wellness find increasing support in emergent biomedical research and "health of every size" advocacy, they are distinct from ideas held by the general population in the global north, where regular exercise and specific diets are directly and almost universally expected to couple with weight loss, thinning, and improved health (Rothblum and Solovay 2009). My intention here is not to review or evaluate the science behind these ideas or to pronounce these positionings as right or wrong, but to outline how these ideas played out in a single locale.

In Metangula, the relative states of becoming larger or smaller (though, again, not necessarily "fat" or "thin" as absolute formulations) were an indication of well- and ill-being (with exceptions, to be discussed below). If a person was in good health, in other words, their body would become plump to its full capacity. For some this may be, say, a BMI of nineteen, and for others a BMI of twenty-six. It was thus not unusual to hear an absolutely thin person told enthusiastically that they were "fat" when regaining strength after a recent bout of poor health, experiencing a financial windfall, or otherwise bigger than they once were. To be called fat was thus a compliment, as increased size was generally not possible without well-being. This could be especially confusing to an outsider because of the similar phrasing that was used to state that an individual was absolutely large (*wojimbala*, an adjective), that they were becoming relatively or absolutely fat, or that they were becoming larger than before (all stated using *kujimbala*, a verb). The adjective for being small bodied (*woonda*) was likewise similar to the verb for becoming relatively or absolutely thin or otherwise smaller than before (*kuonda*). *Mukuonda*, "you are becoming thin," was thus a statement of concern, a smaller (though not necessarily a small) body indicating poor health and distress. It was thus not oxymoronic to hear a rotund person declare their thinness (*ndikuonda*) if they were ill, were in emotional distress, or had otherwise recently decreased in bodily dimension. These descriptions applied regardless of whether a person was absolutely fat, thin, or in between.

That stated, there was a recognized difference between being slim, on the one hand, and emaciation as a clear symptom of serious and potentially life-threatening illness, on the other. Acquaintances distinguished this sort of excessive and always unhealthy thinness both verbally and with body language, the declaration that someone *akuonda bo* (is becoming *really* thin) accompanied by a slight sucking in of cheeks, rolling back of eyes, hunching forward of shoulders, and bending inward of elbows. The same was true for obesity. While the "bigger is beautiful" mantra was palpable in Metangula, there was also widespread agreement that excessive largeness was a sign of ill health. Like *akuonda bo* as an approximation for emaciation, there was no word precisely equivalent to "obesity" in Chinyanja. Acquaintances in Metangula did, however, recognize a difference between *kujimbala* (to become fat) and *kujimbala chimwe* (to become fat *like this*). They used the latter phrase with hands held out about a foot from either side of the body, bent slightly inward to imitate the girth of an obese person's hips, and arms alternately tilted at the shoulder to mimic the forced waddle of a very large person in motion. There was a widespread negative evaluation of *kujimbala chimwe*, but for reasons that did not include the personal blame that dominates fat shaming in the global north. People instead reasoned that individuals of larger dimension tired easily and sweat excessively and were thus prevented from performing care work, and so participating fully in society. Acquaintances frequently asked me about an obese woman I spent a lot of time with—whether she could stand up on her own, farm, cook, or even leave the house. She could, I responded, but with difficulties. What a shame, the inquirers often responded, to be suffering from *bipi*.

In addition to *kujimbala chimwe*, people in Metangula sometimes called obesity *bipi*, referencing the high blood pressure ("BP") they or other large persons (and some small persons) they knew had been diagnosed with. Some, alternatively, called the condition simply by the English word "pressure," or the Portuguese word *tensão*, short for *hypertensão* (hypertension). Rather than understanding *bipi* as a result of obesity (as high blood pressure is in biomedical formulation), acquaintances treated *bipi* as obesity's cause. Specifically, the blood of a person living with *bipi* was foamy, both prejudicing the fluid's movement and its efficacy. Foamy blood also caused bodily swelling, making a person appear large though they were in poor health. Lina, one of the four clinically obese individuals in the dietary survey, explained her body size this way. She emphasized that she was poor and ate poorly and that she had no male partner to provide sexual *vitamina*, and so she lacked blood. "My body," she explained in reference to her larger size, "is simply filled with foam [*thovu*]." Others told me that the body of someone suffering *bipi* could also enlarge with fat (*mafuta*), such that it squeezed the heart and veins. Both of these conditions prevented effective blood circulation and caused poor health.

There were several foods that a person suffering *bipi* could cut out of their diet to improve their condition. A broad range of acquaintances suggested, for example, that eating less salt, oil, and sugar would diminish the foamy swelling, and so improve the health, of someone suffering *bipi*. This knowledge seemingly originated with preventative measures proffered at the health center and spread through word of mouth. The benefits of these changes, however, were not posited by those who explained them to me as the result of improved nutrition leading to decreased weight and body size. Rather, it was a matter of removing the triggers of illness. Just as a *sing'anga* might tell someone with asthma to avoid eating *nkholokolo* fish to prevent respiratory convulsion, someone who suffered *bipi* could reduce their bodily swelling by avoiding salt, oil, and sugar. A person who did not have *bipi* but who avoided these foods in their diet, in other words, could not be expected to improve their health nor to decrease in size. The logic underlining dietary intervention for *bipi* in Metangula thus reflected local foodways as much as it did hospital-proffered nutritional messages.

Aside from *bipi*, the correlation between absolute body size and diet was minimal. A variety of acquaintances told me that while eating well would improve an individual's wellness, and so result in their getting larger, and eating poorly would reduce their wellness, and so lead to a smaller body size, there were no specific foods that a person could eat or avoid to become fat or thin. This was why I received smirks when explaining why I was weighing people as rooted in part in my desire to look for a connection between diet and BMI. "It is fine that you have an interest in our traditions," Lourenço finally said to me one day when I expressed confusion about this reaction. "But what a person eats does not change their body." Words from Verónica, the middle-aged woman whose house was the scene of the lemon-eating incident recounted in chapter 1, echoed Lourenço's positioning. "Some people say that diet makes a person thin or fat. But this is not true." She reasoned, as did many, that she ate the same thing each day as others in her family. Verónica pointed to her adult son, who was a healthy 21.6 BMI. Verónica herself was obese. "A person's body size," she explained, "just comes out that way."

Of note, there *was* little capacity for one obese or overweight individual in a homestead to predict others. Twenty-four percent of homesteads in the dietary survey had a single clinically overweight or obese person, and only 8 percent more than one. In the four cases of obesity (one male and three female), each was the only individual in their homestead to have a BMI greater or equal to thirty. In one case, the spouse was clinically underweight. This could perhaps be explained biomedically by different *amounts* of food consumed by homestead members. Biology might also point to individual metabolic rates as they affect the processing of foods, such that even where household members ate the same amounts and types of foods, the corporeal effect varied. But for my acquaintances in Metangula, while the presence or absence of *vitamina* affected an individual's oscillation toward their own larger or smaller dimensions, whether the extremes of this range reached into absolute states of "fat" and "thin" varied and was independent of dietary quantities. All of this meant that while eating more or fewer *vitamina*-rich foods could enable a person to become fatter or thinner, there were no dietary interventions that could, alone, drastically alter an individual's absolute body size to make them fat or thin.

It is important to note that in addition to circuitous connections between body size and diet, body size and weight were also not directly connected in Metangula. This can be illustrated through an incident where, upon her request, I weighed the children of Fani, a dietary survey participant. Fani stepped onto the scale with her two-month-old son, and then handed him to me and stepped on the scale without him. Through subtraction, we arrived at the weight of four kilograms (nine pounds). Her eleven-year-old nephew then stepped onto the scale, and I read out the weight of twenty-four kilograms (fifty-three pounds). But Fani misheard me and thought that I said "four kilograms" for the second child, too. When she nodded and summed up what had happened, "They weigh the same," I had the opportunity to detect and correct the miscommunication. But still, that it was plausible for her that two children of vastly different dimensions weighed the same was perplexing. While it could have been that Fani was simply showing deference to me as a foreigner or to my aura of medical expertise by carrying around a scale, further encounters would suggest that many people in Metangula perceived there to be no inherent connection between a person's size and their weight. Like two covered pots, one full of water and the other packed with cassava leaves, Amado explained to me one day while we sat together in the market, two persons (or the same person at two different times) could look physically the same but have unequal weights if they were filled with different substances—different qualities or quantities of blood, foam, and fat that were imperceptible on the surface but resulted in distinct weights. When a group of men building bricks each took their turn stepping on my scale (having called me over to have the opportunity to do so), they had also joked that the one who weighed the least was like a sack of maize bran (*thumbo ya gaga*, which is light in comparison to a sack of maize kernels) for being so full bodied but with little weight. The implications for the lightweight man's sex life were perhaps the source of humor in this situation (the connection between body size and sex is addressed below).

The distinction of weight and size is rarely drawn out in anthropological literature, Ira Bashkow's (2006) discussion of the perceived "lightness" of foreigners in Papua New Guinea being a notable exception. While it is possible that the disassociation of size and weight in Metangula is regionally unique, I find this exclusivity unlikely. Justin Sondergaärd, a development consultant working for eight years with a Yaawo population on the border between the Lago and Sanga

Districts in Niassa Province, told me he had witnessed similar confounding at weight in relation to size. Women waiting to have their babies weighed at a health post he regularly visited had suggested to him that the scale clarified health status, and his employees had asked him questions like why an adult weighs more than a child and what weight is at all. He recounted impromptu physics lessons that involved jumping off benches and comparing sticks to trees (personal communication, 1 November 2010). While these anecdotal data do not vastly expand the geographic range in which weight seemed to be disassociated with size, it does suggest that the phenomenon I recorded is not unique to Metangula and that distinctions between body weight and body size are ripe for additional ethnographic interrogation.

Sexual Health

One warm afternoon, I was sitting among a group of women waiting for an OMM meeting to begin. Our backs erect and our legs outstretched before us, we clustered in small groups and chatted. The women I was nearest to were discussing a range of topics, but the focus of their conversation soon became my physical appearance. My chest size had increased since I had been living in Metangula, one offered. Another pointed out that my neck was thicker and was beginning to be lined with rings. Someone poked her finger into my side, noting that it was spilling over the top of my trousers, which I wore beneath my *capulana*. "Arianna," one of the women remarked, "you have really grown fat." The women laughed heartily, clapping their hands together, slapping their thighs, and ululating. I felt like the butt of a joke, but I could not quibble with their observations. While I was still physically thin, I had gained about five pounds, and it was apparently noticeable to more than just me. I sat there feeling dejected as the women continued laughing and touching my body. Then one of them declared, "Arianna's husband must be feeding her well!" Another round of laughter. With this last point, I took issue—it was my research grant that paid the bills, I retorted, and so it was instead me who was feeding my husband well. The women again laughed, this time at my obliviousness to their sexual innuendo ("feeding" was a discrete way of referring to intercourse) and also the contradiction between what I had inadvertently said about "feeding" and cultural knowledge about the physiology of sexual *vitamina*.

Given that sexual fluids (*ubazi*) were just as important as food for contributing to *vitamina* (see chapter 4) and (as discussed above) that body size fluctuated with wellness, it logically follows that a person who has fattened (but, again, not necessarily someone who was absolutely fat) would be someone having regular sexual intercourse—at least, for a woman. While the *vitamina* of a man was necessary for a woman to reach the larger extremes of her body size potential, the *vitamina* of a woman was not necessary for a man to fatten. In fact, *lack* of sexual activity made a man softer and larger as his body filled with unreleased sexual fluids. This happened if a man did not have sex at least once every six months by some accounts and at least once every week by others.

People pointed especially to the round bellies of male government officials whose families had not traveled with them to Metangula as evidence that male abstinence led to rotundity. When I appealed that some were also thin, like Samuel, the government employee debating the meaning of tastiness while drinking *kacholima* in the opening vignette of chapter 1, I was just reminded that everyone's potentials are different—and, further, Samuel had become "sick with thinking" after the death of his wife several years previous, causing him to lose his appetite. Crucially, though, the abstinent men who fattened did so most prominently in the stomach; they did not fatten as excessively in their arms, neck, or back, the regions typically evaluated when gauging largeness. A man's paunch was thus not a sign of *vitamina* or good health. It simply indicated sexual ennui.

It is important to note also that *ubazi* did not always result in a woman's fattening. Specifically, where a man's and woman's blood "disagreed," leading them to constant quarreling and dislike of one another, sexual relations would not contribute to bodily dimension. In this sense *ubazi* operated much as food did—while both types of "eating" were necessary for sufficient blood supply, vitality, and well-being, they did not result in weightiness and fattening without grounding in the solid, intimate, and sanguine relations that enabled pleasure and satisfaction. I frequently heard this same language of blood being "in agreement" used to explain the strength of platonic relationships as well. Monica, for example, told me that we got along so well because our blood agreed with one another's, making us "like this" (*chimwe*)—she interlocked her two index fingers, then kept them together as she pulled her hands apart. We were one—inseparable. In the market also, the salt sellers, the soap sellers, and the tomato sellers often spoke of blood as the reason for the pacific relations between them, sometimes wondering aloud if such sanguinity mapped on to the blood typology of A, B, and O they had studied in school. But such close-knit friendships did not make them fat.

It does not take much of an imagination to consider that this connection of sexual activity and relative bodily dimension and the use of bodily dimension as a measure of wellness for both health and life circumstance had potentially grave implications for the spread of sexually transmitted diseases (STDs). Specifically, if the receipt of sexual fluids within the body was necessary for well-being, women would be reluctant to have sex using a condom. In fact, condoms were not viewed positively in Metangula. While vendors sold many in the market and health professionals gave away many more at the health center, the end use was often children filling the condoms with air and using them as balloons or wrapping them in plastic bags and string to form homemade soccer balls. "My friend asked me to have sex with him with a condom, just to know what it was like,"

Monica once told me. "But I refused. With a condom on, you might as well not have sex." Others used familiar analogies like "eating a banana with the peel on" to explain their repugnance for condoms.

Regional literature suggests that beyond having a stigma for reducing pleasure, condoms are sometimes feared for *spreading* STDs or causing sterilization, and sexual partners often refuse condoms or see their use as signaling lack of trust (Juma 2006; Kasulo 2006; Mbeye 2007; Piano 2007). When the Estamos volunteers who helped with public health programming delivered a lecture at the Metangula Health Center suggesting condom use as the best method of STD prevention, I approached them afterward and asked, "But how is a woman supposed to get her *vitamina* if she uses a condom?" The three volunteers looked to one another for answers and finally excused themselves from answering, justifying their silence with the fact that this matter had not been a part of their training materials. They referred me instead to their former supervisor, who, it turned out, was equally perplexed at the conundrum. After some contemplation, he finally suggested that faithful marriage is really the only practical solution for STD prevention.

But early sexual debut and the frequency of extramarital sexual encounters suggest that faithful marriage alone was an unlikely fix. In a small, unpublished study of fifty-three respondents between fifteen and twenty-three years of age in two Metangula neighborhoods (Seli and Thungo), social scientist Wisdom Malata (2007) found that all but one respondent was sexually active, with intercourse beginning on average at nine and a half years of age. Forty-three percent of Malata's respondents had no knowledge of sexually transmitted diseases, 64 percent had had sex with multiple partners, and eleven of the twenty-seven female respondents had been pregnant at least once. While statistics on extramarital sexual encounters in Metangula are not available, local banter suggests that they were a common occurrence, especially for men, but also for women. Reports from Malawi, though dated, suggest plausibility for such claims. In a large survey in southern Malawi, 25 percent of men and 9 percent of women reported having had an extramarital affair in the previous six months (Kornfield and Namate 1997). In a smaller study in Zomba (Chaphera 2007), men justified extramarital liaisons primarily as a reaction to a wife's insular behavior, but also for reasons of peer pressure, disposable income, a woman's attractiveness, inebriation, lack of sexual satisfaction at home, taboos that prevented having sex with his wife, and the wife's barrenness. Women explained their behavior primarily as a reaction to a husband's failure to financially support her, but also because of physical distance from her husband, the husbands' barrenness, lack of self-control, the love of money, the influence of friends, or for revenge.

"The moment a young woman's husband is in Lichinga, there is another man in her bed," Florinda, the woman who took me to her neighbor's house to watch the video of witches eating human flesh, once told me. Her daughter-in-law, Luana, whose husband was away at military training, was within earshot. She continued, "This is why there is so much disease these days." She was not talking about HIV/AIDS or *mgosyo*, but *mapinga*. Florinda and other acquaintances told me that a woman with multiple sexual partners within or outside of marriage developed this illness from the mixing of the *ubazi* of multiple men in her body. The illness caused dizziness, blacking out, and fainting.[3] Such a woman further risked being labeled a whore (*hule*), which would dramatically decrease her chances of finding a stable partner. Men did not become ill by having sexual relations with multiple women. People did, however, consider it important for a husband to be faithful to his wife when she was pregnant. This was for two reasons. First, a man having extramarital sexual relations while his wife was pregnant could cause her to suffer the illness of *sanjiko* (from the verb *kusanjika*, "to stack"). This could bring about spontaneous abortion or cause the baby to be born covered in wounds. Second, continued sexual intercourse was necessary until the seventh month of pregnancy to ensure that the fetus matured. This was because the man's semen "fed" the baby.[4] This nourishment was not direct. Instead, by having sex with the mother of his child, a man provided her with the *vitamina* she needed to produce extra blood, which the woman passed on to the child in utero. It is thus the father of the child who provided its blood, not the mother. "The woman," as Jose put it, "acts like a sack. But it is the man who provides the maize inside."[5]

Without repetitive sexual intercourse during pregnancy, called "to nurture the child" (*kulera mwana*), acquaintances explained that babies were born small, anemic, or without the strength to live beyond several days. Women said that at the hospital mothers of small babies were always asked if they were lacking a husband, implying that it was because the women had not engaged in regular sexual intercourse that their children were unhealthy, small, and lightweight. A birth attendant at the health center confirmed that this was sometimes the diagnosis, adding that other times a baby was small because the mother had not been eating well and thus had no blood to provide the embryo (possibly related to lacking a husband, also) or because the baby was born prematurely. The importance of sexual activity for producing a healthy baby was, in fact, a topic on which I encountered some discordance. Several women belittled the connection based on their own personal experience of delivering a healthy baby without sex "nurturing the child" during their pregnancies, though others within earshot always met their saying so with derision. One woman waiting to deliver at the health center clandestinely pointed to her own swollen belly, saying that while she was poor and eating just one meal a day, her monthly exams showed progressive growth and healthy development of her baby. She suggested that the necessity for sex was similar, such that some could deliver healthy babies without it and others could not. "How this can be," she said, "is just a secret of God." Despite elaborate measures to avoid misfortune and otherwise control outcomes, life was, ultimately, unpredictable.

Conclusion

A positive view of largeness has been recorded not only across the African subcontinent, but more broadly across the global south (Sobal and Stunkard 1989), a fact some researchers attribute to a history of scarcity—where food supplies are low and energy expenditure is high, fat becomes a sign of wealth and the absence of disease (Gremillion 2005). In like manner, others suggest explanatory importance for the adaptive function of fat in regulating fertility. Underweight women are at greater risk for amenorrhea and spontaneous abortion (Brink 1995), and children have traditionally been one of the few forms of social security available in many parts of the world. In functionalist logic, then, larger female size, as a sign of childbearing ability, would be desirable. But in a review of anthropological literature on the body, Helen Gremillion (2005) suggests that all too often such adaptational aspects of fat are stressed alone. While there may be a connection between scarcity, fertility, and positive perceptions of largeness, in other words, this does not preclude contextualization in local value systems, nor does it dictate that these positive evaluations will reverse if their original stimulus dissipates. Culture change is infrequently so predictable, and looking beyond functional explanations can always enrich analysis.

This chapter both confirmed and complicated the "big is beautiful" characterization of African corporeal perceptions by presenting Metangula as a case study. Here, the population indeed evaluated bigger bodies primarily as a signal of well-being, rather than vilifying fat as a product of moral failing and determinant of poor health, as it is widely interpreted in the global north. It was not, however, whether a person was large or small, but whether they were larger or smaller in comparison to their own former body size that mattered. Each person had their own potential range of bodily contours, and determining an individual body's reflection of wellness had to be considered case by case. Bigger was thus yoked with wellness in Metangula, yes, but not necessarily being fat. And smaller was met with anxiety and derision, but not necessarily being thin.

Further, whereas biomedicine posits body size and weight as resulting from the content and quantity of dietary consumption (in combination with exercise), in Metangula these lines of causation were less clear. Eating would enable a person to fatten and to gain weight only where paired with wellness. This was because a sick body could not amass the *vitamina* that generally drove weight gain and bodily enlargement without first addressing the underlying malady. The content of meals was largely irrelevant; so long as foods were satisfying and pleasurable to consume, a healthy body garnered *vitamina*. And, there was nothing a person could "eat," with the mouth or the sexual organs, that could make them absolutely fat or thin. All of this made the solution of Plumpy'Nut to address a child's malnutrition moot without attention also to the underlying cause of illness. Mothers in Metangula, like Elisa, thus sought pills and other direct medical interventions to address their children's weight loss. They were more averse to food-based solutions.

Corporeal contour as a point of individual range and reflection of circumstance is not unique to Metangula. It is, in fact, widely remarked upon in embodiment literature from African and African diasporic contexts. Elisa Janine Sobo (1997), for example, found that Jamaicans of African descent clearly saw fat and thin as dependent on circumstance rather than diet: fatness signaled happiness and engagement in reciprocal relationships, while thinness reflected meanness, stinginess, and anomie. Antisocial, worried, and unhappy people lacked energy and "*drew down*" (got thin) regardless of food intake, fat simply "melting off" their bodies. Brad Weiss (1996) similarly recorded "growing fat" and "wasting away" as processes that indexed wealth, levels of anxiety, and general well-being among the Haya in Tanzania. Dietary intake was of little import, and even where a person had an insatiable appetite, this did not necessarily lead to physical largeness where there was no element of satisfaction or fullness achieved. Voracity indicated lack of self-control, and hunger social impotence. Jean Comaroff (1985) also discusses the ability of negative social circumstances like repression to "depress" or reduce one's physical dimensions for the South African Tswana, while socially affirming acts like Zionist healing rituals could "make heavy" and augment the physical space a person occupied. In a later work, she and John Comaroff use such examples to support Tswana and broader African perceptions of individual bodies as not bounded, but waxing and waning in response to subjective experience (Comaroff and Comaroff 1992). Such distinctions in the connections of bodies, health, and diet have important implications for dietary interventions, as demonstrated in Ramah McKay's (2018) study of food aid in southern Mozambique. McKay argues that where care for those who are ill is fashioned through both medicine and complex social and nutritional relations, food alone cannot effect medical recovery.

In Metangula, similarities in vocabulary masked distinctions between biomedical and local physiological knowledges, as did practices such as the health center providing medicines when sick babies lost weight (supporting cultural knowledge of malnutrition as treated with medicine, rather than dietary intervention), encouraging consumption of bean soup and multi-ingredient porridge to increase "vitamins" (meaning for one party a balanced diet, and for the other enhanced blood quantity and quantity through enhanced satisfaction and pleasure in eating), and asking women who delivered small babies if they had a husband at home (suggestive to these new mothers of the need for continued sexual relations for healthy fetal development). It was, as such, that distinctions and misunderstandings easily elided perception in the realm of public health. At the same time, the unyoking of diet from weight and body size, and weight and body size from one another, along with insistence on individual bodies as respondent to internal experience as much as social circumstance, and each body with its own potential range of sizes where larger is not by definition unhealthy or bad, provides an important opportunity for self-reflection by practitioners of and adherents to bionutrition. The benefits of ethnography are not only in learning about other places and people, but in doing so revealing the cultural scaffolding that shapes one's own practices and knowledge and so learning about oneself.

Notes

1. Sobo is a soft drink manufactured in Malawi, similar to Fanta in its flavor options. Orange-flavored Sobo was the most widely available in Metangula. The sweetness of the beverage meant that it was strongly associated with *vitamina*.
2. Statistics on obesity and overweight have been extracted from the Global Health Observatory Data Repository, available online at http://apps.who.int/gho/data/?theme=main, and specifically from the categories "Prevalence of Overweight among Adults, BMI ≥ 25, Age Standardized" and "Prevalence of Obesity among Adults, BMI ≥ 30, Age Standardized."
3. Alister Chaundumuka Munthali (2002b) suggests biomedicine would classify the illness of *mapinga* as preeclampsia.
4. Christopher C. Taylor (1992, 67–68), T. O. Beidelman (1993, 33), J. W. M. van Breugel (2001, 182), and Alister Munthali (2002b, 158; 2007, 142) among others have also discussed the role of semen in "feeding" a child or the importance of repeated sexual relations to ensure a healthy pregnancy.
5. Hugh S. Stannus (1922) similarly reports that the Nyanja and the Yaawo believed a child developed from the man's semen alone, though the fetus's growth was connected with the mother.

Conclusion

The church is like the lake	Mu mpingo muli ngati nyanja
Which keeps fish	Yomwe imasunga nsomba
Many kinds of fish	Za mitundumitundu nsomba
Different kinds	Zosiyanasiyana
But you should not forget	Koma musayiwalire
That among the fish	Mkatikati mwa nsombamo
There is a small fish of a certain type	Muli kansomba kenakake
Called *nkholokolo*	Dzina lake nkholokolo
You should really look	Muzikapenyesetsa inu
At the *nkholokolo* fish	Kansomba ka nkholokolo
When it arrives among other fish	Kakafika pa zinzake
Its thorns go like this [outward]	Minga yake imatere
The other fish swim away	Nsomba zinzake zimathawa
In fear of being stung	Kuwopa kubayidwa
With the painful thorns	Ndi minga ija ya ululu
The thorns of the *nkholokolo*	Minga yake nkholokolo
Your behavior, woman [mother]	Khalidwe lanu inu mayi
Your behavior, man [father]	Khalidwe lanu inu bambo
The behavior from your home	Khalidwe la kunyumba kwanu
You have brought it to the church	Mwabweretsa mumpingo
What you are showing [at church]	Zomwe mukuwonetsa
Even at your home	Ngakhalenso kunyumbako
When your friends arrive	Akafika azinzanu
Your heart looks like this [big, meaning selfish]	Chimtimacho ngati apa
But when you leave	Koma mukangochoka inu
People eat and become satisfied [full]	Anthu amadya ndi kukhuta
It is [you who is] that painful thorn	Ndi [inu] minga ija ya ululu
The thorn of the *nkholokolo*[1]	Minga yake nkholokolo

Nkholokolo (*Synodontis njassae*) is a spotted catfish endemic to Lake Niassa. The fish sports sharp dorsal fin rays (referred to as *minga*, or "thorns," in the song lyrics above), it is nocturnal, and it prefers to hide in rocks and caves (often positioned upside down) rather than to swim about. It is also known among local fishers, as well as aquarium enthusiasts around the world, for quarreling with other catfish that cross its path. In these ways, the fish exemplifies a range of traits associated with improper human behavior—it is solitary, aggressive, and harmful to its fellows. The moral of the song—sung, as recorded above, by members of a church choir in the town of Cóbuè in 2007—is that a person should not be like the *nkholokolo*. More specifically, the song implores listeners to not resemble in their behavior the fish's sharp and poisonous "thorns," which threaten and cause pain for others. Because of this feature, it is only when the *nkholokolo* fish leaves that its "friends"—all of the other fish—may eat their food and find satisfaction in their meal.

In reminding us of the close connection between sociality, alimentation, pacific relations, and nourishment, the quotidian ways in which moral constitution can be enacted or evaded, the similitude between humans and animals, and the disruption and destruction affected by causing pain and enacting harm, the *nkholokolo* song offers a fitting conclusion to this volume, an ethnography about foodways in the lakeshore town of Metangula, Mozambique. In the preceding chapters I have outlined and described how mutuality, compassion, intelligence, generative labor, and consideration for others defined humanity in Metangula and how individual efforts at being and becoming a person to the full extent of one's potentiality were embedded in everyday (quotidian) and every day (continuous) beliefs and behaviors surrounding production, distribution, preparation, consumption, and definition of food. Eating good things in life-enhancing contexts provided the energy (*vitamina*) and broader vitality (*thanzi*) to establish, sustain, and deepen interdependence with the living and the dead. Food, then, enabled individuals to not only *have* life, but to partake in it, and those who did well ate well, regardless of their diets. They were also fatter and weightier, though not necessarily fat or heavy.

While neither discrediting the importance of eating for sustaining physical life nor asserting an exclusive role for alimentation in pursuits of being and becoming human, this study forcefully confirms that foodways play an important role in the meaning and making of humanity as a moral orientation of benevolence, a designation for biological species, and a marker of social personhood. The case study thus highlights how selling, exchanging, sharing, pouring, cooking, eating, digesting, and abstaining from food can be meaningful beyond their garnering of calories and micronutrients—even where people have little in the way of material wealth, and alimentary choices seem few. Foodways, in Metangula, nourished life. The present volume ethnographically situates and traces the contours of these pursuits as I recorded them in the opening decade of the twenty-first century.

It is apt, though of pure coincidence, that my research for this volume took place in a town named for some of the very ideas underlying my findings. The moniker "Metangula" comes from incidents surrounding the death of the town's founding chief, Chilombe Uandionerapati. This first Chilombe was one of five "brothers" who set off from Nkhunga (just north of Nkhotakota in Malawi) in the mid-nineteenth century, aiming to settle on the eastern side of Lake Niassa (Mazula 1970, 31).[2] As each brother grew tired on the journey, he was left behind to settle the land. This was how Uandionerapati came to find himself in what would become Metangula (Mazula 1970, 39–40; Umali 1996, 6; 2006, 2). His task of starting a village and attracting dependents, however, was made difficult because of frequent attacks by slave raiders, which led to the de-peopling of villages and the loss of property and agricultural crops. It was in fleeing from one such attack that Uandionerapati was wounded. He ran to a river, where he collapsed within the shade of a cave-like rock. He was alone there, debilitated and bleeding. After the raid, remaining villagers regrouped and searched for him. But when they finally located their founding chief, three days later, he was exhausted and lying nearly lifeless. They attempted to feed him porridge but he was too weak to consume it, and he was too exhausted to walk. He had lost too much blood, and he died. The rock where all of this took place was thereafter called *mwala watenguka*—"rock of exhaustion and lifelessness." This was eventually adopted as the village name, shortened as M'tenguka, later corrupted as Mtengula, and then finally in the colonial era becoming Metangula. The root verb *kutenguka* refers to debilitation and total draining of vitality. Not only did this characterize Chilombe Uandionerapati in his loss of blood and purpose, but also the villagers who were distraught at his passing (Umali 1996, 56). Life, as considered in this historical account, was tied up in interdependence, alimentation, peaceable relations, and sanguinity—just as it was in Metangula's foodways.

In my framing of alimentation as an arena for the constant, continuous, and fraught lived experience of negotiating and living out what it means to be human through daily action and inaction, this volume can be considered an existentially grounded ethnography, though one very different from the phenomenological style advocated and advanced by Michael Jackson and Albert Piette (2015). While I have sought to present individuals as more than Durkheimian passive vehicles for expression and affirmation of collective norms and values or as Bourdieuian unconscious and unreflexive automatons (Jackson and Piette 2015, 14–16), the present volume concentrates on broad patterns of belief and behavior, rather than individual biographies. What I have ethnographically documented, then, is how indeterminate existence was explicitly moralized and woven into daily life through physiology, market principles, taboo, everyday ritual, social institutions, spiritual practices, and market principles, such that humanity was a status to be achieved rather than ascribed, enacted with agency rather than through habitus, and perpetually developed rather than permanently achieved—existentialism, in other words, as lived practice.

In this way, the volume builds upon other ethnographies that are attentive to concrete and material practices through which individuals are brought together and so made into persons as they wrestle with conflicting needs and desires for togetherness and separation (e.g., Geissler and Prince 2010; Holtzman 2009; Taylor 1992). But the ethnographic study I have presented here is also heavily indebted to African philosophical thinking and writing about Ubuntu as a moral principle for prioritizing pro-social, unifying, generative, and revitalizing acts over those that privilege insulation, selfishness, greed, and apathy (and especially Masolo 2010; Ogude 2019b; Ramose 2007).[3] This body of work makes clear that perceptions of "becoming" human as a social process of unfoldment, rather than a static or ascribed state, and the association of humanity with mutuality, intelligence, labor, and compassion are not unique to Metangula. Rather, they are reflective of widespread cultural knowledge in Africa, where the individual does not precede or stand apart from their social relations but is emergent through them in everyday and every day practices. While not unique to Africa, these understandings are palpably distinct from populations where the dominant (and dominative) ontological orientation presupposes society as a derivative product, resulting from the association of predefined individuals who are independent from and primordial to the whole, their relationships contractual rather than organic and based on rights rather than obligations and duties. This atomized conception of what it means to be a person in the world has been naturalized in much of the global north, inclusive of its central place in the operating principles of biomedicine (Gordon 1988), and thus science-driven notions of health, physiology, etiology, and nutrition. Attention to alternative configurations can reveal the cultural underpinnings of these familiar institutions and understandings, often posited to be neutral and value free, and also perhaps to inspire relating to one another through connection, caring, and responsibility as universal capacities that have perhaps not been fully realized everywhere (Weidtmann 2019a, 141).

The origins of the study of African philosophy are often traced to Placide Tempels, a missionary who resided in the Belgian Congo (now Democratic Republic of Congo) between 1933 and 1962 (Mudimbe 1983). Neither African nor a philosopher, Tempels's residency among and interactions with a Luba population led him to compose *Bantoe-filosofie* in 1945, which was soon after translated from Flemish to French as *La Philosophie bantoue*, and then to English as *Bantu Philosophy* in 1952. The volume outlined local perceptions of human beings as interconnected with the spirit world, plants, and animals through an energy, or "vital force," that could be strengthened or diminished through interaction, emotion, and tapping into the strength of others. Tempels argued that "force" (inclusive of intelligence and will) was the sustenance of "being." Rather than being as a simple matter of that which was, in other words, being was that which had force. This point undergirded local customs and rituals meant to acquire, maintain, and strengthen force, which could be sapped through enmity and a host of misfortunes (inclusive of illness, wounds, disappointments, depression, fatigue, injustice, and failure), thus enabling one's being to wax and wane through circumstance, experience, and affect. This meant that no individual was truly independent, that force depended on one's own actions as well as those of others, and that "being" was a state distinct from physical life.

These observations have clear resonance with concepts that I have discussed in this volume, and especially the nourishing qualities of *vitamina* (alimentary and sexually acquired energy reflected in quantity and quality of blood) and *thanzi* (vitality). Tempels, in fact, himself suggested that his observations were not only characteristic of the Luba, but of Bantu language-speaking populations more broadly, a proclamation that has since been widely debated. In fact, the legacy of Tempels's work is often evaluated negatively. Shortcomings include his writing style, which was paternalistic and full of depersonalizing and authoritative declarations. He is also accused of presenting "African personhood" in a dichotomizing fashion, systemizing his findings to fit with Christian ideas, and attributing the label "philosophy" to concepts not subjected to ongoing internal debates or critical reflection within African societies themselves.[4] Particularly damning, Tempels put forth that the Luba had not articulated their philosophy themselves because they were of weak intelligence, and the final chapter in his seminal volume, titled "Bantu Philosophy and Our Mission to Civilize," makes crystal clear both the intended audience of his work and the ethnocentric biases with which he approached it (Songolo 1981).

Despite these shortcomings in motivations and in content, Tempels was a pioneer in outlining an African ontology that rivaled Europeans' in its sophistication. This was, at the time of *Bantu Philosophy*'s publication, quite a radical proclamation (Hellweg and Miller 2019). Others credit Tempels for breaking new ground in seeking out broad philosophical principles in African lifeways. Stephen O. Okafor (1982), for example, finds that in "vital force" Tempels was on the right track of identifying an inner structure to African cosmology. Where Tempels went wrong, Okafor suggests, was in the exotifying diversion of calling this principle "vital force." He suggests instead a core framework of life (the meaning of the universe being the meaning of life itself), commensality (through which the goodness in life is reflected and concretized in peace and harmony among the living and the dead), and what he terms "phenomenon-aura" (metaphysical auras emitted in every phenomenon, which can be manipulated to affect life for good or ill).[5] Such modeling also resonates with that which I have presented here.

More recently, Niels Weidtmann (2019b) has nuanced Tempels's work by infusing vital force with the transformative power of affect. Here Weidtmann's approach is somewhat reminiscent of Victor Turner and Edith Turner's notions of "communitas" as a sense of togetherness, belonging, and joy that can be felt when the lives of a group of individuals take on collective meaning (E. Turner 2012; V. Turner 1969; 1974). Though Weidtmann's assessment is centered in the everyday, rather than ritual states of being "betwixt and between," he is focused, like the Turners, on lived experience and affect as sources of revitalization and meaning. Vital force for Weidtmann is thus not a concept to discard, but to reimagine as the enlivening power of solidarity and intimacy that emerges when humanity is deepened and extended through the experience of multidimensionality. To maintain vitality, then, it is necessary to not only participate in the community, but also to be a part of its perpetual reconstitution. With this reformulation, Weidtmann distances vital force not only from the supernatural, but also from its construction as a cultural belief specific to the Luba or the broader corpus of Bantu-speaking peoples that Tempels held that it applied to. For Weidtmann, vital force is a universal sense of humanity that is experienced most fully through mutuality. This is precisely the sense in which I have made use of the concept of vitality and *vitamina* in documenting Metangula's foodways: as bound up in individual, intentional, and everyday efforts at being and becoming human through interdependence, and (so) in nourishing life.

Considering foodways for their role in the project of defining what makes us human builds on a rich tradition of anthropological literature. Claude Lévi-Strauss (1969) took special interest in the heating of foodstuffs in the distinction of humanity, culminating in the author's "culinary triangle," as discussed in chapter 1. The same point is also made less abstractly by biological anthropologist Richard Wrangham (2010), who contends that controlled fire was the key innovation for human evolution in making previously inedible foods edible through cooking, thus allowing proto-humans to process enough calories to develop the bigger brains that characterize our species today. Cooking also frees our species from the time other animals must devote to chewing and internally processing their foods, which allows us to provision one another and engage in non-subsistence pursuits. Suffice to say, it is not only for the people of Metangula that cooking distinguishes humans from other animals. But where Lévi-Strauss's declarations were in the realm of cognition, and Wrangham's were embedded in a project of biological differentiation, the present volume has considered cooking, and more broadly foodways, as a part of the everyday making and meanings of humanity through individual, perpetual, and fraught negotiations of one's place among others in the world.

To make this case, we began with a consideration of *vitamina* as distinct from its English equivalent, "vitamins." Whereas "vitamins" represent a set of stable nutritional properties contained within foods and with universal applications for promoting health, *vitamina* was mercurial and could manifest or become assuaged through contextualized experiences of alimentation colored by emotional and physical states (well-being, ill-being) and individual corporeal responses (e.g., pleasure, appetite stimulation, satiation). It was such that affect was a more reliable indicator of *vitamina* than diet. *Vitamina* was also distinct from vitamins in its impact on an individual's quality and quantity of blood, which was the source of their vitality, an animating force that enabled living, but not life. Thus *vitamina*—while deceptively similar to scientific explication of biological processes and bionutritional understandings of food, implicating some of the same organs, general processes, and vocabulary—was distinct. It was only through ethnographic contextualization that we could begin to differentiate local understandings of eating and circulatory processes from their biomedical counterparts, and see how these two bodies of knowledge entangled with one another rather than existing in separate realms. Through the exploration of these contours, *vitamina* and its relation to animating or "vital force" (*thanzi*) emerged as the first essential building blocks for tracing the contours of Metangula's foodways.

From blood, vitality, and *vitamina*, we moved on to the cultural importance of generative labor, or hard work directed toward pro-social aims, in order to elucidate why *vitamina* was so integral to the categorization of foodstuffs. This contextualization centered on the idea that laboring was an essential part of achieving and retaining status as a human person, which required active contributions toward the maintenance, reproduction, and revitalization of society. These activities necessitated energy from *vitamina*, without which an individual would become tired and thus unable to partake in (a) nourishing life. Considering the centrality of humanity for self-worth and the connection between labor and personhood, it makes sense that the fuel to achieve the status of "human person" (energy, in the form of *vitamina*) would take central stage in food categorization. But energy alone was not enough. Being and becoming human also required compassion (*lisungu*) and intelligence (*njeru*) that directed creative potentialities toward sustaining life, rather than depleting it. These orientations had direct implications for the practice of market-based exchange, which in a capitalist logic relies on acquisition and accumulation rather than caring and connectivity. But, as scholars have noted across the African continent, the marketplace in Metangula pushed pro-social endeavors along with profits. Those who prioritized the latter too overtly or with too much success would see their gains crumble, like Marco or Sancho had. Or they might be ousted as a witch.

Differentiations between humans and witches, and humans and animals, were by no means absolute. This is because humans were not born persons, nor was it possible to "be" a person as if a finite and permanent state. Humans, rather, constantly and continuously *became* human persons in Metangula through intentional acts that demonstrated positive valuation of the self within society, rather than apart from it, and the suppression of the natural and attractive characteristics associated with alterity. Rather than being positioned as an *opposite* of humanity, then, animals and witches exemplified very familiar human tendencies such as envy, jealousy, spite, indignation, contempt, and selfish accumulation. Humanity was about controlling or repressing (or at least appearing to control and repress) these antisocial sentiments in favor of those that were pro-social. Lest, could an individual truly be a human person? As Brian Morris posited for

Maravi populations broadly, "A human being who is isolated from others, who is ungenerous, unhelpful, melancholy, individualistic and with 'a bad heart' is not a real person" (1998, 66). This does not mean that an individual who resembled a witch or an animal necessarily became or was one, nor that such leanings represented a permanent or unalterable state. The semblance, however, insinuated that the individual was declaring autonomy, and thus giving up both humanity and community. Those who acted like animals and witches in their methods for procuring, preparing, consuming, and sharing foods might, like the Chinese contractors in Michumwa that Pedro was so concerned about, have their status as human persons debated.

Persons, in Metangula, also did not eat other persons. Importantly, this was not conceived to be for lack of want or a gut-level reaction of disgust. People hypothesized human flesh to be, in fact, good-tasting. Eating it was scorned, derided, and posited as reviling because it meant accumulation and consumption of vitality for selfish aims and was therefore a nefarious act. The construction of humanity as distinct from its alters—animals and witches—was, in fact, broadly articulated through food. That this should be the case should not surprise us, given the distinct qualities of "food as food," characterized by Jon Holtzman (2009) as the simultaneously symbolic, social, and material character of edibles, and thus their inherent place as a site of crossover for causality and meaning. Beth Forrest and Deirdre Murphy (2013) more specifically call out food as privileged for meaning making because it provides a way in which individuals can sustain the individual self (through nourishment), participate in culture, and so affirm their place in society. Deborah Lupton (1996) draws attention also to the capacity of eating to remind us of our animality and the entropy of living matter, marking alimentation as particularly apt for experiencing, expressing, and formulating ambivalence. A similar if more theological point is made by Norman Wirzba (2011), who notes that alimentation is about joining human beings to the earth, to fellow creatures, and to God. That some things must die in order for others to live connects us in an unending sharing and receiving of each other—a sort of cannibalism in itself, Francis B. Nyamnjoh (2018) would surely point out—making alimentation an apt place to make room for others to find life by sharing ourselves and to discover and commune with the sources of life itself. Taken together, it is not surprising that foodways operate as one domain in which humanity is prominently defined, enacted, evaded, and experienced.

In Metangula, being and becoming human was enmeshed in sustained and active relations of care, compassion, and nourishment. These values underlay *mgosyo*, a set of rules that were embedded in common activities like sex, visiting, mourning, and cooking. The banality of these practices made the rules easy to forget, and yet the dramatic consequences of neglect made following them each day imperative for ensuring the health of others, particularly those who were deemed vulnerable due to their liminality or sexual inactivity. As "everyday rituals," *mgosyo* thus revitalized mutuality through action (rather than mere belief) and asserted individuals' belonging among those for whom they cared. In this way, each person was always and inescapably part of something greater than themselves. The obligation to care for others was a definitive part of being human, imparted upon the species by God following the "rubbing together of sticks" as a primordial sexual and incendiary act. Sexual relations thereafter became imperative for the physical reproduction of our species and the physiological vitalization of our labor. But sex, like fire, and also like *dawa* and like salt, had the potential to direct transformative potentiality in both generative and destructive ways. *Mgosyo* was not about controlling such contingencies, but about living with them on a journey of perpetual unfoldment, propelled through revitalizing actions. In the early twenty-first century, new uncertainties brought about through neoliberalism, marginalization, and other elements of "modernity" spurned active engagement and creative response, similar to earlier generations though with different barriers to surmount in nourishing life. The capacities for the spirit realm to intervene and resolve disparities and misfortunes in this new world were uncertain, not necessarily as a faltering of belief but of diminished unity in action.

The volume concluded by considering the literal embodiment of humanity via body size and weight. Distinct from mainstream biomedical understandings of human bodies as shaped by diet and exercise, acquaintances in Metangula envisioned each individual to have a unique range in corporeal dimension that both responded to and indexed their physical and emotional well-being, as well as their broad engagement in both gustatory and sexual pleasures. This meant that relative evaluations of "larger" and "smaller" bodies were of more salience than absolute measures like fat and thin, and that fluctuations in girth evidenced life circumstance. Likewise, increase and decrease in weight measured wellness, though this could also fluctuate independent of body size due to the different substances with which a body could fill (such as foam and fat). These distinctions have potential implications for both nutritional and sexual health, particularly where food cannot nourish a sickly body back to health without medical interventions, and condoms are positioned to impede rather than to promote general health. Such findings provide useful contributions for the planning and implementation of public health programming beyond the advocacy of bean soup and enriched porridge to combat malnutrition and the advocacy of "safe sex" to thwart the spread of HIV/AIDS.

While this ethnography outlines and supports the important value people in Metangula placed on interdependence, caring for others, and showing compassion for human fellows, this is in no way meant to imply that Metangula represents a sort of evolutionary (emergent or antiquated) utopia of social harmony. As dominant as pro-social values may have been in the moral imagination, they were actively cultivated rather than implicit, self-evident, determinative, or predictive. And pro-sociality was at times clearly masked, dismissed, and overridden in favor of other pursuits—like domination, selfishness, insensitivity, abusiveness, violence, and so forth. Scholars note that such results come about not only when the principle of participation is negated, but also at times as a direct result of relationality itself. Humans can come together and experience vitality as a group to promote heinous acts, such as genocides and lynchings. Let us remember also that the country of Mozambique was caught up in war for twenty-eight years, ending just two decades before this research took place. The point is that humanity is, by its nature, both beautiful and ugly, virtuous and wicked, generative and destructive, compassionate and self-absorbed—not one or the other, and there is value to be found and attraction in both extremes, and tremendous potential for generative creativity, vitality, and meaning in the struggle between them.

While I have argued that people in Metangula as I encountered them in the twenty-first century valued compassion and privileged mutuality over self-interest, then, this does not mean that everyone enacted these idealized behaviors at all times. This point is especially important to emphasize, given that the people of Metangula did not have much in the way of capitalist notions of wealth. In no way have I intended to imply, utilize, or support a "poor-but-happy" lens through which the state of poverty is both trivialized and made negligible for well-being or romanticized as life enhancing. Such dangerous positioning can excuse and justify material inequalities and relieve us of duties to identify, assess, and redress global gaps and inequalities (Simpson 2004). People in Metangula *did* mind living in poverty, and doing so in no way made pro-sociality rote, default, or given. As examined in chapter 4, these conditions, if anything, made pro-social orientations difficult to enact and to maintain. But a moral imperative toward life-enhancing rather than life-diminishing sentiments, intentions, and actions held true in Metangula, and as I have aimed to articulate in this volume, the cultivation, demonstration, and evaluation of this positioning underlay the character of Metangula's foodways.

It is in the consciousness of the constantness of negotiation at the fraught and fuzzy boundaries of humanity that this small place offers a window and point of reflexivity for what "we"—and here I mean "we" in the sense of global community, but also "we" as in you and I, because I am right there with you—are doing in our own lives to actively embody, embrace, cultivate, and deepen our humanity. Is it enough to just "be" human, or must we earn that distinction? How can our every day and everyday lives transform our humanity from a state of being into a lived practice? What are we doing in our lives now that might inadvertently negate such projects? And where can we insert connection, caring, and responsibility into our notions of morality? I am not advocating that we look to the people of Metangula for answers to the existential question of what it means to be human. But we can take inspiration from the deliberate nature of their approach, through which humanity becomes expected routine without dissipating into habitus, mutuality is experienced as enriching because of (rather than despite) the fact that it binds us together, and moral values in compassion and kindness are positioned to give life meaning. Food for thought as I close out this volume on the foodways of an African town—on the surface perhaps a boring and monotonous affair of *ntchima* and *ndiwo*, born out of poverty and dictated by biological imperative. A closer look reveals, I hope, something that is nourishing.

Notes

Transcription and translation of the *nkholokolo* song was assisted by Patrick Chimutha and Experencia Madalitso Jalasi.

1. Museu Local, Metangula, Oral Traditions Collection (LAG2007.072, 24:28–26:28). Recorded in Cango (northern Cóbuè) on 10 July 2007 with Faith Ambross, Costancia Dama, Maria Dama, Helieti Kalande, Anna Kapombe, Edga Kapombe, Liz Kapombe, Paulo Kapombe, Alicia Movera, Evelyn Mazi, Elena Nkwinda, and Jesi Zimba. Of note, north of the village of Ngoo (the last major village before Cóbuè), the Chinyanja dialect is more akin to Chichewa than it is in Metangula, hence use of the word *nsomba* rather than *nchomba* for "fish," and so forth.
2. Maravi chiefs are typically linked to one another through ties of perpetual kinship, such that greater chiefs are referred to as the older brothers of lesser chiefs (Schoffeleers 1968, 30, 155, 168–69).
3. Additional perspectives on African philosophy are to be found in the volume *African Philosophy as Cultural Inquiry* (2000), edited by Ivan Karp and D. A. Masolo, along with Masolo's *African Philosophy in Search of Identity* (1994) and other classics like Kwasi Wiredu's *Philosophy and an African Culture* (1980) and *Cultural Universals and Particulars* (1996), Paulin J. Hountondji's *African Philosophy: Myth and Reality* (1983 [1976]), John S. Mbiti's *African Religions and Philosophy* (1969), Augustine Shutte's *Philosophy for Africa* (1993), and Kwame Anthony Appiah's *In My Father's House: Africa in the Philosophy of Culture* (1992).
4. Critique of the work of Placide Tempels is widespread and too vast to address here. See, for example, V. Y. Mudimbe's *The Invention of Africa: Gnosis, Philosophy, and the Order of Knowledge* (1988), which also contributes to broader questions about the making and meaning of "ethnophilosophy" in relation to African moral reasoning, a debate succinctly summarized in the second chapter in D. A. Masolo's *Self and Community in a Changing World* (2010).
5. Stephen O. Okafor's framework for African cosmology (1982) is one of many alternative formulations to Tempels's. Others, for example, include that penned by Alexis Abbé Kagame (1976), who focused on *ntu* as a universal cosmic force, and Ernst Wendland (1990), who outlined seven core principles in traditional life and thought that made up the Bantu thought world. See Aloo Osotsi Mojola (2019) for additional details about these studies and an accounting of the shift from a consideration of Ubuntu as a set of values to a broader worldview (also discussed in Gade 2011).

Glossary

afiti	Witches (singular, *mfiti*).
basera	A small addition to a customer's purchase, serving as a gift from the seller.
bipi	Illness characterized by high blood pressure and bodily swelling.
bolos	Dough fritter.
capulana	Cloth panel, commonly worn as women's clothing or used as a sling to carry a child on one's back. Known in Chichewa as *chitenge*.
celeste	Unsoaked maize flour with bran removed, used for making *ntchima*.
chai	"Tea," though sometimes made without tea leaves and thus simply hot water, usually served with sugar.
Chuanga	Village in Lago District, coastal and just north of Metangula.
Cóbuè	Village in Lago District, coastal and opposite Likoma Island.
colorão	Red, powdered food coloring.
dawa	Medicinal substance, used to heal or to harm.
Estamos	Mozambican NGO based in Niassa Province (in Portuguese, literally "we are").
foodways	Beliefs and behaviors surrounding production, distribution, preparation, consumption, and definition of food, bound up with emotional evaluations, affective experiences, and the broader negotiation of well-being.
gaga	Bran flour, composed of the maize pericarp removed when making more refined flours for cooking *ntchima*.
kabanga	Locally brewed beer.

kacholima	Locally brewed spirits.
kamu	Group, ethnicity, or generation.
kujimbala	To be fat, fatter than a person once was, or fattening.
kujimbala chimwe	To be obese, or becoming very fat.
kukoma	To be pleasurable, sweet, or tasty.
kulemera	To be heavy, have weight, be rich, or be valuable.
kuonda	To be thin, thinner than a person once was, or thinning.
kuonda bo	To be emaciated, or becoming very thin.
kuwawa	To be painful, bitter, or unpleasant.
Lago	District in the Niassa Province in Mozambique, where Metangula is located (in Portuguese, literally "Lake").
Lichinga	Capital of Niassa Province in Mozambique.
Likoma	Island in Lake Niassa, just off the Mozambican shore, under the jurisdiction of Malawi.
lisungu	Empathy and compassion for those who are suffering.
mafuta	Lipids (fats) in liquid or solid form.
Maputo	Capital of Mozambique, known previously as "Lourenço Marques."
Maravi	Bantu-speaking matrilineal peoples living in southeast Africa, including the Chewa, Nyanja, Mang'anja, Chipeta, Mbo, Nsenga, and Zimba.
matcheza	Seasoning made by pouring hot water through ashes, akin to salt.
mbamu	Small portion of *ntchima*, dipped into *ndiwo* side dishes.
Metangula	Capital of Lago District in Mozambique's Niassa Province, also known for a short time as Augosto Cardoso.
meticais	Monetary unit in Mozambique (singular, "metical").
mgosyo	Prescriptive actions and illnesses associated with sexual activity and salt pouring.
Michumwa	Village in Lago District, slightly inland and north of Metangula.
mizimu	Those who are physically dead, but continue to impact the world of the living, often referred to in English as "ancestors."
moyo	Physical life.
ndiwo	Side dish that accompanies *ntchima* or any other staple.
ngaiwa	Unsoaked maize flour with bran, used for making *ntchima*.

Niassa	Province in Mozambique, situated in the far northwest corner, where Lago District and its capital Metangula are situated.
njeru	Knowledge (as a matter of cumulative experience) and wisdom (as a matter of reflection, sound judgment, and the capacity for reason).
nsipuko	Love medicine, meant to keep a husband from finding other lovers.
nsuni	Saucy or liquid component of *ndiwo*.
ntamiko	Love medicine, meant to keep a husband at home.
ntchima	Thick polenta-like gruel made through skillful combination of flour with boiling water, served as a main dietary staple.
nthaka	Illness befalling and caused by women who lose a fetus or small child.
nyama	Animal, or the meat, organs, and marrow from an animal (non-fish).
phala	Porridge.
sadaka	Remembrance ceremony for the deceased.
sing'anga	Traditional healer (plural, *ang'anga*).
tchire	Bush, indicating wildness, remoteness, or location outside of human living spaces.
thanzi	Vitality, residing in the blood and enabled through *vitamina*.
thovu	Foam, a substance or consistency of blood that can fill the body, making a person large but with little weight.
ubazi	Sexual fluids, nutritive and provisioning of *vitamina* to sexual partners.
Ubuntu	Worldview in which humanity is conceived as multidimensional, participatory, and continuously unfolding through relationships with and responsibilities to others.
ufa woyera	A soaked maize flour without bran, popular for making *ntchima*. Literally "white flour."
usipa	Small, sardine-like fish
vidule	Seasoning made by pouring hot water through ashes, akin to baking soda.
vijukulu mavi	Grandchildren of grandchildren (singular, *chijukulu mavi*).
vitamina	Energy that enables *thanzi*, accessed through eating and sexual relations in life-affirming, pleasurable circumstances.
vungu	Worms; in the context of this ethnography cerebral *vungu* providing moral guidance for humanity.

References

Ahlberg, Beth Maina. 1994. "Is There a Distinct African Sexuality? A Critical Response to Caldwell." *Africa* 64(2): 220–42.
Akombi, Blessing J., Kingsley E. Agho, Dafna Merom, Andre M. Renzaho, and John J. Hall. 2017. "Child Malnutrition in Sub-Saharan Africa: A Meta-Analysis of Demographic and Health Surveys (2006–2016)." *PLOS ONE* 12(5): e0177338.
Ali, Sandra, Tony Nyirenda, and Malcom MacLachlan. 1998. "The Influence of Traditional Beliefs and Practices on Contemporary Chamba (Marijuana) Use in Malawi." *Journal of Psychology in Africa* 8(1): 70–83.
Alpers, Edward A. 1969. "Trade, State, and Society among the Yao in the Nineteenth Century." *Journal of African History* 10(3): 405–20.
Altuna, Raul Ruiz de Asúa. 2006. *Cultura tradicional bantu*. Luanda: Paulinas.
Ambali, Augustine. 1916. *Thirty Years in Nyasaland*. Westminster: UMCA.
Amide, João Baptista. 2008. *"Wayao'We" no conhecido Niassa: os valores culturais e a globalização*. Maputo: Diname.
Ammerman, Nancy Tatom. 2007. *Everyday Religion: Observing Modern Religious Lives*. Oxford: Oxford University Press.
Anderson-Morshead, Anne Elizabeth Mary. 1897. *The History of the Universities Mission to Central Africa, 1859–1896*. London: Office of the Universities' Mission to Central Africa.
Anigbo, Osmund A. C. 1987. *Commensality and Human Relationship among the Igbo: An Ethnographic Study of Ibagwa Aka, Igboeze L.G.A. Anambra State, Nigeria*. Nsukka: University of Nigeria Press.
António, Alexandre, and Lúcia Laurentina Omar. 2007. *Alguns usos e costumes matrimonias dos povos Yao e Nyanja da Província do Niassa*. Lichinga: CIEDIMA.
Appiah, Anthony. 1992. *In My Father's House: Africa in the Philosophy of Culture*. New York: Oxford University Press.
Archambault, Julie Soleil. 2017. *Mobile Secrets: Youth, Intimacy, and the Politics of Pretense in Mozambique*. Chicago: University of Chicago Press.
Arens, William. 1979. *The Man-Eating Myth: Anthropology and Anthropophagy*. New York: Oxford University Press.
Arnfred, Signe, ed. 2004. *Re-thinking Sexualities in Africa*. Stockholm: Almquist & Wlksell Tryckeri.

———. 2007. "Sex, Food and Female Power: Discussion of Data Material from Northern Mozambique." *Sexualities* 10(2): 141–58.

———. 2011. *Sexuality & Gender Politics in Mozambique: Rethinking Gender in Africa*. Oxford: James Currey.

Arnold, David. 1988. "Introduction: Disease, Medicine, and Empire." In *Imperial Medicine and Indigenous Societies in the Nineteenth and Twentieth Centuries*, edited by David Arnold, 1–26. Manchester: Manchester University Press.

Ashforth, Adam. 2005. *Witchcraft, Violence, and Democracy in South Africa*. Chicago: University of Chicago Press.

Bagnol, Brigitte. 2017. "The Aetiology of Diseases in Central Mozambique: With a Special Focus on HIV/AIDS." *African Studies* 76(2): 205–20.

Bagnol, Brigitte, Matthew Chersich, Isabelle François, Francisco Mbofana, Esmeralda Mariano, and Adriane Martin Hilber. 2015. "Determinants of Vaginal Cleansing, Application, and Insertion in Tete Province, Mozambique, and Products Used." *International Journal of Sexual Health* 27 (3): 324–36.

Banerjee-Dube, Ishita, ed. 2016. *Cooking Cultures: Convergent Histories of Food and Feeling*. Delhi: Cambridge University Press.

Barnard, Alan. 2000. *History and Theory in Anthropology*. Cambridge: Cambridge University Press.

Baro, Mamadou, and Tara F. Deubel. 2006. "Persistent Hunger: Perspectives on Vulnerability, Famine, and Food Security in Sub-Saharan Africa." *Annual Review of Anthropology* 35: 521–38.

Bashkow, Ira. 2006. *The Meaning of Whitemen: Race and Modernity in the Orokaiva Cultural World*. Chicago: University of Chicago Press.

Beachey, Ray W. 1976. *A Collection of Documents on the Slave Trade of Eastern Africa*. London: Rex Collings.

Beattie, John. 1980. "Representations of the Self in Traditional Africa." *Africa: Journal of the International African Institute* 50(3): 313–20.

Beidelman, T. O. 1993. *Moral Imagination in Kaguru Modes of Thought*. Washington, DC: Smithsonian Institution Press.

Bekoff, Marc, and Jessica Pierce. 2009. *Wild Justice: The Moral Lives of Animals*. Chicago: University of Chicago Press.

Berry, Veronica, and Celia Petty. 1992. *The Nyasaland Survey Papers 1938–1943: Agriculture, Food, and Health*. London: Academy Books.

Bimwenyi-Kweshi, Oscar. 1982. *Alle Dinge erzählen von Gott. Grundlegung afrikanischer Theologie*. Freiburg: Herder.

Biruk, Crystal. 2018. *Cooking Data: Culture and Politics in an African Research World*. Durham: Duke University Press.

Bledsoe, Caroline H. 2002. *Contingent Lives: Fertility, Time, and Aging in West Africa*. Chicago: University of Chicago Press.

Bloch, Maurice, and Jonathan Parry, eds. 1982. *Death and the Regeneration of Life*. Cambridge: Cambridge University Press.

Boehm, Christopher. 2012. *Moral Origins: The Evolution of Virtue, Altruism, and Shame*. New York: Basic Books.

Bogost, Ian. 2018. "The Myth of 'Dumbing Down.'" *Atlantic*, 26 October.

Bonate, Liazzat. 2006. "Matriliny, Islam and Gender in Northern Mozambique." *Journal of Religion in Africa* 36(2): 139–66.
Brantley, Cynthia. 2002. *Feeding Families: African Realities and British Ideas of Nutrition and Development in Early Colonial Africa*. Portsmouth: Heinemann.
Breithaupt, Fritz. 2019. *The Dark Sides of Empathy*. Translated by Andrew B.B. Hamilton. Ithaca: Cornell University Press.
Brewis, Alexandra A., Amber Wutich, Ashlan Falletta-Cowden, and Isa Rodriguez-Soto. 2011. "Body Norms and Fat Stigma in Global Perspective." *Current Anthropology* 52(2): 269–76.
Brink, Pamela J. 1995. "Fertility and Fat: The Annang Fattening Room." In *Social Aspects of Obesity*, edited by Igor de Garine and Nancy J. Pollock, 71–85. London: Taylor & Francis.
Brown, Judith E., and Richard C. Brown. 2000. "Traditional Intravaginal Practices and the Heterosexual Transmission of Disease: A Review." *Sexually Transmitted Diseases* 27(4): 183–87.
Burgard, Deb. 2009. "What Is 'Health at Every Size'?" In *The Fat Studies Reader*, edited by Esther Rothblum and Sondra Solovay, 41–53. New York: New York University Press.
Caballero, Benjamin, and Barry M. Popkin, eds. 2002. *The Nutrition Transition: Diet and Disease in the Developing World*. Amsterdam: Academic Press.
Caplan, Pat. 1987. Introduction to *The Cultural Construction of Sexuality*, edited by Pat Caplan, 1–30. New York: Routledge.
Carsten, Janet. 1995. "The Substance of Kinship and the Heat of the Hearth: Feeding, Personhood, and Relatedness among Malays in Pulau Langkawi." *American Ethnologist* 22(2): 223–41.
Chaphera, Madalitso. 2007. "Factors That Influence Married People to Engage in Extramarital Sexual Affairs Despite Their Negative Effects: The Case of Chikanda, Zomba." BA thesis, University of Malawi, Chancellor College.
Chimwaza, Beatrice Mary. 1982. "Food and Nutrition in Malawi." PhD diss., Faculty of Science, University of London.
Chingota, Felix L. 1998. "Sacraments and Sexuality." *Religion in Malawi* 8: 34–40.
Chrzan, Janet. 2013. "Nutritional Anthropology." In *Routledge International Handbook of Food Studies*, edited by Ken Albala, 48–64. London: Routledge.
Ciekawy, Diane, and Peter Geschiere. 1998. "Containing Witchcraft: Conflicting Scenarios in Postcolonial Africa." *African Studies Review* 41(3): 1–14.
Clark, Gracia. 1994. *Onions Are My Husband: Survival and Accumulation by West African Market Women*. Chicago: University of Chicago Press.
Cliggett, Lisa. 2005. *Grains from Grass: Aging, Gender, and Famine in Rural Africa*. Ithaca: Cornell University Press.
Cole-King, P. A., and Mapopa O. J. Chipeta. 1987. *Lake Malawi Steamers*. Lilongwe: Ministry of Education and Culture, Department of Antiquities.
Comaroff, Jean. 1985. "Bodily Reform as Historical Practice: The Semantics of Resistance in Modern South Africa." *International Journal of Psychology* 20(3/4): 541–67.
———. 1993. "The Diseased Heart of Africa: Medicine, Colonialism, and the Black Body." In *Knowledge, Power and Practice: The Anthropology of Medicine and Everyday Life*, edited by Shirly Lindenbaum and Margaret M. Lock, 305–29. Berkeley: University of California Press.
Comaroff, John, and Jean Comaroff. 1992. *Ethnography and the Historical Imagination*. Boulder: Westview Press.

———. 1993. *Modernity and Its Malcontents: Ritual and Power in Postcolonial Africa*. Chicago: University of Chicago.

———. 2001. "On Personhood: An Anthropological Perspective from Africa." *Social Identities* 7(2): 267–83.

Cooper, Elizabeth, and David Pratten, eds. 2015. *Ethnographies of Uncertainty in Africa*. Basingstoke: Palgrave Macmillan.

Counihan, Carole. 1999. *The Anthropology of Food and Body: Gender, Meaning, and Power*. New York: Routledge.

Coutinho, João de Azevedo. 1931 [1893]. *Do Nyassa a Pemba: os territorios da Companhia do Nyassa, o futuro porto commercial da região dos Lagos*. Lisbon: Livaria Triunfo.

DeGabriele, Joseph. 1999. "When Pills Don't Work: African Illnesses, Misfortune and Mdulo." *Religion in Malawi* 9: 9–23.

de Garine, Igor. 1997. "Food Preferences and Taste in an African Perspective: A Word of Caution." In *Food Preferences and Taste: Continuity and Change*, edited by Helen M. Macbeth, 187–207. New York: Berghahn Books.

De Groote, Hugo, and Simon Chege Kimenju. 2008. "Comparing Consumer Preferences for Color and Nutritional Quality in Maize: Application of a Semi-Double-Bound Logistic Model on Urban Consumers in Kenya." *Food Policy* 33(4): 362–70.

de Luna, Kathryn M. 2016. *Collecting Food, Cultivating People: Subsistence and Society in Central Africa*. New Haven: Yale University Press.

De Matteis, Allesandro. 2006. "Report of Baseline Survey of Food Security and Nutrition in Mozambique." Maputo: SETSAN.

de Villiers, Jacques. 2019. "Approaching the Uncertain Turn in African Video-Movies: Subalternity, Superfluity, and (Non-)Cinematic Time." In *A Companion to African Cinema*, edited by Kenneth Harrow and Carmela Garritano, 44–68. Hoboken: Wiley Blackwell.

de Waal, Alex. 1997. *Famine Crimes: Politics & Disaster Relief Industry in Africa*. Oxford: James Currey.

Devisch, René. 1990. "The Human Body as a Vehicle for Emotions among the Yaka of Zaire." In *Personhood and Agency: The Experience of Self and Other in African Cultures*, edited by Michael Jackson and Ivan Karp, 115–33. Washington, DC: Smithsonian Institution Press.

———. 1991. "Symbol and Symptom among the Yaka of Zaire." In *Body and Space: Symbolic Models of Unity and Division in African Cosmology and Experience*, edited by Anita Jacobson-Widding, 283–302. Stockholm: Almqvist and Wiksell.

Diallo, Rozenn N., and Estienne Rodary. 2017. "The Transnational Hybridisation of Mozambican Nature." *African Studies* 76(2): 188–204.

Dicks, Ian D. 2012. *An African Worldview: The Muslim Amacinga Yawo of Southern Malawi*. Zomba: Kachere.

Dirks, Robert, and Gina Hunter. 2013. "The Anthropology of Food." In *Routledge International Handbook of Food Studies*, edited by Ken Albala, 3–13. London: Routledge.

dos Santos, Nuno Valdez. 1964. *O desconhecido Niassa*. Lisbon: Minerva.

Douglas, Mary [Tew]. 1950. *Peoples of the Lake Nyasa Region: East Central Africa, Part 1*. Oxford: Oxford University Press.

———. 1980 [1966]. *Purity and Danger: An Analysis of Concept of Pollution and Taboo*. London and New York: Routledge.

Drake, Ann Minick. 1976. "Illness, Ritual and Social Relations among the Chewa of Central Africa." PhD diss., Duke University.

Draper, Catherine E., Kesiah J. Davidowitz, and Julia H. Goedecke. 2016. "Perceptions Relating to Body Size, Weight Loss and Weight-Loss Interventions in Black South African Women: A Qualitative Study." *Public Health Nutrition* 19(3): 548–56.
Ellen, Roy. 2016. "The Cultural Cognition of Time: Some Anthropological Perspectives." In *Conceptualizations of Time*, edited by Barbara Lewandowska-Tomaszczyk, 125–50. Amsterdam: John Benjamins.
Englund, Harri. 2002. *From War to Peace on the Mozambique-Malawi Borderland*. Edinburgh: Edinburgh University Press.
———. 2018. Preface to *Eating and Being Eaten: Cannibalism as Food for Thought*, edited by Francis B. Nyamnjoh, ix–x. Mankon Bamenda: Langaa Research & Publishing Common Initiative Group.
Erdal, Marta Bivand, and Kaja Borchgrevink. 2017. "Transnational Islamic Charity as Everyday Rituals." *Global Networks* 17(1): 130–46.
Evans-Pritchard, E. E. 1939. "Nuer Time-Reckoning." *Africa* 12(2): 189–216.
———. 1976 [1937]. *Witchcraft, Oracles, and Magic among the Azande*. Malden: Blackwell.
Eyre, C. B. 1902. "Letter from Rev. C. B. Eyre, 23 April 1902." Oxford, Bodleian Libraries, USPG Archive, UMCA/TC/G2.
Fabian, Johannes. 1991. *Time and the Work of Anthropology: Critical Essays, 1971–1991*. Philadelphia: Harwood Academic Publishers.
FAO, IFAD, UNICEF, WFP, and WHO. 2018. *The State of Food Security and Nutrition in the World 2018: Building Climate Resilience for Food Security and Nutrition*. Rome: FAO.
Farrell, Amy Erdman. 2011. *Fat Shame: Stigma and the Fat Body in American Culture*. New York: New York University Press.
Fassin, Didier. 2012. "Introduction: Toward a Critical Moral Anthropology." In *A Companion to Moral Anthropology*, edited by Didier Fassin, 1–18. Hoboken: Wiley Blackwell.
Feierman, Steven. 2000. "Explanation and Uncertainty in the Medical World of Ghaambo." *Bulletin of the History of Medicine* 74(2): 317–44.
Feierman, Steven, and John M. Janzen, eds. 1992. *The Social Basis of Health and Healing in Africa*. Berkeley: University of California Press.
Ferguson, James. 2006. *Global Shadows: Africa in the Neoliberal World Order*. Durham: Duke University Press.
———. 2013. "Declarations of Dependence: Labour, Personhood, and Welfare in Southern Africa." *Journal of the Royal Anthropological Institute* 19(2): 223–42.
Flax, Valerie L. 2015. "'It Was Caused by the Carelessness of the Parents': Cultural Models of Child Malnutrition in Southern Malawi." *Maternal & Child Nutrition* 11(1): 104–18.
Flynn, Karen Coen. 2005. *Food, Culture, and Survival in an African City*. New York: Palgrave Macmillan.
Forrest, Beth, and Deirdre Murphy. 2013. "Food and the Senses." In *Routledge International Handbook of Food Studies*, edited by Ken Albala, 352–63. New York: Routledge.
Fortes, Meyer. 1987. *Religion, Morality and the Person: Essays on Tallensi Religion*, edited by Jack Goody. Cambridge: Cambridge University Press.
Freidberg, Susanne. 2004. *French Beans and Food Scares: Culture and Commerce in an Anxious Age*. New York: Oxford University Press.
Gade, Christian B. N. 2011. "The Historical Development of the Written Discourses on Ubuntu." *South African Journal of Philosophy* 30(3): 303–29.
Gaesser, Glenn A. 2002. *Big Fat Lies: The Truth about Your Weight and Your Health*. Carlsbad: Gürze Books.

Geissler, Paul Wenzel, and Ruth Jane Prince. 2010. *The Land Is Dying: Contingency, Creativity and Conflict in Western Kenya*. New York: Berghahn Books.
Gell, Alfred. 1979. "Reflections on a Cut Finger: Taboo in the Umeda Conception of the Self." In *Fantasy and Symbol: Studies in Anthropological Interpretation: Essays in Honor of Georges Devereux*, edited by R. H. Hook, 133–48. London: Academic Press.
Geschiere, Peter. 1997. *The Modernity of Witchcraft: Politics and the Occult in Postcolonial Africa*. Charlottesville: University Press of Virginia.
———. 2003. "Witchcraft as the Dark Side of Kinship: Dilemmas of Social Security in New Contexts." *Etnofoor* 16(1): 43–61.
Gilbert, Juliet. 2018. "'They're My Contacts, Not My Friends': Reconfiguring Affect and Aspirations through Mobile Communication in Nigeria." *Ethnos* 83(2): 237–54.
Gilman, Sander L. 2010. *Difference and Pathology: Stereotypes of Sexuality, Race, and Madness*. Ithaca: Cornell University Press.
Goebel, Allison. 2002. "'Men These Days, They Are a Problem': Husband-Taming Herbs and Gender Wars in Rural Zimbabwe." *Canadian Journal of African Studies* 36(3): 460–89.
Goldstone, Brian, and Juan Obarrio, eds. 2017. *African Futures: Essays on Crisis, Emergence, and Possibility*. Chicago: University of Chicago Press.
Good, Charles M. 1991. "Pioneer Medical Missions in Colonial Africa." *Social Science & Medicine* 32(1): 1–10.
———. 2004. *The Steamer Parish: The Rise and Fall of Missionary Medicine on an African Frontier*. Chicago: University of Chicago Press.
Goody, Jack. 1982. *Cooking, Cuisine and Class: A Study in Comparative Sociology*. Cambridge: Cambridge University Press.
Gordon, Deborah R. 1988. "Tenacious Assumptions in Western Medicine." In *Biomedicine Examined*, edited by Margaret M. Lock and Deborah R. Gordon, 19–56. Dordrecht: Kluwer Academic Publishers.
Gregory, Chris A. 1982. *Gifts and Commodities*. New York: Academic Press.
Gremillion, Helen. 2005. "The Cultural Politics of Body Size." *Annual Review of Anthropology* 34: 13–32.
Gupta, Pamila, and Estienne Rodary. 2017. "Opening-up Mozambique: Histories of the Present." *African Studies* 76(2): 179–87.
Guyer, Jane I., ed. 1987. *Feeding African Cities: Studies in Regional Social History*. Bloomington: Indiana University Press.
Guzman, Isabel. 2006. "Manual de orientação para a mudança de habitos e práticas alimentares negativas, com base nas principais constatações nas regiões sul, centro e norte de Moçambique." Maputo: Ministry of Health, Department of Community Health, Nutrition Sector.
Hafkin, Nancy Jane. 1973. "Trade, Society, and Politics in Northern Mozambique, C.1753–1913," PhD diss., Boston University.
Hahn, Robert A., and Arthur Kleinman. 1983. "Biomedical Practice and Anthropological Theory: Frameworks and Directions." *Annual Review of Anthropology* 12: 305–33.
Ham, Jessica R. 2017. "Cooking to Be Modern but Eating to Be Healthy: The Role of Dawa-Dawa in Contemporary Ghanaian Foodways." *Food, Culture & Society* 20(2): 237–56.
Hanlon, Joseph, and Teresa Smart. 2008. *Do Bicycles Equal Development in Mozambique?* Rochester: James Currey.
Hannig, Anita. 2017. *Beyond Surgery: Injury, Healing, and Religion at an Ethiopian Hospital*. Chicago: University of Chicago Press.

Hansen, Karen Tranberg. 1999. "The Cook, His Wife, the Madam and Their Dinner: Cooking, Gender and Class in Zambia." In *Changing Food Habits: Case Studies from Africa, South America and Europe*, edited by Carola Lentz, 73–90. Amsterdam: Harwood Academic.

Hanson, Stephanie. 2018. "African Agriculture. A Report of the Council on Foreign Relations." Council on Foreign Relations. https://www.cfr.org/backgrounder/african-agriculture.

Haram, Liv., and Bawa Yamba. 2009. *Dealing with Uncertainty in Contemporary African Lives*. Stockholm: Nordic Africa Institute.

Harris, Marvin. 1977. *Cannibals and Kings: The Origins of Cultures*. New York: Vintage Books.

Heald, Suzette. 1995. "The Power of Sex: Some Reflections on the Caldwells' 'African Sexuality' Thesis." *Africa* 65(4): 489–505.

Hellweg, Joseph, and Jesse C. Miller. 2019. "Power, Meaning, and Materiality in the Anthropology of African Religions South of the Sahara: A Dialogue with Religious Studies." In *A Companion to the Anthropology of Africa*, edited by Stephen C. Lubkemann, Christopher B. Steiner, and Euclides Gonçalves, 119–144. Hoboken: Wiley.

Hodgson, A. G. O. 1933. "Notes on the Achewa and Angoni of the Dowa District of the Nyasaland Protectorate." *Journal of the Royal Anthropological Institute of Great Britain and Ireland* 63: 123–64.

Holtzman, Jon. 2009. *Uncertain Tastes: Memory, Ambivalence, and the Politics of Eating in Samburu, Northern Kenya*. Berkeley: University of California Press.

Honwana, Alcinda. 2012. *The Time of Youth: Work, Social Change, and Politics in Africa*. Boulder: Kumarian Press.

Horak, Ivan G. 2005. "Parasites of Domestic and Wild Animals in South Africa. XLVI. Oestrid Fly Larvae of Sheep, Goats, Springbok and Black Wildebeest in the Eastern Cape Province." *Onderstepoort Journal of Veterinary Research* 72(4): 315–20.

Hountondji, Paulin J. 1983 [1976]. *African Philosophy: Myth and Reality*. Translated by Henri Evans and Jonathan Rée. Bloomington: Indiana University Press.

Howard, Mary, and Ann V. Millard. 1997. *Hunger and Shame: Child Malnutrition and Poverty on Mount Kilimanjaro*. New York: Routledge.

Howard, Robert. 1904. *A Report to the Medical Board of the Universities' Mission on the Health of the European Missionaries in the Likoma Diocese. Including an Historical Survey from the Commencement of Work in Nyasaland*. London: UMCA.

Howell, Katharine R. 2017. "'When You Leave, They Will Kill Me': Navigating Politics in and of the Field in Northern Mozambique." In *XXVII European Society of Rural Sociology Congress: Final Proceedings*, 146–47. Krakow, Poland.

Howes, David. 1991. *The Varieties of Sensory Experience: A Sourcebook in the Anthropology of the Senses*. Toronto: University of Toronto Press.

———. 2019. "Multisensory Anthropology." *Annual Review of Anthropology* 48: 17–28.

Hughes, Charles. 1978. "Ethnomedicine." In *Health and the Human Condition: Perspectives on Medical Anthropology*, edited by Michael Logan and Edward Hunt, 150–58. North Scituate: Duxbury Press.

Huhn, Arianna. 2012. "Sustenance and Sociability: Foodways in a Mozambican Town." PhD diss., Boston University.

———. 2013. "The Tongue Only Works without Worries: Sentiment and Sustenance in a Mozambican Town." *Food and Foodways* 21(3): 186–210.

———. 2015. "¿Qué es humano? Tabús alimentarios y antropofagia en el noroeste de Mozambique." Translated by Ramón Cota Meza. *Estudios de Asia y África* 50(3): 721–47.

———. 2016. "Body, Sex, and Diet in Mozambique." In *The Routledge Handbook of Medical Anthropology*, edited by Lenore Manderson, Elizabeth Cartwright, and Anita Hardon, 54–58. New York: Routledge.

———. 2017. "Enacting Compassion: Hot/Cold, Illness and Taboos in Northern Mozambique." *Journal of Southern African Studies* 43(2): 299–313.

Hutchinson, Sharon. 1992. "The Cattle of Money and the Cattle of Girls Among the Nuer, 1930–83." *American Ethnologist* 19(2): 294–316.

———. 2000. "Identity and Substance: The Broadening Bases of Relatedness among the Nuer of Southern Sudan." In *Cultures of Relatedness: New Approaches to the Study of Kinship*, edited by Janet Carsten, 55–72. Cambridge: Cambridge University Press.

Hyden, Goran. 1980. *Beyond Ujamaa in Tanzania: Underdevelopment and an Uncaptured Peasantry*. Berkeley: University of California Press.

Ikpe, Eno Blankson. 1994. *Food and Society in Nigeria: A History of Food Customs, Food Economy, and Cultural Change, 1900–1989*. Stuttgart: Franz Steiner Verlag.

Ingold, Tim. 1994. Introduction to *What Is an Animal?*, edited by Tim Ingold, 1–16. London and New York: Routledge.

Ingstad, Benedicte, Frank J. Bruuns, and Sheila Tlou. 1997. "AIDS and the Elderly Tswana: The Concept of Pollution and Consequences for AIDS Prevention." *Journal of Cross-Cultural Gerontology* 12(4): 357–72.

Instituto Nacional de Estatística. 2011. *Anuário Estatístico 2010 – Moçambique*. Maputo: Instituto Nacional de Estatística. Available online at http://www.ine.gov.mz/estatisticas/publicacoes/anuario/nacionais/anuario-estatistico_2010/at_download/file.

Isichei, Elizabeth. 1997. *A History of African Societies to 1870*. Cambridge: Cambridge University Press.

———. 2002. *Voices of the Poor in Africa*. Rochester: University of Rochester Press.

Jackson, Michael. 1990. "The Man Who Could Turn Into an Elephant: Shape-Shifting among the Kuranko of Sierra Leone." In *Personhood and Agency: The Experience of Self and Other in African Cultures*, edited by Michael Jackson and Ivan Karp, 59–78. Washington, DC: Smithsonian Institution Press.

———. 2005. *Existential Anthropology: Events, Exigencies, and Effects*. New York: Berghahn Books.

———. 2011. *Life Within Limits: Well-Being in a World of Want*. Durham: Duke University Press.

Jackson, Michael, and Ivan Karp, eds. 1990. *Personhood and Agency: The Experience of Self and Other in African Cultures*. Washington, DC: Smithsonian Institution Press.

Jackson, Michael, and Albert Piette. 2015. "Anthropology and the Existential Turn." In *What Is Existential Anthropology?*, edited by Michael Jackson and Albert Piette, 1–29. New York: Berghahn Books.

Jacobson-Widding, Anita. 1990. "The Shadow as an Expression of Individuality in Congolese Conceptions of Personhood." In *Personhood and Agency: The Experience of Self and Other in African Cultures*, edited by Michael Jackson and Ivan Karp, 310–58. Washington, DC: Smithsonian Institution Press.

Jansson, Johanna, and Carine Kiala. 2009. *Patterns of Chinese Investment, Aid and Trade in Mozambique*. Briefing Paper Prepared for World Wide Fund for Nature (WWF)." Available online at https://wwf.panda.org/?unewsid=190465.

Janzen, John M. 1978. *The Quest for Therapy: Medical Pluralism in Lower Zaire*. Berkeley: University of California Press.

Jeal, Tim. 2013. *Livingstone*. New Haven: Yale University Press.
Johnson, Jennifer Lee. 2014. "Fishwork in Uganda: A Multispecies Ethnohistory about Fish, People, and Ideas about Fish and People." PhD diss., University of Michigan.
———. 2017. "Eating and Existence on an Island in Southern Uganda." *Comparative Studies of South Asia, Africa and the Middle East* 37(1): 2–23.
Johnson, Jessica. 2018. "Feminine Futures: Female Initiation and Aspiration in Matrilineal Malawi." *Journal of the Royal Anthropological Institute* 24(4): 786–803.
Johnson, Michelle C. 2016. "'Nothing Is Sweet in My Mouth': Food, Identity, and Religion in African Lisbon." *Food and Foodways* 24(3/4): 232–54.
Johnson, William Percival. 1969[1922]. *Nyasa the Great Water: Being a Description of the Lake and Life of the People*. New York: Negro University Press.
Johnston, Harry Hamilton. 1897. *British Central Africa: An Attempt to Give Some Account of a Portion of the Territories Under British Influence North of the Zambezi*. London: Methuen & Co.
Juma, Martha Ulemu. 2006. "Intravaginal Agents Cultural Beliefs and Practices among Chewa Women of Lilongwe." BS thesis, Kamuzu College of Nursing.
Junod, Henri A. 1912. *The Life of a South African Tribe*. Vol. 1. Neuchatel: Imprimerie Attinger Freres.
Kagame, Alexis. 1976. *La philosophie bantu comparée*. Paris: Présence Africaine.
Kahn, Miriam. 1986. *Always Hungry, Never Greedy: Food and the Expression of Gender Relations in a Melanesian Society*. Cambridge: Cambridge University Press.
Kanyike, Edward. 2004. *The Principle of Participation in African Cosmology and Anthropology*. Balaka: Montfort Media.
Kaphagawani, Didier N. 1998. "Themes in a Chewa Epistemology." In *The African Philosophy Reader*, edited by P. H. Coetzee and A. P. J. Roux, 240–44. London: Routledge.
Karp, Ivan. 1997. "Person, Notions Of." In *Encyclopedia of Africa South of the Sahara*, vol. 3, edited by John Middleton, 392–96. New York: Charles Scribner's Sons.
Karp, Ivan, and D. A. Masolo. 2000. *African Philosophy as Cultural Inquiry*. Bloomington: Indiana University Press.
Kaspin, Deborah. 1996. "A Chewa Cosmology of the Body." *American Ethnologist* 23(3): 561–78.
Kasulo, Catherine Kapelemera. 2006. "Use, Safety, Acceptability and Availability of Safer Sex Practices among Young People of Lilongwe Technical College." BS thesis, Kamuzu College of Nursing, Lilongwe.
Katto, Jonna. 2019. *Women's Lived Landscapes of War and Liberation in Mozambique: Bodily Memory and the Gendered Aesthetics of Belonging*. London: Routledge.
Kayange, Grivas Muchineripi. 2019. *Meaning and Truth in African Philosophy: Doing African Philosophy with Language*. Cham: Springer.
Keim, Curtis, and Carolyn Somerville. 2018. *Mistaking Africa: Curiosities and Inventions of the American Mind*. 4th ed. New York: Routledge.
Kincaid, Jamaica. 1988. *A Small Place*. New York: Penguin.
Kinyanjui, Mary Njeri. 2019. *African Markets in Nairobi: The Utu-Ubuntu Business Model, 'African Metropolis' and Cultural Villages*. Cape Town: African Minds.
Klaits, Frederick. 2010. *Death in a Church of Life: Moral Passion during Botswana's Time of AIDS*. Berkeley: University of California Press.
Klugman, Jeni. 2011. *Human Development Report 2011: Sustainability and Equity: A Better Future for All*. United Nations Development Programme-Human Development Reports

Office (UNDP-HDRO) Human Development Reports. Available at SSRN: http://ssrn.com/abstract=2294671.
Kopytoff, Igor. 1971. "Ancestors as Elders in Africa." *Africa: Journal of the International African Institute* 41(2): 129–42.
Kornfield, Ruth, and Dorothy Namate. 1997. *Cultural Practices Related to HIV/AIDS Risk Behavior: Community Survey in Phalombe, Malawi*. US Agency for International Development, Support to AIDS and Family Health (STAFH) Project 612-238, Report No. 10.
Korsmeyer, Carolyn. 2005. *The Taste Culture Reader: Experiencing Food and Drink*. New York: Berg.
Korsmeyer, Carolyn, and David Sutton. 2011. "The Sensory Experience of Food." *Food, Culture & Society* 14(4): 461–75.
Leach, Edmund. 1989. *Claude Lévi-Strauss*. Chicago: University of Chicago Press.
Lentz, Carola. 1999. "Changing Food Habits: An Introduction." In *Changing Food Habits: Case Studies from Africa, South America and Europe*, edited by Carola Lentz, 1–26. Amsterdam: Harwood Academic.
Lévi-Strauss, Claude. 1969. *The Raw and the Cooked*. New York: Harper and Row.
Lévy-Bruhl, Lucien. 1925. *How Natives Think*. Translated by Lilian A. Clare. New York: Knopf.
Littlewood, Roland, ed. 2007. *On Knowing and Not Knowing in the Anthropology of Medicine*. Walnut Creek: Left Coast Press.
Livingston, Julie. 2005. *Debility and the Moral Imagination in Botswana*. Bloomington: Indiana University Press.
Livingstone, David, and Charles Livingstone. 1865. *Narrative of an Expedition to the Zambesi and Its Tributaries; And of the Discovery of the Lakes Shirwa and Nyassa, 1858–1864*. London: John Murray.
Lock, Margaret M., and Deborah R. Gordon, eds. 1988. *Biomedicine Examined*. Dordrecht: Kluwer Academic Publishers.
Logan, Michael H. 1977. "Part Five: Anthropological Research on the Hot-Cold Theory of Disease: Some Methodological Suggestions." *Medical Anthropology* 1(4): 87–112.
Lupton, Deborah. 1996. *Food, the Body and the Self*. London: Sage.
———. 2018. *Fat*. 2nd ed. New York: Routledge.
Machava, Benedito. 2019. "Reeducation Camps, Austerity, and the Carceral Regime in Socialist Mozambique (1974–79)." *Journal of African History* 60(3): 429–55.
Makawa, Moses. 2010. "Umakwiya Chani." *Khuzumule*. Vol. 2. DVD distributed by RHEM Records, Lilongwe.
Malata, Wisdom. 2007. Untitled Report on Research into Sexuality. Metangula: Khalidwe.
Manderson, L. 1987. "Hot-Cold Food and Medical Theories: Overview and Introduction." *Social Science & Medicine* 25(4): 329–30.
Manderson, Lenore, Elizabeth Cartwright, and Anita Hardon, eds. 2016. *The Routledge Handbook of Medical Anthropology*. New York: Routledge.
Martinez, Francisco Lerma. 2009. *O povo Macua e a sua cultura: análise dos valores culturais do povo Macua no ciclo vital, Maúa, Moçambique 1971–1985*. 2nd ed. Maputo: Paulinas.
Marwick, Max G. 1965. *Sorcery in Its Social Setting: A Study of the Northern Rhodesian Cewa*. Manchester: Manchester University Press.
Masolo, D. A. 1994. *African Philosophy in Search of Identity*. Bloomington: Indiana University Press.

———. 2010. *Self and Community in a Changing World*. Bloomington: Indiana University Press.
———. 2019a. "Crafting Ideal Conditions: Ubuntu and the Challenges of Modern Society." In *Ubuntu and the Reconstitution of Community*, edited by James Ogude, 40–72. Bloomington: Indiana University Press.
———. 2019b. "Everyday and Other Days: What's the Difference?" In *Ubuntu and the Everyday in Africa*, edited by James Ogude and Unifer Dyer, 25–63. Trenton: Africa World Press.
Mazula, Assahel Jonassane. 1970. *História dos Nianjas*. Lourenço Marques [Maputo]: Minerva Central.
Mbeye, Nyanyiwe Masingi. 2007. "Sexual Behavior and Future Childbearing Intentions of HIV Infected Women Receiving Antiretroviral Therapy (ART) in Lilongwe." MA thesis, University of Malawi, College of Medicine.
Mbiti, John S. 1969. *African Religions and Philosophy*. London: Heinemann.
———. 1970. *Concepts of God in Africa*. New York: Praeger Publications.
McCann, James C. 2012. "Writing on the African Pot: Recipes and Cooking as Historical Knowledge." In *Writing Food History: A Global Perspective*, edited by Kyri W. Claflin and Peter Scholliers, 199–208. New York: Berg.
McGuire, Meredith B. 2008. *Lived Religion: Faith and Practice in Everyday Life*. Oxford: Oxford University Press.
McKay, Ramah. 2018. *Medicine in the Meantime: The Work of Care in Mozambique*. Durham: Duke University Press.
Medeiros, Eduardo da Conceição. 1997. *História de Cabo Delgado e do Niassa: c.1836–1929*. Maputo: Central Impressora.
Meneses, Maria Paula. 2018. "Singing Struggles, Affirming Politics: Mozambique's Revolutionary Songs as Other Ways of Being (in) History." In *Mozambique on the Move: Challenges and Reflections*, edited by Sheila Pereira Khan, Maria Paula Meneses, and Bjørn Enge Bertelsen, 254–278. Leiden: Brill.
Menkiti, Ifeanyi A. 1984. "Person and Community in African Traditional Thought." In *African Philosophy: An Introduction*, edited by Richard Wright, 171–82. Lanham: University Press of America.
Mennell, Stephen. 1996. *All Manners of Food: Eating and Taste in England and France from the Middle Ages to the Present*. 2nd ed. Urbana: University of Illinois Press.
Messer, Ellen. 1984. "Anthropological Perspectives on Diet." *Annual Review of Anthropology* 13: 205–49.
Middleton, John, and E. H. Winter. 2004 [1963]. Introduction to *Witchcraft and Sorcery in East Africa*, edited by John Middleton, John Beattie, and E. H. Winter, 1–26. London: Routledge.
Miers, Suzanne, and Igor Kopytoff, eds. 1977. *Slavery in Africa: Historical and Anthropological Perspectives*. Madison: University of Wisconsin Press.
Mills, Dora S. Yarnton. 1933. *A Hero Man: The Life and Adventures of William Percival Johnson Archdeacon of Nyasa*. Westminster: UMCA.
Mintz, Sidney W. 1985. *Sweetness and Power: The Place of Sugar in Modern History*. New York: Penguin Books.
Mintz, Sidney W., and Christine M. Du Bois. 2002. "The Anthropology of Food and Eating." *Annual Review of Anthropology* 31: 99–119.
Mogensen, Hanne Overgaard. 1997. "The Narrative of AIDS among the Tonga of Zambia." *Social Science & Medicine* 44(4): 431–39.

Mohanty, Chandra Talpade. 1984. "Under Western Eyes: Feminist Scholarship and Colonial Discourses." *Boundary 2* 12(3)/13(1): 333–58.
Mojola, Aloo Osotsi. 2019. "Ubuntu in the Christian Theology and Praxis of Archbishop Desmond Tutu and Its Implications for Global Justice and Human Rights." In *Ubuntu and the Reconstitution of Community*, edited by James Ogude, 21–39. Bloomington: Indiana University Press.
Moore, Henrietta L., and Todd Sanders. 2001. *Magical Interpretations, Material Realities: Modernity, Witchcraft and the Occult in Postcolonial Africa*. New York: Routledge.
Morris, Brian. 1998. *The Power of Animals: An Ethnography*. Oxford: Berg.
———. 2000. *Animals and Ancestors: An Ethnography*. Oxford: Berg.
———. 2016. *An Environmental History of Southern Malawi: Land and People of the Shire Highlands*. Cham: Springer.
Mousalimas, S. A. 1990. "The Concept of Participation in Levy-Bruhl's Primitive Mentality." *Journal of the Anthropological Society of Oxford* 21(1): 33–46.
Mtembezeka, Memory M. 1994. "Dietary Habits of the Elderly People in Villages around Bunda College of Agriculture." BS thesis, University of Malawi, Bunda College, Lilongwe.
Mudimbe, V. Y. 1983. "African Philosophy as an Ideological Practice: The Case of French-Speaking Africa." *African Studies Review* 26(3/4): 133–54.
———. 1988. *The Invention of Africa: Gnosis, Philosophy, and the Order of Knowledge*. Bloomington: Indiana University Press.
Mulago, Vincent. 1969. "Vital Participation: The Cohesive Principle of the Bantu Community." In *Biblical Revelation and African Beliefs*, edited by Kwesi A. Dickson and Paul Ellingworth, 137–58. London: Lutterworth
Müller, Julian, John Eliastam, and Sheila Trahar. 2019. *Unfolding Narratives of Ubuntu in Southern Africa*. New York: Routledge.
Munn, Nancy D. 1992. "The Cultural Anthropology of Time: A Critical Essay." *Annual Review of Anthropology* 21: 93–123.
Munthali, Alister C. 2002a. "After Delivery: Attempts to Protect Children from Tsempho in a Rural Malawian Village." *Society of Malawi Journal* 55(1): 24–37.
———. 2002b. "Change and Continuity: Perception about Childhood Diseases among the Timbuka of Northern Malawi." PhD diss., Rhodes University.
———. 2007. "Beliefs about Pregnancy, Childbearing, and Newborn Infants in a Rural District in Northern Malawi." In *Childrearing and Infant Care Issues: A Cross-Cultural Perspective*, edited by Pranee Liamputtong, 141–54. New York: Nova Science.
Murcott, Anne. 1988. "Sociological and Social Anthropological Approaches to Eating." *World Review of Nutrition and Dietetics* 55: 1–40.
Murray, Colin, and Peter Sanders. 2005. *Medicine Murder in Colonial Lesotho: The Anatomy of a Moral Crisis*. Edinburgh: Edinburgh University Press.
Musopole, Augustine Chingwala. 1984. "The Chewa Concept of God and Its Implications for the Christian Faith." MA thesis, University of Malawi.
———. 1998. "Needed: A Theology Cooked in an African Pot." In *Theology Cooked in an African Pot*, edited by Klaus Fiedler, Paul Gundani, and Hilary Mijoga, 7–47. Zomba: Association of Theological Institutions in Southern and Central Africa.
Muzhingi, Tawanda, Augustine S. Langyintuo, Lucie C. Malaba, and Marianne Banziger. 2008. "Consumer Acceptability of Yellow Maize Products in Zimbabwe." *Food Policy* 33(4): 352–61.

Myhre, Knut Christian. 2018. *Returning Life: Language, Life Force, and History in Kilimanjaro*. New York: Berghahn.
Naval Intelligence Division. 1969. *A Handbook of Portuguese Nyasaland*. New York: Negro University Press.
Neil-Tomlinson, Barry. 1977. "The Nyassa Chartered Company: 1891–1929." *Journal of African History* 18(1): 109–28.
Newitt, Malyn. 2009 [1995]. *A History of Mozambique*. London: Hurst.
Nielsen, Morten. 2012. "Roadside Inventions: Making Time and Money Work at a Road Construction Site in Mozambique." *Mobilities* 7(4): 467–80.
Njal, Jorge. 2012. *Chinese Aid to Education in Mozambique*. Conference Paper No. 24. III Conferência Internacional Do Instituto de Estudos Sociais e Económicos (IESE). 4 and 5 September, 2012. IESE: Maputo.
Nyamnjoh, Francis B. 2001. "Expectations of Modernity in Africa or a Future in the Rear-View Mirror?" *Journal of Southern African Studies* 27(2): 363–69.
———. 2018. "Introduction: Cannibalism as Food for Thought." In *Eating and Being Eaten: Cannibalism as Food for Thought*, edited by Francis B. Nyamnjoh, 1–98. Mankon Bamenda: Langaa Research & Publishing Common Initiative Group.
Nyarwath, Oriare. 2019. "Entrenching the Moral Value of Ubuntu in Everyday Life." In *Ubuntu and the Everyday in Africa*, edited by James Ogude and Unifer Dyer, 65–87. Trenton: Africa World Press.
Obosu-Mensah, Kwaku. 1999. *Food Production in Urban Areas: A Study of Urban Agriculture in Accra, Ghana*. Aldershot: Ashgate.
Ocholla-Ayayo, A. B. C. 1976. *Traditional Ideology and Ethics among the Southern Luo*. Uppsala: Scandinavian Institute of African Studies.
Ogude, James, ed. 2018. *Ubuntu and Personhood*. Trenton: Africa World Press.
———. 2019a. Introduction to *Ubuntu and the Reconstitution of Community*, edited by James Ogude, 1–20. Bloomington: Indiana University Press.
———. 2019b. *Ubuntu and the Reconstitution of Community*. Bloomington: Indiana University Press.
Ogude, James, and Unifer Dyer, eds. 2019. *Ubuntu and the Everyday in Africa*. Trenton: Africa World Press.
Okafor, Stephen O. 1982. "'Bantu Philosophy': Placide Tempels Revisited." *Journal of Religion in Africa* 13(2): 83–100.
O'Neill, Sarah, Susan Dierickx, Joseph Okebe, Edgard Dabira, Charlotte Gryseels, Umberto d'Alessandro, and Koen Peeters Grietens. 2016. "The Importance of Blood Is Infinite: Conceptions of Blood as Life Force, Rumours and Fear of Trial Participation in a Fulani Village in Rural Gambia." *PLoS ONE* 11(8): e0160464.
Osseo-Asare, Fran. 2005. *Food Culture in Sub Saharan Africa*. Westport: Greenwood Press.
Pagel, Mark. 2012. *Wired for Culture: Origins of the Human Social Mind*. New York: W. W. Norton & Co.
Parkin, David. 1985. "Reason, Emotion, and the Embodiment of Power." In *Reason and Morality*, edited by Joanna Overing, 134–49. London: Tavistock Publications Ltd.
Parman, Susan. 2002. "Lot's Wife and the Old Salt: Cross-Cultural Comparisons of Attitudes toward Salt in Relation to Diet." *Cross-Cultural Research* 36(2): 123–50.
Parry, Jonathan P., and Maurice Bloch, eds. 1989. *Money and the Morality of Exchange*. Cambridge: Cambridge University Press.

Paul, John. 1975. *Mozambique: Memoirs of a Revolution*. Harmondsworth: Penguin Books.
Perani, Judith, and Fred T. Smith. 1998. *The Visual Arts of Africa: Gender, Power, and Life Cycle Rituals*. Upper Saddle River: Prentice Hall.
Peters, Pauline E., Peter A. Walker, and Daimon Kambewa. 2008. "Striving for Normality in a Time of AIDS in Malawi." *Journal of Modern African Studies* 46(4): 659–87.
Peterson, Bhekizizwe. 2019. "The Art of Personhood: Kinship and Its Social Challenges." In *Ubuntu and the Reconstitution of Community*, edited by James Ogude, 73–97. Bloomington: Indiana University Press.
Phillips, Kristin D. 2018. *An Ethnography of Hunger: Politics, Subsistence, and the Unpredictable Grace of the Sun*. Bloomington: Indiana University Press.
Piano, António José. 2007. "HIV/SIDA em Moçambique: o impacto psicológico e cultural do uso do preservativo, caso de ovens do distrito do Meconta." Licenciatura thesis, Universidade Pedagógica, Nampula.
Pietilä, Tuulikki. 2007. *Gossip, Markets, and Gender: How Dialogue Constructs Moral Value in Post-Socialist Kilimanjaro*. Madison: University of Wisconsin Press.
Platt, Benjamin S. 1939. "Report of a Nutrition Survey in Nyasaland." Unpublished document filed at the Documentation Centre of the Centre for Social Research at the University of Malawi, Chancellor College, Zomba, Malawi.
Popkin, Barry M. 1998. "The Nutrition Transition and Its Health Implications in Lower-Income Countries." *Public Health Nutrition* 1(1): 5–21.
———. 2015. "Nutrition Transition and the Global Diabetes Epidemic." *Current Diabetes Reports* 15(9): 64, 1–8.
Popkin, Barry M., Linda S. Adair, and Shu Wen Ng. 2012. "Global Nutrition Transition and the Pandemic of Obesity in Developing Countries." *Nutrition Reviews* 70(1): 3–21.
Pottier, Johan. 1985. *Food Systems in Central and Southern Africa*. London: School of Oriental and African Studies, University of London.
Premawardhana, Devaka. 2018. *Faith in Flux: Pentecostalism and Mobility in Rural Mozambique*. Philadelphia: University of Pennsylvania Press.
Quinn, Victoria. 1994. *Nutrition and National Development: An Evaluation of Nutrition Planning in Malawi from 1936 to 1990*. PhD diss., Wageningen University.
Ramose, Mogobe. 1999. *African Philosophy through Ubuntu*. Harare: Mond Books.
Rangeley, W. H. J. 1948. "Notes on Cewa Tribal Law." *Nyasaland Journal* 1(3): 5–68.
Ranger, Terence Osborn. 1982a. "Medical Science and Pentecost: The Dilemma of Anglicanism in Africa." In *The Church and Healing*, edited by W. J. Sheils, 333–65. Oxford: Basil Blackwell.
———. 1982b. "Race and Tribe in Southern Africa: European Ideas and African Acceptance." In *Racism and Colonialism: Essays on Ideology and Social Structure*, edited by Robert Ross, 121–42. Dordrecht: Springer.
———. 2007. "Scotland Yard in the Bush: Medicine Murders, Child Witches and the Construction of the Occult: A Literature Review." *Africa* 77(2): 272–83.
Ransford, Oliver. 1966. *Livingstone's Lake: The Drama of Nyasa*. London: John Murray.
Reed, Danielle R., and Amanda H. McDaniel. 2006. "The Human Sweet Tooth." *BMC Oral Health* 6(Supplement 1): S17.
Reis, Jaime Batalha. 1889. *Os Portuguezes na região do Nyassa*. Lisbon: Imprensa Nacional.
Rennick, Agnes. 2003. "Church and Medicine: The Role of Medical Missionaries in Malawi 1875–1914." PhD diss., University of Stirling.

Richards, Audrey I. 1932. *Hunger and Work in a Savage Tribe*. London: Routledge.
———. 1939. *Land, Labour, and Diet in Northern Rhodesia: An Economic Study of the Bemba Tribe*. London: Oxford University Press.
Riesman, Paul. 1986. "The Person and the Life Cycle in African Social Life and Thought." *African Studies Review* 29(2): 71–138.
Rita-Ferreira, António. 1966. *Os Cheuas da Macanga*. Lourenço Marques [Maputo]: Memórias Do Instituto de Investigação Científica de Moçambique.
Roberts, Allen F. 1995. *Animals in African Art*. New York: Museum for African Art.
Rodrigues, Eugénia. 2014. "Eating and Drinking at the Royal Hospital of Mozambique Island: Medicine and Diet Change between the End of the 18th and the Early 19th Century." *Afriques: Débats, méthodes et terrains d'histoire* 5. Online publication available at https://doi.org/10.4000/afriques.1553.
Rothblum, Esther D, and Sondra Solovay, eds. 2009. *The Fat Studies Reader*. New York: New York University Press.
Ruel, Malcolm. 1997. *Belief, Ritual and the Securing of Life: Reflexive Essays on a Bantu Religion*. New York: Brill.
Saguy, Abigail C, and Rene Almeling. 2008. "Fat in the Fire? Science, the News Media, and the 'Obesity Epidemic.'" *Sociological Forum* 23(1): 53–83.
Sahlins, Marshall. 1976. *Culture and Practical Reason*. Chicago: University of Chicago Press.
Said, Edward W. 1978. *Orientalism*. New York: Pantheon Books.
Salo, Elaine R. 2018. *Respectable Mothers, Tough Men and Good Daughters: Producing Persons in Manenberg Township South Africa*. Mankon Bamenda: Langaa Research & Publishing Common Initiative Group.
Sanders, Todd. 2003. "Reconsidering Witchcraft: Postcolonial Africa and Analytic (Un)Certainties." *American Anthropologist* 105(2): 338–52.
Scherz, China. 2018. "Stuck in the Clinic: Vernacular Healing and Medical Anthropology in Contemporary Sub-Saharan Africa." *Medical Anthropology Quarterly* 32(4): 539–55.
Schoffeleers, Matthew J. 1968. "Symbolic and Social Aspects of Spirit Worship among the Manganja." PhD diss., Oxford University.
———. 1992. *River of Blood: The Genesis of a Martyr Cult in Southern Malawi, c. AD 1600*. Madison: University of Wisconsin Press.
Schoffeleers, Matthew J., and Adrian A. Roscoe. 1985. *Land of Fire: Oral Literature from Malawi*. Limbe: Montfort Press.
Setel, Philip W. 1999. *A Plague of Paradoxes: AIDS, Culture, and Demography in Northern Tanzania*. Chicago: University of Chicago Press.
Shaw, Rosalind. 1997. "The Production of Witchcraft/Witchcraft as Production: Memory, Modernity, and the Slave Trade in Sierra Leone." *American Ethnologist* 24(4): 856–76.
———. 2002. *Memories of the Slave Trade: Ritual and the Historical Imagination in Sierra Leone*. Chicago: University of Chicago Press.
Shih, Shu-Mei. 2008. "Comparative Racialization: An Introduction." *PMLA* 123(5): 1347–62.
Shipton, Parker. 1989. *Bitter Money: Cultural Economy and Some African Meanings of Forbidden Commodities*. Washington, DC: American Anthropological Association.
———. 1990. "African Famines and Food Security: Anthropological Perspectives." *Annual Review of Anthropology* 19: 353–94.
———. 2007. *The Nature of Entrustment: Intimacy, Exchange, and the Sacred in Africa*. New Haven: Yale University Press.

Shutte, Augustine. 1993. *Philosophy for Africa*. Milwaukee: Marquette University Press.
Simoons, Frederick J. 1994. *Eat Not This Flesh: Food Avoidances from Prehistory to the Present*. 2nd ed. Madison: University of Wisconsin Press.
Simpson, Kate. 2004. "'Doing Development': The Gap Year, Volunteer-Tourists and a Popular Practice of Development." *Journal of International Development* 16(5): 681–92.
Smith, James H. 2019. "Witchcraft in Africa." In *A Companion to the Anthropology of Africa*, edited by Roy Richard Grinker, Stephen C. Lubkemann, Christopher B. Steiner, and Euclides Gonçalves, 63–79. Hoboken: Wiley.
Sobal, Jeffery, and Albert J. Stunkard. 1989. "Socioeconomic Status and Obesity: A Review of the Literature." *Psychological Bulletin* 105(2): 260–75.
Sobo, Elisa Janine. 1993. *One Blood: The Jamaican Body*. New York: State University of New York Press.
———. 1997. "The Sweetness of Fat: Health, Procreation, and Sociability in Rural Jamaica." In *Food and Culture: A Reader*, edited by Carole Counihan and Penny Van Esterik, 256–71. New York: Routledge.
Songolo, Aliko. 1981. "Muntu Reconsidered: From Tempels and Kagame to Janheinz Jahn." *Ufahamu* 10(3): 92–100.
Stannus, Hugh S. 1922. "The Wayao of Nyassaland." In *Harvard African Studies*, vol. 3, edited by E. A. Hooton and Natica I. Bates, 229–372. Cambridge: African Department of the Peabody Museum.
Steinforth, Arne S. 2009. *Troubled Minds: On the Cultural Construction of Mental Disorder and Normality in Southern Malawi*. Frankfurt: Peter Lang.
Stevano, Sara. 2014. "Women's Work, Food and Household Dynamics: A Case Study of Northern Mozambique." PhD diss., SOAS, University of London.
Stoller, Paul. 1989. *The Taste of Ethnographic Things: The Senses in Anthropology*. Philadelphia: University of Pennsylvania Press.
Stoller, Paul, and Cheryl Olkes. 1986. "Bad Sauce, Good Ethnography." *Cultural Anthropology* 1(3): 336–52.
———. 2005. "Thick Sauce: Remarks on the Social Relations of the Songhay." In *The Taste Culture Reader*, edited by Carolyn Korsmeyer, translated by K. Hunter, 131–42. Oxford: Berg.
Stuart, Richard Grey. 1974. "Christianity and the Chewa: The Anglican Case, 1885–1950." PhD diss., University of London.
Sutton, David E. 2001. *Remembrance of Repasts an Anthropology of Food and Memory*. New York: Berg.
———. 2010. "Food and the Senses." *Annual Review of Anthropology* 39: 209–23.
Tamele, Viriato, and João Armando Vilanculo. 2003. *Algumas danças tradicionais na zona norte de Moçambique*. Maputo: ARPAC.
Taylor, Christopher C. 1992. *Milk, Honey and Money: Changing Concepts in Rwandan Healing*. Washington: Smithsonian Institution Press.
Tempels, Placide. 1952. *Bantu Philosophy*. Translated by Colin King. Paris: Présence Africaine.
Tengatenga, James. 2010. *The UMCA in Malawi: A History of the Anglican Church, 1861–2010*. Zomba: Kachere.
Thompson, T. Jack. 2013. "Lake Malawi, I Presume? David Livingstone, Maps and the 'Discovery' of Lake Nyassa in 1859." *Society of Malawi Journal* 66(2): 1–15.
Trentini, Daria. 2016a. "'The Night War of Nampula': Vulnerable Children, Social Change and Spiritual Insecurity in Northern Mozambique." *Africa* 86(3): 528–51.

———. 2016b. "'Muslims of the Spirits'-'Muslims of the Mosque': Performing Contested Ideas of Being Muslim in Northern Mozambique." *Journal for Islamic Studies* 35: 70–106.
Turner, Edith. 2012. *Communitas: The Anthropology of Collective Joy*. New York: Palgrave Macmillan.
Turner, Victor. 1967. *The Forest of Symbols: Aspects of Ndembu Ritual*. Ithaca: Cornell University Press.
———. 1969. *The Ritual Process: Structure and Anti-structure*. Chicago: Aldine.
———. 1974. *Dramas, Fields, and Metaphors: Symbolic Action in Human Society*. Ithaca: Cornell University Press.
Umali, Daniel Chedreque. 1996. *História de Nyanjas*. Lichinga: Accord.
———. 2006. "A história do régulo Massumba." Unpublished document, filed at Museu Local, Metangula.
United Nations Population Division. N.d. "Infant Mortality Rate, for Both Sexes Combined (Infant Deaths per 1,000 Live Births)." Accessed 22 December 2019. http://data.un.org/Data.aspx?d=PopDiv&f=variableID%3A77#PopDiv.
Universities' Mission to Central Africa. 1952. *His Marvellous Works: An Account of the Work of the Mission*. London: UMCA.
Vail, Leroy. 1976. "Mozambique's Chartered Companies: The Rule of the Feeble." *Journal of African History* 17(3): 389–416.
van Beek, Walter E. A., and William C. Olsen. 2016. "Introduction: African Notions of Evil: The Chimera of Justice." In *Evil in Africa: Encounters with the Everyday*, edited by William C. Olsen and Walter E. A. van Beek, 1–26. Bloomington: Indiana University Press.
van Breugel, J. W. M. 2001. *Chewa Traditional Religion*. Blantyre: CLAIM.
van den Borne, Francine. 2005. *Trying to Survive in Times of Poverty and AIDS: Women and Multiple Partner Sex in Malawi*. Amsterdam: Het Spinhuis.
Van der Meer, Erwin. 2013. "Child Witchcraft Accusations in Southern Malawi." *Australasian Review of African Studies* 34(1): 129–44.
van Koevering, Helen E. P. 2005. *Dancing Their Dreams: The Lakeshore Nyanja Women of the Anglican Diocese of Niassa*. Zomba: Kachere.
Vaughan, Megan. 1991. *Curing Their Ills: Colonial Power and African Illness*. Stanford: Stanford University Press.
Versfeld, Anna. 2012. "Generational Change in Manenberg: The Erosion of Possibilities for Positive Personhood." *Agenda* 26(4): 101–13.
Vibeke, Steffen, Richard Jenkins, and Hanne Jessen. 2005. *Managing Uncertainty: Ethnographic Studies of Illness, Risk and the Struggle for Control*. Chicago: University of Chicago Press.
Vincent, Louise. 2008. "New Magic for New Times: Muti Murder in Democratic South Africa." *Studies of Tribes and Tribals* 2: 43–53.
Visser, Margaret. 2005. "Salt, the Edible Rock." In *The Taste Culture Reader: Experiencing Food and Drink*, edited by Carolyn Korsmeyer, 105–9. Oxford: Berg.
von Poser, Anita. 2013. *Foodways and Empathy: Relatedness in a Ramu River Society, Papua New Guinea*. New York: Berghahn Books.
Wainaina, Binyavanga. 2005. "How to Write about Africa." *Granta* 92: 91–96.
Waller, Horace. 1874. *The Last Journals of David Livingstone in Central Africa from 1865 to His Death. Continued by a Narrative of His Last Moments and Sufferings, Obtained from His Faithful Servants Chuma and Susi*. Vol. 1. London: John Murray.

Wegher, Luís. 1995. *Um olhar sobre o Niassa*. Vol. 1. Maputo: Paulinas.
———. 1999. *Um olhar sobre o Niassa*. Vol. 2. Maputo: Paulinas.
Weidtmann, Niels. 2019a. "The Historical Dimension of Ubuntu in Everyday Life." In *Ubuntu and the Everyday in Africa*, edited by James Ogude and Unifer Dyer, 135–55. Trenton: Africa World Press.
———. 2019b. "The Philosophy of Ubuntu and the Notion of Vital Force." In *Ubuntu and the Reconstitution of Community*, edited by James Ogude, 98–113. Bloomington: Indiana University Press.
Weiss, Brad. 1996. *The Making and Unmaking of the Haya Lived World: Consumption, Commoditization, and Everyday Practice*. Durham: Duke University Press.
———. 1998. "Electric Vampires: Haya Rumors of the Commodified Body." In *Bodies and Persons: Comparative Perspectives from Africa and Melanesia*, edited by Michael Lambeck and Andrew Strathern, 172–96. Cambridge: Cambridge University Press.
Welling, Menno. 1999. "Verkenningen in Maravi Kleurensymboliek. Een beschouwing over doden-, regen- en genezingsrituelen [Explorations of Maravi color symbolism: A discussion of funeral, rain, and healing rituals]." MA thesis, University of Leiden.
Wendland, Ernst R. 1990. "Traditional Central African Religion." In *Bridging the Gap: African Traditional Religion and Bible Translation*, edited by Philip C. Stine and Ernst R. Wendland. New York: United Bible Societies.
Werner, Alice. 2010 [1933]. *Myths & Legends of the Bantu*. London: Abela Publishing.
West, Harry G. 1997. "Mozambique: Peoples and Cultures." In *Encyclopedia of Africa South of the Sahara*, edited by John Middleton, 3:198–202. New York: Simon & Schuster.
———. 2005. *Kupilikula: Governance and the Invisible Realm in Mozambique*. Chicago: University of Chicago Press.
White, Landeg. 1987. *Magomero: Portrait of an African Village*. Cambridge: Cambridge University Pres.
White, Luise. 2000. *Speaking with Vampires: Rumor and History in Colonial Africa*. Berkeley: University of California Press.
Whitehead, Neil L., and Robin Wright, eds. 2004. *In Darkness and Secrecy: The Anthropology of Assault Sorcery and Witchcraft in Amazonia*. Durham: Duke University Press.
Whyte, Susan Reynolds. 1989. "Anthropological Approaches to African Misfortune, from Religion to Medicine." In *Culture, Experience and Pluralism: Essays on African Ideas of Illness and Healing*, edited by Anita Jacobson-Widding and David Westerlund, 289–301. Stockholm: Almqvist & Wiksell International.
———. 1997. *Questioning Misfortune: The Pragmatics of Uncertainty in Eastern Uganda*. Cambridge: Cambridge University Press.
Wiegink, Nikkie. 2013. "Why Did the Soldiers Not Go Home? Demobilized Combatants, Family Life, and Witchcraft in Postwar Mozambique." *Anthropological Quarterly* 86(1): 107–32.
Williamson, A. C. 1972. "Notes on Some Changes in the Malawian Diet over the Last 30 Years." *Society of Malawi Journal* 25(2): 49–54.
Williamson, Jessie. 1954. "Legumes in the Diet of the Nyasaland African, with Notes on Cooking and Palatability." *Nyasaland Journal* 7(1): 19–29.
———. 1956. "Salt and Potashes in the Life of the Cewa." *Nyasaland Journal* 9(1): 82–87.
Willis, Roy, ed. 1990. *Signifying Animals: Human Meaning in the Natural World*. Boston: Unwin Hyman.

Wiredu, Kwasi. 1980. *Philosophy and an African Culture*. New York: Cambridge University Press.

———. 1996. *Cultural Universals and Particulars: An African Perspective*. Bloomington: Indiana University Press.

Wirzba, Norman. 2011. *Food and Faith: A Theology of Eating*. Cambridge: Cambridge University Press.

Wolf, Angelika. 2001. "AIDS, Morality and Indigenous Concepts of Sexually Transmitted Diseases in Southern Africa." *Africa Spectrum* 36(1): 97–107.

World Bank. 2018. *Poverty and Shared Prosperity 2018: Piecing Together the Poverty Puzzle*. Washington, DC: World Bank.

Wrangham, Richard W. 2010. *Catching Fire: How Cooking Made Us Human*. London: Profile Books.

———. 2019. *The Goodness Paradox: The Strange Relationship between Virtue and Violence in Human Evolution*. New York: Pantheon Books.

Wylie, Diana. 2001. *Starving on a Full Stomach: Hunger and the Triumph of Cultural Racism in Modern South Africa*. Charlottesville: University Press of Virginia.

Zamparoni, Valdemir. 2000. "Monhés, Baneanes, Chinas e Afro-maometanos. Colonialismo e racismo em Lourenço Marques, Moçambique, 1890–1940." *Lusotopie* 7(1): 191–222.

———. 2017. "Leprosy: Disease, Isolation, and Segregation in Colonial Mozambique." *História, Ciências, Saúde-Manguinhos* 24(1): 13–39.

Zigon, Jarrett. 2008. *Morality: An Anthropological Perspective*. New York: Berg.

Index

afiti (witches), 92–93, 186. *See also* witches and witchcraft
Africa, sub-Saharan: alimentation in, 7–8; ancestors in, 75; cuisine and diets, 7–8; food, anthropology and, 3–17; foodways of, 7; malaria in, 34; markets in, 84–85; modernity in, 140–41; obesity in, 152–53; philosophy in, 178–80; sex and sexuality in, 128–29, 132–33; subsistence farming in, 7; Ubuntu in, 62–65, 127, 178; undernutrition in, 151; witches and witchcraft in, 92
African cosmology, 86n4, 179, 185n5
African personhood, 4, 61–62, 65, 77, 86n3, 179
Afro-Jamaicans, 56
AIDS/HIV, 2, 34, 155, 183
alimentation, 177; African, 7–8; cannibalism and, 182; nourishment, 3–6, 8, 24; personhood and, 63; *vitamina* and, 37, 61, 133; weight and, 155–57
Altuna, Raul Ruiz de Asúa, 77
Ambali, Augustine, 70
AMETRAMO. *See* Associação dos Médicos Tradicionais de Moçambique
ancestors (*mizimu*), 75–76, 87n10, 87n12, 122, 127, 133, 143
anemia, 34, 54–55, 130, 159
ang'anga. *See* sing'anga
animals: humanity and, 23, 91, 103–14, 116, 133, 136; as meat (*nyama*), 14;

ntchima and, 109; salt and, 136; witches and, 109, 181
anthropology, food and, 3–17
anthropomorphic anthropophagy, 103–8, 115
Archaeological and Cultural Patrimony Project (Projecto Património Arqueológico e Cultural), xi, 17–18
Archambault, Julie, 64
Associação dos Médicos Tradicionais de Moçambique (AMETRAMO), 96, 114
The Atlantic, 22

baboons, 104–5
Bantoe-filosofie (*Bantu Philosophy*) (Tempels), 178–79
Bantu languages, xvi–xvii, 62
Barnard, Alan, 43
basera (gift), 41, 83–85, 186
Bashkow, Ira, 167
beer (*kabanga*), 17, 186
Berlin Conference, 1884–85, 70
biomedicine, 30, 35, 55, 57n2, 135, 153, 157; on diet, 172; personhood and, 178
bipi, 165–66, 186
Bledsoe, Caroline H., 33, 140
blood, 28–30; body and, 32, 34; food and, 32, 56–57; milk and, 34–35; sex and, 129–33, 169; vitality and, 33–34, 129–31, 160, 169, 177, 180–81; *vitamina* and, 33–35, 38, 42, 56, 58n7, 133, 155–56, 180–81

BMI. *See* body mass index
body: blood and, 32, 34; interdependence and, 64–65; in Judeo-Christian ethics, 153; self and, 59n16
body mass index (BMI), 21, 152, 154, 163–64, 166
body size: diet and, 23–24, 166–67, 173–74; larger and smaller, 163–68, 172–73, 183; Metangula, 164–68, 172, 183; *vitamina* and, 167–69; weight and, 153, 167–68, 172, 183
Bogost, Ian, 22
boiling, 43
bolos, 13, 20, 43, 186
Botswana, 64, 141
Brantley, Cynthia, 33
bread, 43, 52, 111–12
bush (*tchire*), 35, 109, 188

Cabo Delgado Province, 70, 98
cannibalism, 23, 90–91, 96–106, 115–16, 181–82
capitalism, compassion and, 77–85
capulana, 11–12, 14, 16, 74, 122, 143, 161, 186
Carsten, Janet, 5–6
catfish, 14
celeste, 110, 186
chai, 40, 49–50, 52, 186
Chewa populations, 11–12, 32, 50, 65, 70, 75
Chichewa language, 31, 78, 92–93
children, in Metangula, 11, 16–17; undernutrition and overnutrition of, 152; *vitamina* and, 37; weight and body size of, 167
Chilombe, Barnabe Mpalila, 95–96, 107
Chilombe, Uandionerapati, 176–77
Chimwaza, Beatrice Mary, 50, 52
Chinese people, 89–91, 114, 116n1
chingabwe (tea without sugar), 49–50
Chingota, Felix, 134
Chinyanja language, xvi–xvii, 11, 20, 33, 53, 64, 69, 78, 80; life and living in, 31–32; *nyama* in, 44; taste in, 49–50; weight in, 154; witches in, 92–93

chipeta, 137
Chiyaawo language, 20–21, 127, 161
Christianity, 67–68, 78, 81
Chuanga, 9, 15, 89, 160, 186
circumstance, *vitamina* and, 34–39
Clinton Foundation, 45
Colonial period in Mozambique, x, 69–71
colorão, 46, 186
Comaroff, Jean, 62, 65–66, 173
Comaroff, John, 62, 65–66
commensality, 5–6, 32, 63, 179
communitas, 179
community: global, 184; in humanity, 61–62, 66; individualism and, 64, 86n3, 115; moral, 75; vitality and, 180
compassion (*lisungu*), 98, 114, 180, 187; capitalism and, 77–85
composite personhood, 23
condoms, 169–70
connectivity, 6, 64, 181
cooked versus raw food, 42–43
cooking the child (*kumphika mwana*), 123, 138
cuisine and diets, African, 7–8
culinary triangle, 43, 180

dawa, 23, 38–39, 94, 96–97, 120, 186; love medicines as, 137–39, 188; *matcheza* and, 138–40; *mgosyo* and, 124, 135, 146; salt and, 134–40, 183
de Luna, Kathryn, 110
de Villiers, Jacques, 140
Democratic Republic of Congo, 56–57
Descartes, René, 104
Devisch, René, 56–57, 59n16
Dicks, Ian, 98
diet, 7–8; biomedicine and, 172; BMI and, 154, 166; body size and, 23–24, 166–67, 173–74; in Malawi, nutrition and, 33; variety in, 47–48; wealth, BMI and, 154
dietary interventions, 166–67, 173
digestion, 52, 135
Diocese of Nyasaland, 69. *See also* Universities' Mission to Central Africa
disability, 38, 73–74, 80
domestic abuse, 38–39

dos Santos, Nuno Valdez, x

eating, humanity and, 108–14, 116
energy: Metangula, food and, 60–61; sex and, 130. *See also* vitality; *vitamina*
Estamos, 44, 163, 170, 186
ethnomedicine, 57n2
everyday rituals. *See mgosyo*
extramarital affairs, 170

feces grandchildren (*vijukulu mavi*), 144, 188
Ferguson, James, 141
fire, 67, 133, 180, 183
fish and fishing, ix, 12–14, 39, 40, 42–43, 51–52, 66, 175–76, 188
flour, *ntchima* and, 80, 110–12, 186, 188
food: animals, humans and, 103–14, 116; in anthropology and Africa, 3–17; blood and, 32, 56–57; cooked versus raw, 42–43; eating, humanity and, 108–14, 116; memory and, 37; raw, 42–43, 109, 112; sex, energy and, 130; sharing, 109, 113–14, 120, 162. *See also Metangula, food in*; *vitamina*; *specific topics*
food aid, 6, 173
food groups, 157, 159, 160
food taboos, 103–8, 115–16
foodways, 7, 186; humanity and, 109, 120, 180, 182–84; personhood and, 3, 86; Samburu, 6. *See also* Metangula, foodways in
foraging, 109–10
The Forest of Symbols (Turner, V.), 58n7
Forrest, Beth, 182
Frelimo, 73

gaga, 38, 80, 186
Geissler, Paul Wenzel, 6, 32, 62, 72, 129
Gell, Alfred, 116
gender, work and, 70
Geschiere, Peter, 97
Ghana, 56
gift (*basera*), 41, 83–85, 186
Goebel, Allison, 138
Gremillion, Helen, 172

Hanlon, Joseph, 141
Haya, of Tanzania, 6, 32, 50, 173
Heald, Suzette, 129
heat, as responsibility, 128–34
hippopotamus, 107–8
HIV/AIDS, 2, 34, 155, 183
Hodgson, A. G. O., 70
Holtzman, Jon, 6, 50, 56, 58n12, 182
Hughes, Charles, 57n2
human-animal relations, 103–7
humanism, 63
humanity: *afiti* as failed, 93; animals and, 23, 91, 103–14, 116, 133, 136; in anthropology, 61; as becoming, 24, 61–62, 108, 178, 181; cannibalism and, 103, 115–16; community in, 61–62, 66; conditions of, African, 140; eating and, 108–14, 116; in ethnography, 25–26; foodways and, 109, 120, 180, 182–84; in global community, 184; in Metangula, 3–4, 8, 71, 91, 141, 176, 182–83, 184; morality and, 24–25; mutuality and, 93, 178; nonpersons versus, 90; principle of participation in, 62; Ubuntu, 62; *vitamina* and, 71, 85; witches, witchcraft and, 23, 115, 181–82
human-lions, 106–7
hunger, 6–7; being full and, 53–54
Hutchinson, Sharon, 32

illness: anemia, 34, 54–55, 130, 159; asthma, 65, 80, 94, 166; bipi, 165–66, 186; healing and, 64–65; *mapinga*, 171; *nthaka*, 120–21, 123–24, 127, 188; *sanjiko*, 119, 171; *vitamina* and, 158–59, 163; weight and, 156, 158, 164–65. *See also mgosyo*; sexually transmitted diseases
individualism, community and, 64, 86n3, 115
infant mortality, 119–21
intelligence (*njeru*), 87n9, 110, 181, 188; plan making and, 71–77
interconnectivity, 64
interdependence, 4, 23–24, 61–65, 183
intersubjectivity, 63
Islam, 81, 87n16, 105

Jackson, Michael, 24, 59n15, 127, 146, 177
Jalasi, Experencia Madalitso, 72
Janson, Charles, 69
Johnson, Jennifer Lee, ix, 59n15
Johnson, Michelle C., 56
Johnson, William Percival, 69
Junod, Henri, 72

kabanga (beer), 17, 186
kacholima (spirits), 17, 28, 169, 187
Kagame, Abbé Alexis, 77
Kahn, Miriam, 6
kaminga, 36–37
kamu, 143–45, 187
Kaphagawani, Didier N., 87n9
Katto, Jonna, x–xi
Kenya, 6, 32, 50, 56
kinship, 97
Kinyanjui, Mary Njeri, 84–85
Klaits, Frederick, 141
kopili, 78
kujimbala, 164–65, 187
kujimbala chimwe, 165, 187
kukhoma, 57n1
kukoma, 49–50, 57n1, 135, 187
kukosya, 127
kulemera, 154, 187
kumphika mwana (cooking the child), 123, 138
kuonda, 164, 187
kuonda bo, 165, 187
kutafuna, 112
kutenguka, 177
kuwawa, 50, 135, 187

labor, 65–70, 77–79, 82, 85–86, 181
Lago District, 9, 33, 70, 83, 157, 161–62, 167–68, 187
Lake Niassa, 9–10, 15; fish and, 14, 176; naming of, 9–10, 26n5
Lake Niassa region, x, 3, 8, 22, 106; UMCA in, 68–70; work and productivity in, 68–71. *See also* Niassa Province
Lake Victoria, ix

Land Labour and Diet in Northern Rhodesia (Richards), 5
Leach, Edmund, 43
lemon (*ndimu*), 54–55
Lévi-Strauss, Claude, 42–43, 180
Lichinga, 15–16, 44, 51–52, 80–81, 130, 187
Likoma, 68–69, 187
lions, humans and, 106–7
lisungu (compassion), 98, 114, 181, 187; capitalism and, 77–85; pain and, 59n15, 81
Livingston, Julie, 64
Livingstone, David, 9–10, 68–70
love medicine, 137–39, 188
Luba populations, 76, 178–79
Luo populations, 32, 72
Lupton, Deborah, 59n14, 153, 182

mafuta, 165–66, 187
Makawa, Moses, 99–101, 115
Makhuwa populations, x–xi, 64, 125
malaria, 34
Malata, Wisdom, 170
Malawi, 10, 12, 15, 20; alcohol and cigarette advertisements in, 31–32; bread in, 52; Chewa in, 50; diet and nutrition in, 33; extramarital affairs in, 170; *mdulo* in, 125; *mizimu* in, 75; work in, 70; worms in, 72–73
Malaysia, 5–6
malnutrition, 4, 145, 151–52, 172–73, 183
Mang'anja populations, 68, 70
mapinga, 171
Maputo, 44, 126, 187
Maravi populations, 11–12, 27n7, 68, 104, 121, 128, 135, 187; creation myth, 133–34; *mgosyo* and, 133–34; personhood in, 181–82
market: African, 84–85; in Metangula, 13–15, 40–44, 76–77, 79, 82–85, 181; in Tanzania, 85
market economy, 61, 77, 79, 85
Masolo, D. A., 62, 77
matcheza, 136, 138–40, 187

mbamu, 46–47, 58n8, 58n10, 187
Mbiti, John S., 61–62
McCann, James C., 7, 26n2
McKay, Ramah, 6, 173
mdulo, 125, 147n7
meat (*nyama*): craving for, 43–44, 103; in Metangula, 14, 44, 102; *vitamina* and, 44
meat taboos, 103–8
medicine. *See dawa*
medicine murder, 94
Melanesia, 6
memory, food and, 37
men: alcohol and, 16, 17; fishing, ix, 12–13; gender norms, 16–17; sex, blood and, 129–32; sex, body size and, 168–69
Mennell, Stephen, 43
Mercader, Julio, xi, 44, 83
Metangula, vii–ix, xi, 3, 187; ancestors in, 75, 87n10, 127, 133, 143; body size in, 164–68, 172, 183; cannibalism and, 98, 115–16, 182; children in, 16–17; Chinyanja language in, 11, 20; Chiyaawo language in, 20–21; fire and, 133; founding of, 127, 176–77; humanity in, 3–4, 8, 71, 91, 141, 176, 182–83, 184; landscape of, 8–9; lions and humans in, 106–7; malnutrition in, 151–52, 172–73; market, 13–15, 40–44, 76–77, 79, 82–85, 181; *mgosyo* in, 122, 125–28, 145; multidimensionality of humanity in, 3–4; Newcastle disease in, 105–6; *ntamiko* in, 139; Nyanja creation myth, 67–68; OMM in, 142–43; Portuguese language in, 11, 20–21, 33; poverty in, 141–42, 184; principle of participation in, 63; productivity and work in, 65–67; relationality in, 66; ritual events in, 19; sex and sexuality in, 129–34, 170–71; unemployment in, 141; *vungu* in, 72–77; witches and witchcraft in, 93–96, 103. *See also specific topics*
Metangula, food in: *colorão* in, 46; dietary variety, 47–48; digestion and, 52; energy and, 60–61; holidays, 53; hunger and being full, 53–54; meat, 43–44; nourishment and, 3, 24; *ntchima* and, 46–47, 110–12; nutritional education, 157–63; oil, onion, and tomato, 39–48; porridge and soup, 159–63, 173; salt, 134–35, 138; sugar and, 30, 40–41, 48–51; taste, 30, 35–36, 48–51; weight and, 155. *See also vitamina*
Metangula, foodways in, ix–x, 22, 176–77, 184; nourishment and, 4, 8; personhood and, 3; *vitamina* and, 34, 85, 180–81
meticais, 13–14, 17, 39, 41, 76, 187
mgosyo: *dawa* and, 124, 135, 146; as everyday ritual, 120–29, 139, 146, 187; *kamu* and, 143–45; Maravi and, 133–34; *matcheza* and, 136, 139–40; *mdulo* and, 125, 147n7; mutuality and, 125, 127, 129, 143; *nthaka* and, 120–21, 123–24, 127; salt and, 124–25, 134–35, 146; sex and, 133–34
Michumwa, 28, 89–91, 114, 116n1, 187
Micuio neighborhood, 81–82
migrant labor, 78
milk, blood and, 34–35
Mintz, Sidney W., 59n14
mizimu (ancestors), 75–76, 87n10, 87n12, 122, 127, 133, 143, 187
Mojola, Aloo Osotsi, 66
monetization, 77–78
money, 77–79, 84, 98. *See also* meticais
morality: evolution and, 24; humanity and, 24–25; personhood and, 30–31
Morris, Brian, 75, 104, 123, 181–82
Mount Chifuli, 8–9, 37
moyo, 31–32, 187
Mozambican Ministry of Health, 56
Mozambique, ix–xii, 184; Chinese nationals in, 116n1; colonial period in, x, 69–71; conservation in, xiii; food aid in, 6, 173; food and drinks in, 131; infant mortality in, 119; malnutrition and, 151–52; poverty in, 13–14, 142; rural residents, 141; Tanzania and, 10; *vungu* in, 72. *See also* Metangula
Mtembezeka, Memory M., 52
multidimensionality, 3–4, 62
Municipality of Metangula, 9

Murcott, Anne, 43
Murphy, Deirdre, 182
mushrooms, 14, 40–41
Musopole, Augustine, 65–66
mutuality, 18–19, 25–26, 61–62, 64; humanity and, 93, 178; *mgosyo* and, 125, 127, 129, 143; sex and, 129, 133; vitality and, 95
MV Ilala, 15–16
mwiiko, 125
Mythologies (Lévi-Strauss), 42

Nchenga neighborhood, 9, 42
ndaka, 125, 127
ndimu (lemon), 54–55
ndiwo, 35, 37, 40–42, 45–51, 58nn10–11, 136–37, 187; *ntchima* and, 66, 111, 120, 185; salt and, 124, 135, 146; *vitamina* and, 135
Newcastle disease, 105–6
Newitt, Malyn, 87n7
ngaiwa, 110–11, 187
Niassa Province, 187; ethnographies on, x–xi, xivn3; Lichinga in, 15–16, 187; naming of, 9–10; Portuguese government in, 70–71; remoteness of, x; vitamins, energy, and blood in, 56; weight and size in, 154, 167–68. See also Lake Niassa region
njeru (intelligence), 87n9, 110, 181, 188; plan making and, 71–77
nkholokolo, 176
nourishment: commensality and, 5–6; in Metangula, food and, 3, 24; in Metangula, foodways and, 4, 8; social relations and, 5–6. See also alimentation
nsipuko (love medicine), 137–39, 188
nsuni, 37, 40–41, 45–46, 188
ntamiko (love medicine), 139, 188
ntchima, 13–15, 35, 46–47, 51, 58n8, 58n10, 188; animals and, 109; flour and, 80, 110–12, 186, 188; *ndiwo* and, 66, 111, 120, 185; *vitamina* and, 37–39
nthaka, 188; infant mortality and, 119–20; *mgosyo* and, 120–21, 123–24, 127; salt and, 120

Nuer populations, 32
nutrition, 7–8; in Malawi, diet and, 33; malnutrition, 4, 145, 151–52, 172–73, 183; overnutrition, 152; undernutrition, 151–52
nutritional anthropology, 5
nutritional education, 157–63
nyama (meat), 14, 43–44, 102–8, 188
Nyamnjoh, Francis B., 115, 182
Nyanja, x, 11, 22, 32, 43–44; creation myth, 67–68; meat taboos, 104; UMCA and, 69; work, productivity and, 67–70
Nyassa Chartered Company (Companhia do Nyassa), 70

obesity, 152–53, 163–65
Ocholla-Ayayo, A. B. C., 72
O desconhecido Niassa (dos Santos), x
Ogude, James, 62–63
oil, onion, and tomato, 39–48
Okafor, Stephen O., 179, 185n5
Olkes, Cheryl, 58n11
OMM. See Organização das Mulheres Moçambicanas
onion, oil, and tomato, 39–48
"Operation Production" in Mozambique, x
Organização das Mulheres Moçambicanas (OMM), 142–43, 168
Othering, 91
overnutrition, 152

pain: foodways and, 29, 50; *lisungu* and, 59n15, 81
Papua New Guinea, 5, 167
participation, principle of, 61–65, 86n1
Perani, Judith, 59n15
personhood: African, 4, 61–62, 65, 77, 86n3, 179; alimentation and, 63; biomedicine and, 178; cannibalism and, 182; compassion and, 81; composite, 23; foodways and, 3, 86; labor and, 181; morality and, 30–31; mutuality in, 61–62; principle of participation in, 62. See also humanity
persons, as economic beings, 65–71
phala (porridge), 157, 188

214 Index

Phillips, Kristin D., 6–7
Pietilä, Tuulikki, 85
Piette, Albert, 177
plan making, intelligence and, 71–77
Platt, Benjamin S., 58n6
Popkin, Barry M., 152
porridge (*phala*), 157, 188
Portuguese language, 11, 20–21, 30–31, 33, 145
pouring salt, 23, 124, 134
poverty, 13–14, 141–42, 184
Premawardhana, Devaka, x–xi, 64
primates, 104–5
Prince, Ruth Jane, 6, 32, 56, 62, 72, 129
productivity, work and, 65–71
Projecto Património Arqueológico e Cultural (Archaeological and Cultural Patrimony Project), xi, 17–18
pro-sociality, 22–24, 84–85, 120, 138, 178, 181–84
public health, 23

Quinn, Victoria, 33

The Raw and the Cooked (Lévi-Strauss), 43
raw food, 42–43, 109, 112
relationality, 6–7, 62–63, 65–66, 84–85
RENAMO. *See* Resistência Nacional Moçambicana, Mozambican National Resistance
Rennick, Agnes, 57n4
Resistência Nacional Moçambicana, Mozambican National Resistance (RENAMO), 73
Richards, Audrey, 5
Rita-Ferreira, António, 70
rituals: everyday, 120–29, 139, 146, 187; of pouring salt, 23, 124, 134
roasting, 43
Roman Catholic church, 69, 161–62
Rwanda, 59n16

sadaka, 79, 89, 188
salt, 79; animals, humans and, 136; *dawa* and, 134–40, 183; *matcheza* and, 136, 138–39; *mgosyo* and, 124–25, 134–35, 146; *ndiwo* and, 124, 135, 146; *nthaka* and, 120; pouring rituals, 23, 124, 134; sex and, 120, 123; witchcraft and, 138–39
Samburu populations, 6, 50, 56
Samora Machel, 136
Sanga District, 83, 167–68
Sanjala neighborhood, 9, 13, 28–29, 34, 36–37, 49–50, 84
sanjika, 51–52
sanjiko, 119, 171
Schoffeleers, Matthew, 121, 127
Seli neighborhood, 9, 95–96; market, 13–15
sex and sexuality, 119; in Africa, 128–29, 132–33; blood and, 129–33, 169; condoms and, 169–70; as culturally constructed, 128; extramarital affairs, 170; fire and, 133, 135, 183; heat and, 129–34; in Metangula, 129–34, 170–71; *mgosyo* and, 133–34; mutuality and, 129, 133; pregnancy, birth and, 171; salt and, 120, 123; *ubazi* and, 129–32, 168–69, 171, 188; vitality and, 129–31, 133; *vitamina* and, 129–30, 133–34, 153, 168–71; wellness and, 130
sexual fluids (*ubazi*), 129–32, 168–69, 171, 188
sexual health, 168–71
sexually transmitted diseases (STDs), 169–70; HIV/AIDS, 2, 34, 155, 183
sharing food, 109, 113–14, 120, 162
Shaw, Rosalind, 97
Sierra Leone, 59n15, 97, 146
sing'anga (traditional healer), 34, 38, 72, 94–95, 125, 139, 166, 188
slave trade, 68, 177
slimness, 164–65
Smart, Teresa, 141
Smith, Fred T., 59n15
Sobo, Elisa Janine, 56, 173
sociality, 5–6, 56–57; pro-sociality, 22–24, 84–85, 120, 138, 178, 181–84
Sondergaärd, Justin, 167–68
sorcerers, witches versus, 92–93, 186
South Africa, 65–66, 106–7, 111–12, 173
South Sudan, 32
spirits (*kacholima*), 17, 28, 169, 187

starvation, 56–57
STDs. *See* sexually transmitted diseases
Steinforth, Arne, 72, 87n11
Stevano, Sara, 56
Stoller, Paul, 58n11
subsistence farming, 7
suffering, 80–81
sugar, 20, 30, 40–41, 48–51
sweetness, 30, 49–50

taboos: cannibalism and, 23, 103–6, 115–16; food, 103–8, 115–16; meat, 103–8
Tanzania, 6, 10, 32, 50, 56, 85, 173
taste, 30, 35–36, 48–51
Taylor, Chris, 59n16
tchire (bush), 35, 109, 188
tea without sugar (*chingabwe*), 49–50
Tempels, Placide, 178–80, 185n5
Tete Province, 70
thanzi (vitality), 33–39, 56, 129–31, 176, 179, 181, 188; community and, 180; compared to *moyo*, 31–32; mutuality and, 95; sex and, 129–31, 133; witches and, 93, 95. *See also vitamina*
thobwa, 48
thovu, 165, 188
tomato, oil, and onion, 39–48
traditional healer (*sing'anga*), 34, 38, 72, 94–95, 125, 139, 166, 188
Tswana populations, 65–66, 173
Turner, Edith, 179–80
Turner, Victor, 58n7, 147n9, 179–80
Tutu, Desmond, 61–62

ubazi (sexual fluids), 129–32, 168–69, 171, 188
Ubuntu, 62–65, 77, 84–85, 127, 178, 188
ufa woyera, 40, 110–11, 188
Uganda, ix, 59n15
UMCA. *See* Universities' Mission to Central Africa
undernutrition, 151–52
unfoldment, 4, 178, 183
United Nations Development Programme, 13–14

Universities' Mission to Central Africa (UMCA), 68–70, 77–78. *See also* Diocese of Nyasaland
usipa, 14, 42–43, 51–52, 66, 188
utaka, 14, 40
utu-ubuntu, 84–85

van Breugel, J. W. M., 75, 97
van Koevering, Helen E. P., x
vidule, 136–37, 188
vijukulu mavi (feces grandchildren), 144, 188
vimbozi (worms), 72–73
Visser, Margaret, 134–35
vital force, 179–81
vitality (*thanzi*), 33–39, 56, 129–31, 176, 179, 181, 188; community and, 180; compared to *moyo*, 31–32; mutuality and, 95; sex and, 129–31, 133; witches and, 93, 95. *See also vitamina*
vitamina, 22–23, 77, 125, 176, 188; alimentation and, 37, 61, 133; blood and, 33–35, 38, 42, 56, 58n7, 133, 155–56, 180–81; body size and, 167–69; *chai* and, 49; of children, in Metangula, 37; circumstance and, 34–39; *colorão* and, 46; deficiency in, 37–39; dietary variety and, 47–48; foodways and, 34, 85, 180–81; foraging and, 109–10; humanity and, 71, 85; illness and, 158–59, 163; lemons and, 54–55; meat and, 44; *ndiwo* and, 45–46, 135; *ngaiwa* and, 111; *nsuni* and, 45–46; *ntchima* and, 37–39; in nutritional education, 158–60, 163; oil, onion, and tomato, 39–40, 42–48; Portuguese language and, 30–31; sex and, 129–30, 133–34, 153, 168–71; sugar and, 49–50; sweetness and, 49; taste and, 35–36; *tchire* (bush) and, 109; *usipa* and, 42–43; vitality and, 36, 48, 85, 129–30, 133, 180–81; weight and, 155, 172; wellness and, 47, 50, 155–56; women in Metangula and, 45, 168–69. *See also* vitality
von Poser, Anita, 5
vungu (worms), 72–77, 188

War for Independence, 37
wealth, BMI and, 154
Weidtmann, Niels, 62, 75–76, 124–25, 127, 179–80
weight, 153–58, 166; alimentation and, 155–57; body size and, 153, 167–68, 172, 183; illness and, 156, 158, 164–65; obesity and, 152–53, 163–65; *vitamina* and, 155, 172
Weiss, Brad, 6, 32, 50, 173
wellness, 47, 50, 130, 155–57
Whyte, Susan Reynolds, 140
Williamson, Jessie, 58n10, 59n17, 147n7
Wirzba, Norman, 182
witches and witchcraft, 65, 90–97; as *afiti*, 92–93, 186; animals and, 109, 182; as cannibals, 96–103, 115; humanity and, 23, 115, 181–82; *lisungu* and, 98; Makawa music videos and, 99–101, 115; salt and, 138–39; sorcerers versus, 92–93, 186; vitality and, 93, 95
wolemera, 154

women, in Metangula: *capulanas* and, 11–12, 14, 16, 74, 122, 143, 186; cassava washed and sorted by, 67; meal preparation and, 17, 122; sex, blood and, 129–32; tasks of, 11–13, 16–17; *vitamina* and, 45, 168–69; work, money and, 78–79
work: gender and, 12–13, 16–17, 70; industriousness and, 65–71; labor, 65–70, 77–79, 82, 85–86, 181; money and, 78–79
World Health Organization, 152
worms (*vungu*), 72–77, 188
Wrangham, Richard, 180
Wylie, Diana, 57

Yaawo populations, 98, 127
Yaka populations, 56–57

Zigon, Jarrett, 24
Zomba, 170

www.ingramcontent.com/pod-product-compliance
Lightning Source LLC
Chambersburg PA
CBHW051539020426
42333CB00016B/2004